What People Are Saying About This Book

Dr. Ann Gillies' meticulous research, years of counselling, and first-hand experience with gender identity realities and the LGBT agenda make this book a compelling read. Even in a world where "feeling" is everything, there is comfort in a foundation provided by fact, reason and common sense. This book provides such a foundation.

—Jim Burk, B.Sc., M.Ed.
Medicine Hat, Alberta

In writing her book *Closing the Floodgates*, Ann has identified the root cause and dangerous outcomes that have changed mindsets and educational agendas in our public, particularly through the high school systems across our land. There is a growing ignorance in our society, and much of the church, on the topic of gender and sexuality. I think this book is a must-read for every leader, from elected government officials to school board representatives, clergy, and heads of households. It is my prayer that *Closing the Floodgates* will at least cause decision-makers in our government and education field to rethink the direction sex education has taken in the past forty years, and to make positive policies for the future health and wellness of our nation.

—Louie Foster, Lead Pastor
Durham Foursquare Gospel Church

Dr. Gillies' academic expertise, combined with her personal testimony, makes her the perfect voice to speak into the area of gender and sexuality. *Closing the Floodgates* provides a clear message of truth spoken in love—a must-read for generations to come.

—Paul Lucas, Family Ministries Pastor
Gentle Shepherd Community Church
Eugena, Ontario

Ann's latest book is a clarion call to those of us who believe we are challenged to protect, instruct, and inspire the next generation! It is my opinion that *Closing the Floodgates* should be read by every parent, pastor, and educator in Canada. It is a reliable source for accurate, scientific information on a battle that we're all facing, one for the minds and hearts of everyone in our culture. The enemy's schemes are masterfully revealed.

Ann has it right: it's high time to wake up and close the floodgates! May we be characterized like the ancient men of Issachar who *"understood the times and knew what Israel should do..."* (1 Chronicles 12:32, NIV).

—Jim Gordon, author of No-Default Living
Co-author (with his wife Carrie) of The 7-Day Sex Challenge
Founding principal/teacher of a Christian school (twenty years)
Present pastors of the Elora Road Christian Fellowship

D1591061

CLOSING THE
FLOODGATES

SETTING THE RECORD STRAIGHT ABOUT GENDER & SEXUALITY

A. E. GILLIES, PH.D.

Printed in Canada
ISBN: 978-1-4866-1830-9

Word Alive Press
119 De Baets Street Winnipeg, MB R2J 3R9
www.wordalivepress.ca

WORD ALIVE
—P R E S S—

MIX
Paper from
responsible sources
FSC
www.fsc.org FSC® C016245

Cataloguing in Publication information may be obtained through Library and Archives Canada.

This book is dedicated to my children.
Oh, how I wish I could have sheltered you from the evil of this world.
May you continue to be brave and courageous in the midst
of the pain and injustice you have suffered.
You are my inspiration.

To my husband, who is my right arm, my advocate,
my chief supporter and my best friend.
Without you, none of this would ever be possible.

My deepest gratitude to those who have responded so enthusiastically to this manuscript with editorial comments, recommendations, and endorsements.

Table of Contents

You may choose to
Look the other way
But you can never say again
that you did not know.

William Wilberforce

Foreword

I HOPE YOU WILL FIND THIS BOOK PROFOUNDLY DISTURBING. NOT BECAUSE you disagree with the views expressed here—far from it; I trust you will be in substantial or even complete agreement.

No, I hope it disturbs you in a better way. I hope it disturbs you out of your apathy. I hope it disturbs you to the point you decide to become part of an army that needs to be raised to fight what is one of the greatest moral challenges our society faces.

As Dr. Gillies, whom my wife and I have known for over thirty years, repeatedly points out, the real issue is truth. The objectives of the community pushing the agenda she so powerfully describes in this book are opposed by the truth God established his creation upon. In other generations, attacks on truth have come from all sorts of directions. Internally, they have arisen through false teaching invading the church and trying to corrupt it. Externally, they have come from attempts by everyone from radical Muslims to Marxists to destroy God's people outright.

The LGBT agenda, to use the phrase broadly, is simply another one of those attacks. It is insidious because it is not obvious. When the medieval caliphs invaded Europe in an attempt to eradicate Christianity, the threat was clear. When Nazis, Stalinists or Maoists persecuted the church, the threat was clear.

But this threat has arisen slowly and subtly. It has gained enormous traction by disguising its true objectives as the pursuit of legitimate human rights. Any who oppose that are quickly and easily portrayed as narrow-minded bigots.

The truth, which Dr. Gillies clearly sets forth, is that the goal of these activists is primarily to enlarge their sphere of rights at the expense of the rights of others, sometimes even innocent children. In a society where the standard of truth as God defined it has been destroyed, a new standard is being erected, for no society can exist in a moral vacuum.

In the face of such an onslaught, we can feel helpless. Yet that in itself is the goal of the enemy with whom we contend.

In this book, the lies we are being sold today are exposed and destroyed through balanced, careful and clear research. This research comes not only, and indeed not primarily from Christian or religious sources, but generally from psychiatrists, psychologists, and social scientists of the highest repute.

There is a remark of Jesus inscribed on the stonework of Victoria College in the University of Toronto, where I completed my undergraduate degree. The words are these: "The truth shall make you free."

Those words still stand, and will stand when this battle is over. The question is this: will you have taken your place in the battle lines, or will apathy or the cares of this world have rendered you useless to God? He will hold you and me, and all of us, to account for our response.

Read, be disturbed, and respond.

—David H. Campbell, B.A., M.Div., M.Litt
Author & Lecturer

Preface

THE BOOK IS NOT ABOUT ME NOR MY FAMILY, ALTHOUGH WE HAVE LIVED much of what is described herein. Instead, it comes from the deep burden of my heart for Canada, its people, and the crossroads we find ourselves at in our country's 150th year. The foundation of values and morals that Canadians once thought unshakable has crumbled, much as the levees of Louisiana collapsed under the assault of floodwaters from Hurricane Katrina.

The fact that we are no longer shocked and appalled by the sexual climate we live in speaks to a deeper dilemma—that of a desensitized, lost soul. Instead of the love and peace espoused by the Woodstock generation, we are now living in a country of bitter hatred and division. The further we've kicked God out the door and down the street, the more we've degenerated.

The very idea that sex should be confined in any manner, but particularly in a monogamous heterosexual marriage, is looked upon with disdain. The notion that sex is a deeply private and genuinely intimate experience has become foreign to our generation. Overt sexuality is everywhere. When we have no problem taking our children to parades where nudity, sexual gestures, and all kind of depictions of immorality are valued, it is time for a deeper look within. Old taboos have been annihilated in the face of a new norm, but is it better?

As a culture, we've become fixated on sex. It fuels our emotions, our fantasies, and our hedonism, to the great cost of marriage, our children, and family relationships. Pornography has rewired our brains so that our sexuality has become more and more distorted and callous. A pornography addiction does not simply crave more of the same over and over, but it is an addiction that requires more and different expressions continually—it is a curse. What is different sexually can turn violent and deviant quickly—and it has. Sex has simply become a dehumanizing act.

Divine design constitutes male and female—husband and wife producing children within the stability of the family. Even those who accept the theories of evolution, mutation or adaptation have all have espoused the binary categories of male and female. No hint here of biology producing sexual confusion.

Our sexuality is designed for a union between a man and woman within the covenant of marriage—self-giving and faithfully committed, learning and growing together in ever-deepening cycles of love throughout the seasons of our lives. This beautiful ideal of marriage is achievable. It's not out of reach, but it takes work and self-sacrifice, something we are often hesitant to invest in.

As a result, our communities are filled with lonely people seeking connection, oftenturning to pleasures and passions that ensnare and entangle them in a lifetime of deeper loneliness, abandonment, rejection and pain. But even as the floodwaters of the sexual revolution rise, there is hope.

When we understand that truth, it brings freedom; it brings the refreshment to our souls that we long for; it dissipates confusion and has the power to lead us on a new path of restoration.

When we are confused, the vacuum created can be filled relatively easily, and we tend to cling to what the masses believe. It feels safe there somehow. Such is the condition of our culture. Our collective media—news, entertainment and social networks—have filled the vacuum caused by our confusion with their own version of truth. Our minds can become confused and dulled by the constant repetition of such words that we begin to accept propaganda as truth.

If the eyes are truly the windows of the soul, then what we see enters our mind and quickly flows to our heart (spirit). Because behaviour then flows out of the heart, the best way to protect ourselves from brainwashing and behavioural modification is to carefully guard what we allow into our minds—what we allow ourselves to see and experience. Whatever we absorb continually through written word, music, video or television impacts us and has an immense potential to change our worldview.

With a lack of criteria or boundaries, our minds and thoughts can easily be lead astray, and ideas can be promoted which have little or no relevance to the original paradigm. I would suggest that as far as we, the people of Canada, have misunderstood or set aside the historic understanding of the original biological human design, this is the extent to which we are now experiencing the newest wave of the sexual revolution, and it's resulting in extreme sexual confusion.

What we are putting into the minds of our children is setting them on the road to disaster. Instead of challenging young minds with the principles from the stories of the Bible, Mother Goose, or the classics, we are now filling them with sexual thoughts, ideas and pictures that would have been unheard of even ten short years ago.

Thoughts, as you are aware, can very quickly lead to behaviours. In his book, *The 7 Habits of Highly Effective People*, Stephen Covey says this:

> *Sow a thought; reap an action*
> *Sow an action; reap a habit*
> *Sow a habit; reap a character*
> *Sow a character; reap a destiny.*

For some of you, reading that Canada is at the place of denying the biological design of male and female may come as a surprise. The newly popularized idea of sexual fluidity (suggesting that sexuality is experienced on a continuum from totally heterosexual to totally homosexual, along with the innate ability to choose sexual preference depending on who we are with), isn't actually all that new. The concept of plastic (or fluid) sexuality was coined in 1992, but this concept was formulated by Freud and stimulated by Alfred Kinsey.

This perspective speculates that sexual behaviour remains fluid and changeable throughout our lifespan. Of course, this largely accepted concept runs in the face of the "born this way" proponents. I do believe that as human beings we have the ability to choose how we express our sexuality. That doesn't mean that any and all forms of sexual expression are conducive to health and wholeness, to the good of the family or to that of the human community.

Delinking sexuality from the bounds of heterosexual marriage and romantic love allows our society to reframe its meaning—and reframe we have! We are living within a truly risky milieu that has thrown away the long-held scientific understanding of biological male and female in favour of fluid sexuality.

What has happened is that sexual activity has been devalued to an extreme level. As the early 70s song indicates, if you aren't able to win the love of the person you want, "Love the One You're With." Only now there's a twist. It's no longer just about having heterosexual intercourse with the girl or guy beside you; even if you are in a setting with all the same gender, or gender confused individuals, you can go ahead and have sex with anyone any way you want! The "new" doctrine of sexual gratification has actually been percolating for decades. Today's secular perspective on sexuality is not just about the sex drive, but about letting sex drive.

As you will find in the pages of this book, I neither "bash" nor affirm gay people. I simply observe the writing on the wall, compelled to speak the truth. This book is the culmination of nearly two decades of study on sexuality and the LGBT culture, yet the story is far from over. If, perhaps, Canadians had seen the writing on the wall sooner, the story today might be far different; nevertheless, as the saying goes, "It is what it is." My chief focus is not on the past, but on the future. The ever-expanding waters of sexual revolution flooding our land are set to drown us and our children.

I have written this book to heighten your awareness, to illuminate the tsunami that threatens, and to inspire parents and grandparents everywhere to take a very serious second look at the sexualization flooding our land—from sea to shining sea.

So, prepare your minds for action and be self-controlled... (1 Peter 1:13a, paraphrased)

An Overview Of This Book

I FEEL COMPELLED TO WRITE THIS BOOK. THIS COMPULSION COMES FROM being an observer of our nation's moral decline. We are well down the road to becoming a nation without a shared foundation of core values or moral principle. Our "free and democratic society"[1] is giving way to the pressures of a politically correct inclusiveness that threatens any and all who resist. We have become a sexually addicted society, the results of which will be borne on the backs of our youth for many following generations.

This book is meant to be a wake-up call to parents, grandparents, communities, church leaders, and politicians. It is a book focused on where the sexual revolution has brought us, and where, if unimpeded, it will lead us. This book, then, is a warning call to Canada. Not the first, mind you. Lord knows others have tried to bring us to our senses, but perhaps Canadians are now ready to heed the warnings, and to turn the tide for our children and future generations.

Here is a brief summary of what you will find in this book.

Chapter 1: Headwaters of the Sexual Revolution

This chapter will deal with the Kinsey reports of 1949, and the subsequent research that has shaped four generations of the western world. The truth about this research, the sexual abuse of infants and children used to provide "data," and subsequent media misrepresentation will be described. This is the research that propelled

---

[1] Constitution Act (1982)

the American Psychological Association to remove homosexuality as a mental disorder, and it has controlled much of the political agenda in the area of sexuality.

Chapter 2: The Widening Stream – Childhood Sexual Abuse

Exploring the travesty of childhood sexual abuse and its life-long legacy.

Chapter 3: Rushing Rivers – The Indoctrination of Our Children

A brief look at how children are being exposed to the new ideology of sexual identity and expression.

Chapter 4: The Watershed Effect – The Consequences of Early Adolescent Sexuality

A presentation about what is happening in our society and how it is affecting our children.

Chapter 5: The Flood of the Century – Sexual Addiction

A consideration of sexual addiction: what it is, how it begins, and where it leaves us. Along with this we will look at the exponential rise in pornography, the ushering in of homosexuality as normal sexual behaviour, and the 21st century rendition of "anything goes."

Chapter 6: Confluence of Choices – Gay, Lesbian, or Bi-sexual

A comprehensive look at statistical information, sexual behaviour, physical and mental health facts. The numbers are not what you are led to believe.

Chapter 7: Muddied Tributaries – Gender Dysphoria & Transgenderism

An in-depth look at the facts surrounding Gender Dysphoria and the Transgender population, including statistics, media misrepresentation, and the LGBT connection in one of today's most fiercely-debated topics.

Chapter 8: Lost at Sea – The Concept of Intergenerational Intimacy

The disturbing real world of incest and pedophilia. This chapter highlights the not-so-hidden agenda to reclassify pedophilia as a sexual orientation, as well as showing how the Kinsey legacy is propelling society toward embracing the last taboo.

Chapter 9: Societal Storm Waters – What Comes Next?

Has legislating gay marriage and current transgender normalization created an open door for the next steps of this progression?

Chapter 10: Artesian Springs Welling Up: Findings from the New Atlantis Report

This is a fresh breath of empirically sound scientific fact, providing a springboard for addressing the inaccuracy of the LGBT agenda.

Chapter 11: Finding the Source – What Does Attachment Have to Do With It?

A look at healthy attachment in childhood, and the life-long results of insecure attachment and trauma.

Chapter 12: The Flood Plains – A Political Arena

Political clout: what is the reality? Is there a hidden agenda behind what is happening in current legislation? If so, what is it, and how, if left unattended, will it change the lives of Canadians?

Chapter 13: Stemming the Flood – Enough is Enough: Parents Unite

Are you content to allow your children to be swept over the dam to drown in the floodwaters of the sexual revolution?

Chapter 14: Hope on the Horizon

A fresh look at Christianity and its impact on society.

CHAPTER 1
Headwaters of the Sexual Revolution

No one is hated more than he who speaks truth.
Plato

WHAT IF I WERE TO TELL YOU THAT FOR NEARLY SEVEN DECADES OUR NATION has been resting its understanding of human sexuality on false data? What would you say if I were to tell you that the "scientific" research of which I speak has never been replicated nor validated, yet it is the source of our current legislation on sexuality and the resource upon which our educational system bases our children's sex education? Would you believe me? Not likely. Why should you; you would need proof. That's exactly what I plan to give you in these next few chapters.

I don't expect everyone to like what I'm about to tell you, but the importance of truth mandates that it be shared, particularly when it comes to the sexual research that is the basis for training our children. Perhaps the biggest explosion of truth will reverberate from this chapter. We need to turn the tide on the rampant teaching of sexual behaviour that we have witnessed over the last few decades. Let's walk together through this journey.

One of the foremost sources for this chapter comes from Dr. Judith Reisman and her team. I am sharing Dr. Reisman's credentials with you, because as you will see, the information that follows is likely to rock you to the core, and I want you to appreciate the level of credibility of what is presented. Dr. Judith Reisman has written several books and has been listed in:

Who's Who in Sexology (the scientific study of human sexuality utilizing biology, medicine, psychology, epidemiology, sociology and criminality);
Who's Who of Women;
Who's Who in Education, International;
Who's Who in Education;
Who's Who in Society;
Personalities of America: Two Thousand Notable Americans;

Dr. Reisman has been a:
- Consultant to four U.S. Department of Justice administrations, the U.S. Department of Education, and the U.S. Department of Health and Human Services
- Writer, producer, and performance artist for Scholastic Magazine, Milwaukee Public Museum, Cleveland Museum of Art, and CBS television network
- Associate Professor at the University of Haifa, Israel
- Research Full Professor, The American University
- Part of the adjunct faculty of George Mason University
- Guest lectures at the following institutions:
  - Princeton
  - Notre Dame
  - Georgetown
  - Pepperdine
  - University of Jerusalem
  - University of Haifa
  - Tel Aviv University
  - Johns Hopkins University School of Medicine
  - Rutherford Institute
  - Council for National Policy
  - Federal Bureau of Investigation
  - United States Air Force Academy
- Currently the Research Professor and Director of the Child Protection Institute, Liberty University School of Law
- Scientific Adviser, California Protective Parents Association

- Distinguished Senior Fellow, at The Inter-American Institute
- President of the Institute for Media Education[2]

Most importantly here, she has spent over thirty years investigating the work of Alfred Kinsey and the Kinsey Institute of Sex Research. I think you would agree that this is one remarkably accomplished woman!

Here's a map of where we're headed in this chapter.

- Let me introduce you to the world of relevant research! I can almost hear you groaning now. Take heart; it's my job to translate academic jargon into something more palatable. Believe me, doing it has given me a few headaches! When you get past these few details you will be glad you took the time.
- Making sense of the research: What does it mean? Who does it apply to?
- Identifying the impact: Who is affected?
- Mapping the outcome: What results are expected to happen because of the research?

Perhaps no one in modern times has shaped public attitudes on human sexuality more than Alfred Kinsey. Yet, it seems few people realize that the data he presented is not, as he claimed, scientific. In fact, Kinsey's data have been demonstrably proven to have been extremely biased, and his published results fraudulent.[3] From 1948-1956, Kinsey travelled the world advising governments on how to modernize allegedly outdated sex laws. His advice was central to changing sexual attitudes, particularly toward homosexual behaviour.

You will read about statistical data in this book so let me clarify what that is:

Statistical data is the **organization and investigation** of an entire population (in this case men, women and children) from a sampling (the process of choosing a representative sample) of the population. To be significant, the data needs to come from a representative sample of the population. A random sample means that individuals are selected randomly. Here's an example. An unbiased scientist wanting to determine alcohol consumption amongst college students would randomly (without previous knowledge of participants) select four students from each class in several different colleges; interview them or do a survey, and come up with a pretty clear estimate of how much

---

[2] Reisman (2017 p. 1)
[3] Reisman (1999)

alcohol the average college student consumes. This, of course, would not be applicable to every student in the school; nor would it necessarily apply to the general public.

The research I comment on in this chapter comes from studies by Albert Kinsey and his team. What Kinsey did in his studies equates to the scientists in my example above going to a bar filled with inebriated college students, buying them a few more drinks, interviewing them, then applying what they had learned about alcohol consumption in this select group to the entire country! The two study examples illustrate "good" and "bad" scientific research and explain why many of us have difficulty trusting statistics: sometimes you can't trust the

> "The only unnatural sex act is that which you cannot perform."
> Kinsey, 1948

scientist. Such is the case of Albert Kinsey, who stated, "the only unnatural sex act is that which you cannot perform."[4] He took 25% of the male sample he personally selected for his sex study from pedophiles, then set out to prove their sexual behaviour was normative to the entire U.S. population.

Kinsey began making claims about "statistically" common sexual behaviour in the 1940s. Here are some of the early claims he presented:

1. Nearly 70% of US men have sex with prostitutes
2. Between 30 and 45% of husbands have extramarital intercourse.

These bold statements about common sexual behaviour are not even applicable to our highly-sexualized culture today. The percentage of men who hire prostitutes at least once in their life time varies by country. A survey of twenty-one studies that included fifteen countries (Canada not being one of them) found that as of 2010 15-20% of American men have hired a prostitute.

A 2015 poll by Mainstreet Research found that about 13% of Canadian men and 8% of women say they have cheated on their spouse, while 22% have considered it.[5] Now compare these current statistics to Kinsey's 1948 stats (about nearly 70% of men having sex with prostitutes), which were taken in an era of sexual modesty and marital fidelity!

That's where we start with Kinsey's findings, but the most shocking of his reports are those identified in the childhood sexuality sections of his study of males

[4] Kinsey et al (1948)
[5] Mainstreet Research (2015)

in 1948 and females in 1953. He purported that children are sexual beings from infancy onward and that they could and should have pleasurable sexual interaction with adult "partners." His view seemed to be that parents and the public overreact with hysteria about child sexual abuse and this "hysteria" is what damages the child![6]

I have worked with childhood sexual abuse survivors for over 20 years, and I can tell you that Kinsey's research reads like a biography of criminal pedophilia and sexual assault! Perhaps the saddest part of his research is that Kinsey has been described the 'patron saint of sex' and according to sexologist Morton Hunt, he was "the giant on whose shoulders all sex researchers since his time has stood"![7] Astoundingly, he was never charged nor convicted of sexually abusing children, which, as you will soon read, is what transpired during his research.

KINSEY, 1948

Although some of his data was based on participant recall, Kinsey wasn't satisfied with the results. Most of his subjects had only fragmented memories before age six or seven. In looking for more direct sources he decided to interview and experiment with the children themselves. Kinsey began to create situations with children where parents were present. What these "situations" were are not identified. With children acquired from ghetto areas, he dismissed the need for parental accompaniment or consent.[8] His reported results, if true, suggest the perpetration of horrific abuse on children.

KINSEY'S RESEARCH TEAM

Having stacked the deck in favour of his desired results, Kinsey presented skewed statistics as fact and promoted these statistics as pertaining to all of humanity. His research sample of men was highly unrepresentative of society. In addition, many of his own team of student researchers were novices in the field of science and sexology.

Kinsey himself was interested in biology and had undergrad degrees in biology and psychology. He continued to study applied biology at Harvard's Bussey Institute and completed his doctoral thesis on the study of wasps. I have not found any evidence that he had

> Kinsey believed that children are sexual beings from infancy onward and they could and should have pleasurable sexual interaction with adult "partners".

---

[6] Reisman (1998)
[7] Reisman & Eichel (1990)
[8] Pomeroy (1972); Reisman (2003)

previous experience in interviewing adults or children. Based on his descriptions (of children's responses—see the section "Child Sex Experiments - Male" below), he was not interested in human emotion, nor the effects of abuse on children and/ or adults. For further understanding of these responses, see Finkelhor's work.[9]

The essential criteria Kinsey used to select his group of "professionals" came from their sexual experience interviews. Only those with a deviant sexual past were accepted. He also only hired men to interview women about their most intimate sexual feelings and experiences.

Kinsey is reported to have resorted to classifying prostitutes as "married women" to make his female study more acceptable. His criteria for a married woman was one who had lived with a man for a period of one year! A woman in his study therefore did not need to be married to qualify as married.[10] Don't forget that this was 1948. Co-habitation (called fornication in those days) was against the law, which already makes his "evidence" extremely questionable.

Kinsey's team was entirely dependent on him for the advancement of their careers, and therefore highly influenced by him. Although Kinsey was married, he and his wife Clara both participated in recording interviews. They also participated in some of the sex films he produced.[11] He reportedly had at least two regular male lovers who were also part of his team.[12] His sexual behaviour confirmed his position that all human beings are bisexual.

Pomeroy, his assistant, later revealed that Kinsey controlled the staff through fear, intimidation and shame. According to James Jones in his biography on Alfred Kinsey,[13] Kinsey initiated "field" sexual activities which were used as a desensitization process for staff and subjects. It certainly seems to have had that effect on Pomeroy as he later stated that

> *Incest between adults and younger children can also prove a satisfying and enriching* experience. Incestuous relationships can – and do work out well – we find many beautiful and mutually satisfying relationships between fathers and daughters. These may be transient or ongoing, but they *have no harmful effects!*[14] (emphasis added)

Do you believe that *incest has no harmful effect on children?!*

[9] Finkelhor (1979)
[10] Reisman (2003)
[11] Reisman (1990, 2013)
[12] Reisman (2003)
[13] Ibid
[14] Pomeroy (1976 p. 10)

KINSEY'S "RANDOM" SAMPLE

Alfred Kinsey acquired his research subjects from people who volunteered; such situations, when applied to the public, are bound to slant the statistical evidence. There are also differing reports of how many were interviewed. His associate Clyde Martin stated that Kinsey gathered 6,200 male histories, yet the American Statistical Association concluded Kinsey interviewed 4,120 at most.[15] If Martin's number is accurate, where the rest of the interviews went to is still a quandary.

His "random" sample, supposedly made up of over 4,000 men, included nearly 1,000 present and former inmates (25%); many of whom were homosexual and/or pedophiles. As many as 5% of his subjects may have been male prostitutes.[16] Other members of the study who would have provided a statistical bias included those from "Mattachine Society" (a homophile organization), various pedophile organizations, personal friends of individuals known to be sexually deviant, and patients in mental hospitals (Kinsey called them feebleminded).[17]

From this misrepresentative sample, the Kinsey team generalized that:

• 37% of the total male population (in the US) has some sort of overt homosexual experience
• 13% of the population was predominantly homosexual.[18]

Kinsey classified more than 1,400 criminals and sex offenders as a "normal" representation of the general population. His prison sample was biased toward sexual disorders. According to one of his team members, Kinsey sought out the worse sex offenders for his interviews, avoiding more common types of offenses (rape for example).[19]

Kinsey assumed that the experiences of pedophiles and prostitutes could be construed as representative of the entire country. His subjective 1948 statistic that 13% of the general population is gay is a far cry from the 2010 Canadian statistical report that indicates approximately 1% of the population identify as gay and 1% identify as lesbian. I'll discuss this more in chapter 8.

It seems Kinsey's goal was two-fold. Firstly, to change society's view on what "normal" sexuality is, and secondly to establish himself as the world's foremost sex researcher. He accomplished both.

---

[15] Reisman (2003)
[16] Reisman & Eichel (1990)
[17] Eichel & Muir (1990)
[18] DuBay (2001)
[19] Reisman (2003)

During his 1948 study Kinsey was confronted by renowned scientist Abraham Maslow, who had initially been part of Kinsey's team. You may have encountered Maslow's famous "Hierarchy of Needs."[20] When Maslow challenged Kinsey on his bias toward the unconventional sexual behaviour of the subjects who had volunteered for his sex research, Kinsey ended the professional relationship and deliberately ignored Maslow's findings.[21] Maslow subsequently stated in a letter that the volunteer error proved that the whole basis for Kinsey's statistics was unreliable.[22]

A 1953 study to evaluate Kinsey's 1948 report on male sexual behaviour taken by the American Statistical Association (ASA)[23] concluded:

> That *critics are justified in their objections* that many of the most provocative statements in the book are not based on the data presented therein...the conclusions drawn from data presented are often stated by Kinsey, Pomeroy and Martin in much too bold and confident a manner. (emphasis added)

CHILD SEX EXPERIMENTS - MALE

The following information is disturbing, but it is necessary to review in order to understand the depths to which Kinsey and associates would stoop to get the desired results. As you will learn later in this chapter, one of his subjects was a Nazi leader who had been in charge of a Polish concentration camp where he practiced his victimization of children.

Kinsey reportedly used three child-research methods:
1. Adolescents and adults recalling childhood (called the retrospective method)
2. Interviewing children (supposing they were old enough to answer questions about their sexual history);
3. Direct observation (sexual stimulation)

You will notice, in the charts to follow, that boys up to 15 years old were subjected to systematic sexual abuse to gratify Kinsey's quest to support his hypothesis and to advance his sexual agenda. The Kinsey team apparently obtained data on genital stimulation on children through actual observation and

---

[20] Maslow (1943)
[21] Reisman & Eichel (1990)
[22] Reisman & Eichel (1990)
[23] Cochran, Mosteller, & Tukey (1953)

timed orgasms with the second hand of a stop watch! These children ranged in age from two months to fifteen years of age, with the majority being between four and ten years of age.

Kinsey claimed that the results of

homosexual masturbation of young boys (sometimes for 24 hours at a time), is a valuable way to learn about childhood sexuality.[24]

The identity of these children is not clear. There were apparently 317 boys, but possibly more. There is no clear indication of where these children came from, or of written parental consent. As the Kinsey files at the University of Indiana have yet to be revealed, the information on these children remains officially undisclosed.

Kinsey claimed that the data came from a combination of recalled information from child sex abuser interviews and technical information from "trained" observers! What he's saying here is that these histories were recalled with precision, right down to the second! The notion of one person sexually abusing a child in such a way as to be able to time and monitor the event to the second, while concurrently holding the child down and recording such an event in precise detail, would be impossible.

The charts below show the actual observations identified in his report. They include immense detail on the nature of orgasms of children as young as five months of age. As you read these charts, remember that the "trained" observers were his research team.

Kinsey's colleague, Clarence Tripp, suggested that the records of the sodomizing of these children were all carried out scientifically because these men used "stopwatches to record their thing." Documentation in Kinsey's report indicates that nine of his adult male subjects had observed such orgasms.[25]

The data in Kinsey's Table 31 on the following page is extraordinarily disturbing. Kinsey and team claim orgasms were observed in a five-month-old baby! Attempts to achieve orgasms were even made on babies of 2, 3, and 4 months

> Supposedly the records of the sodomizing of these children were all carried out scientifically because these men used "stopwatches to record their thing."

[24] Reisman & Eichel (1990)
[25] Ibid

of age! In five of these cases, observations were made over a period of months or years, continuing until the children were old enough to make sure a true orgasm was involved[26].

This begs the question – where were the parents? Were they not only supportive, but also involved? Were these the "ghetto" children spoken of, who for the purpose of experiment were used for years? Perhaps we'll never know.

Pre-Adolescent Experience in Orgasm – Kinsey, Table 31
(adapted from Kinsey, 1948, p. 176)

Age when Observed	Total Population	Cases not reaching climax	Cases reaching climax	Cumulated population	Cumulated cases to climax	Percent of each reaching climax
2 mon.	1	1	0			
3 mon.	2	2	0			
4 mon.	1	1	0			
5 mon.	2	1	1			
8 mon.	2	1	0			
9 mon.	1	1	3			
10 mon.	4	1	2			
11 mon.	3	1	2			
12 mon.	12	10				
Up to 1 yr.	28	19	9	28	9	32.1
Up to 2 yr.	22	11	11	50	20	
Up to 3 yr.	9	2	7	59	27	
Up to 4 yr.	12	5	7	71	34	57.1
Up to 5 yr.	6	3	3			
Up to 6 yr.	12	5	7	89	44	
Up to 7 yr.	17	8	9	106	53	
Up to 8 yr.	26	12	14	132	67	63.4
Up to 9 yr.	29	10	19	161	86	
Up to 10 yr.	28	6	22	189	108	
Up to 11 yr.	34	9	25	223	133	
Up to 12 yr.	46	7	39	269	172	80.0
Up to 13 yr.	35	7	28	304	200	
Up to 14 yr.	11	5	6	315	206	
Up to 15 yr.	2	2	0	317	206	
TOTAL	317	111	206	317	206	65.0

Kinsey's notorious Table 34 (summarized in Table 2 below) indicates the exact number of orgasms each child had (starting with a five-month-old!) and

---

[26] Kinsey (1948 p. 171)

shows the time involved to reach repeated orgasms. Please read this chart carefully. One needs to assimilate the incredible horror and damage done to these innocent children. The knowledge of who these children were, of whether the data was collected by his team (as some apparently was) or by anecdotal recording of pedophilic "work," is still buried somewhere in his records at the University of Indiana. Kinsey's own colleagues have indicated that they didn't keep records of where the pedophile "diaries" came from! Such statements cast serious doubt upon the scientific relevance of Kinsey's work.

Table 34 presented the number of alleged orgasms of 182 preadolescent boys and the time recorded between each orgasm with 64 of them. Records indicate that three children required less than 10 seconds and 15 of the children 11-15 seconds between orgasms.[27] This table itemizes the ages of each "subject." These charts indicate that these innocent, helpless babies were being criminally sexually abused, and not one person intervened! Where these children came from and disappeared to is shrouded in mystery.

Sexual Behaviour in Human Males – Kinsey, Table 34
(adapted from Kinsey, 1948, p. 180)

Age	No. of Orgasms	Time Involved	Age	No. of Orgasms	Time Involved
5 mon.	3	?	11 yr.	11	1 hr.
11 mon.	10	1hr.	11 yr.	19	1 hr.
11 mon.	14	38 min.	12 yr.	7	3 hr.
2 yr.	7	9 min.	12 yr.	3	3 min.
	11	65 min.		9	2 hr.
2 ½ yr.	4	2 min.	12 yr.	12	2 hr.
4 yr.	6	5 min.	12 yr.	15	1 hr
4 yr.	17	10 hr.	13 yr.	7	24 min
4 yr.	26	24 hr.	13 yr.	8	2 ½ hr.
7 yr.	7	3 hr.	13 yr.	9	8 hr.
8 yr.	8	2 hr.	13 yr.	3	70 sec.
9 yr.	7	68 min.		11	8 hr
10 yr.	9	52 min.		26	24 hr.
10 yr.	14	24 hr.	14 yr.	11	4 hr.

Here is Kinsey's description of what happened with the children who were manipulated into orgasm:

---

[27] Reisman & Muir (1990)

- Extreme tension with violent convulsion
- Gasping, eyes staring
- Mouth distorted, sometimes with tongue protruding
- Whole body or parts of it spasmodically twitching
- Throbs or violent jerking of the penis
- Groaning, sobbing or more violent cries
- Masochistic (deriving sexual gratification from one's own pain or humiliation) reactions
- Frenzied movements
- Extreme trembling
- Loss of colour
- Fainting
- Pain or frightened
- Some would fight away from the "partner" (pedophile?) making violent attempts to avoid climax

> Kinsey claimed that the results of homosexual masturbation of young boys – sometimes for 24 hours at a time – is a valuable way to learn about childhood sexuality.

Kinsey's claim again: *homosexual masturbation of young boys is a valuable way to learn about childhood sexuality!* According to Kinsey, Table 34 is alleged to document "*typical cases" of the orgasmic potential* of male infants and children, yet these behaviours are direct expressions of intense pain and suffering.[28]

KINSEY'S MALE STUDY CONCLUSIONS

I had to read this material over a couple of times before the impact of the information worked its way through my state of shock.

According to Pomeroy,[29] Kinsey's own research had produced some material about adolescent male fertility (actively collecting sperm); and reported that there were mature sperm even in the first ejaculation!

Kinsey's evaluation was that

these children derive definite pleasure from the situation[30].

[28] Perry (2003 p. 13)
[29] Reisman & Eichel (1990); Pomeroy (1972 p. 315)
[30] Reisman & Eichel (1990); Kinsey (1948 p. 161)

He declared that

sexuality is a component present in the human animal from earliest infancy[31].

He further held that *younger pre*-adolescents needed the help of older, more experienced persons to discover masturbatory techniques that are sexually effective. What he's stating here is that pedophilia is good for the child! We can only conclude that Kinsey considered these examples of child molestation to be scientifically legitimate, and for decades his conclusions went unchallenged.

What kind of an individual could come to this conclusion after witnessing what happened to these children? Yet, this is the very person our society looks up to as an expert on sexuality! These assumptions now pervade our governments, and, in particular, the sex-education programs in our schools.

Existing evidence highlights how a group of men, hand-picked by Kinsey, were coerced into delinquency and even blatant criminality. Kinsey's strong, authoritarian approach to his team ensured their obedience. This kind of blind obedience has been documented in research such as the Milgram Experiment.

THE MILGRAM EXPERIMENT

The Milgram Experiment study of 1963[32] focused on the conflict between obedience to authority and personal conscience. Milgram wanted to investigate whether WWII German soldiers were particularly obedient to authority, as their defense suggested at the Nuremberg War Crimes trials. He wanted to see how far people would go in obeying instruction if it involved harming another person.

The conclusion of Milgram's study found that ordinary people are likely to follow orders, given by an authority figure, even to the point of killing an innocent human[33]! When authority was pitted against the subject's moral imperatives against hurting others, even with the victim's screams ringing in their ears, authority won out more often than not[34].

Given such an understanding of human nature helps one understand the power and control Kinsey held over his "research assistants." Such control would silence their concerns or objections about the abuse of children that they were witnessing.

---

[31] Ibid p. 180
[32] McLeod (2007)
[33] Ibid
[34] Milgram (1974)

KINSEY'S FEMALE REPORT

In 1953 Kinsey and his team published their alleged findings on female sexuality. These data resulted from reportedly interviewing over 5,900 girls and women, seven of them under 4 years of age. As with the male study, Kinsey used a non-randomized sample and then attempted to apply the findings to the entire female population.

Kinsey indicated that the achievement of orgasm in women is a learned process. This statement seems incompatible with his prior theory that sexual intercourse and orgasm is something humans do not have to learn[35].

> "Some of the pre-adolescent contacts had provided emotional satisfactions which had conditioned the female for the acceptance of later sexual activities."
> Kinsey, 1953

Two main areas of female child sexuality were examined in his 1953 study:

1. Preadolescent sexual response and orgasm
2. Preadolescent contacts with adult males

Kinsey's Female Study Data
(Female, p 127)

"Table 10. Accumulative Incidence: Pre-Adolescent Orgasm from Any Source"

AGE	% OF TOTAL SAMPLE	CASES
3	-	*5908
5	2	5862
7	4	5835
9	6	5772
10	8	5,76 2

*UNEXPLAINED FLUCTUATING SAMPLE SIZE

Adapted from Reisman, 2003, pg 154

According to Reisman & Fink,[36] the Kinsey team used the same three research methods identified in the male section:

1. Recalled information in interviews
2. Interviews with children
3. Direct observation of and experimentation on children

---

[35] Reisman & Eichel (1990 p. 63)
[36] Reisman & Fink (1990 p. 58)

Kinsey further stated that some of the pre-adolescent contacts *"had provided emotional satisfactions which had conditioned the female for the acceptance of later sexual activities"* (my emphasis).[37] (Notice he does not call what is happening "sex," instead calling it "contacts," thereby attempting to minimize sexual abuse.)

Kinsey also had a very positive perspective on incest, suggesting that it was a mutually positive experience for both the child and the adult! Kinsey is uninformed (or on the other hand, uncaring) of the devastation of incest. He acknowledges the effects as "complications," but blames them on parental overreaction as well as law enforcement and societal "hysteria."

Most abuse survivors that have traversed through the immeasurably complex and painful healing process necessary to recover from the horror of incest have never disclosed the abuse to parents, nor told police. Kinsey continually pressed to make his work socially acceptable—and he succeeded.

Reisman & Fink[38] relate that Kinsey gave details about a three-year-old girl who was observed during masturbation and subsequent orgasm. He also reported on an orgasm of a female baby of four months of age. This seems to be the only information given about the seven girls under four years of age in Kinsey's female study.

One of the sections of the Female Report was entitled Preadolescent Contacts with Adult Males. Notice again the wording, used previously in describing his team of "trained persons." He indicates that 75% of these preadolescent girls had sexual activity with adult males. His term *sexual activity is a misnomer;* it was *sexual abuse,* yet Kinsey was determined to minimize its effect and naturalize "sexual activity" in pre-adolescence!

Kinsey's criteria for sex offender may also shock some of you. The male had to be over 15 and at least 5 years older than the victim at the time of the incident. This would mean that an 8-year-old girl who was raped by a 13-year-old boy would not have been classified as a victim of sexual abuse; instead it would be just adolescent sex play. Does that sit well with you?

Another of Kinsey's distortions is that in the case of repeated "sexual activity" (abuse and incest) it was the child who had become interested and therefore sought out the 'activity'! He calls this sexual abuse "repetitions of the experience."[39]

Well-documented and well-researched studies in attachment theory[40] show a very different perspective of what happens to a child who experiences sexual

---

[37] Kinsey (1953 p. 115)
[38] Reisman & Fink (1990 p. 64)
[39] Ibid (75)
[40] Eagle (2013)

activity in their early life. Attachment theory has long recognized the need for early childhood trust and security in the parental or caregiver relationship. Childhood sexual abuse disrupts secure attachment; this finding is counter-intuitive to Kinsey's research as it highlights the consequential behavioural reactions of children after being abused.

STOCKHOLM SYNDROME

Stockholm syndrome could be used to describe what happened to some of these children. This syndrome came to the forefront of public awareness after the kidnapping of Patty Hearst in 1974. Patty herself seemed to become a willing participant in a robbery. Her lawyer used the defence of brainwashing or "Stockholm Syndrome." This syndrome is now often used to describe the seemingly irrational feeling of protection and/or association that some captives develop for their captors. Such behaviour is often observed in incest survivors who attempt to protect their parent, due to the deep desire to be loved—even though the cost of such "love" is repeated sexual abuse.

KINSEY'S STANCE

Kinsey has been identified as anti-female and anti-child in his manner and treatment of this group, whether it was with female staff, participants in the study, or even his own wife. His posture was one of personal self-fulfillment, no matter the cost to anyone else, and especially to women and children. He denied the physical damage caused by child rape. Kinsey distanced himself from reality by using innocent scientific terminology that didn't relate to his research in any way.

He acknowledged that some adults did physical damage to children with whom they had attempted sexual "contacts," but indicated that these cases were in a minority and the public should differentiate between them and serious contacts (sex) with other adults who are not likely to do "the child any appreciable harm... if the child's parents do not become disturbed"[41] (emphasis added). He indicated that his data showed only a small number of cases in which physical harm was done to the child. In fact he describes only one case of serious injury, and a

> Kinsey's data showed one clear-cut case of serious injury, and a very few instances of vaginal bleeding, "which however did not appear to do any appreciable damage"!

[41] Reisman & Fink (1990 p. 64)

very few instances of vaginal bleeding, which *according to Kinsey, did not appear to do any appreciable damage!*[42]

It is a well-established fact that young children can be severely injured both physically and psychologically because of rape; and even more extreme is the psychological damage caused by incest. I speak more to this in the chapter on sexual abuse. Clearly Kinsey was fixated on childhood orgasm.

Given the societal norms of the early 1950s, the sexual content of the study would have made it extremely difficult for Kinsey to come up with a representative sample on which to base his findings of childhood orgasm.

Kinsey's Girl Masturbation Data
(Female, p, 177 & 180)

AGE	PERCENTAGE	ORGASM
	(table 21, p. 177)	(table 25, p. 80
3	1% (of 5,913)	0% (of 5,913)
5	4% (of 5,8 66)	2% of (5,866)
7	7% (of 5,841)	4% (of 5,838)
10	13% (of 5,808)	8% (of 5,802)
12	19% (of 5,784)	12% (of 5,778)

*Unexplained fluctuating totals

Adaped from Reisman, 2003, p.154

Seven of the girls were directly observed, and according to this table four of these children had experienced orgasm at less than a year of age! It is unimaginable that a child could remember such a thing through recall at this age; therefore these abuses either happened "on-site" with some of Kinsey's experienced "trained staff" (child molesters) or were compiled in the diaries of the pedophiles he interviewed. Whatever the case, do these diaries accurately represent Kinsey's claim of childhood sexuality from infancy onward? Or do they rather point to the effect of pedophilic abuse on the child?

CONTROVERSIAL SEX RESEARCH

To participate in, and observe sex acts, Kinsey took the utmost care in the construction of a soundproof lab at his university, where staff, invited guests and his wife joined him while engaging in sex acts. All the sexual histories of his research subjects were taken within the prison-like confines of this lab. The "lab" was soundproofed to 80 decibels (a level which blocks out rock

---

[42] Ibid (p. 75)

music!)[43] Windows were fitted with metal grills and special locks installed. Such a thorough soundproofing could cover the screams of both adults and children being abused.

Kinsey's assistant, Wardell Pomeroy, stated that Kinsey possessed the ability to observe actual sexual behaviour with objectivity. This is called emotional detachment, which is something that seems to be evident throughout Kinsey's life. Emotional detachment is the shutting off of external emotional reactions. There is an emotional withdrawal from the reality of the situation. The individual often appears distant and unaware of the current emotional reality. Even if Kinsey appeared objectively detached, though, the fact that he participated in his own research would be enough to have his study thrown out of scientific journals today.

Kinsey created video recording studios in both his home and at the university where he recorded some of the earliest videos that documented rape, sexual abuse, and wife swapping.[44] The lack of objectivity was astounding. Included in the research were co-workers, peers, employees, their wives and even the cameraman.

Samuel Stewart (later to become a well-known psychologist) describes a filming at the Kinsey institute where a sadist (someone who derives sexual gratification from inflicting pain or humiliation on others) had handcuffed a masochist (someone who derives sexual gratification from their own pain or humiliation) and burned his nipples with a cigarette. The sadist then took a lit candle and dripped the hot wax onto the other man's genitals, sending him into spasms of anguish.

Pomeroy asserted that *brutality to the genitals can be loving and sexually exciting!*[45] I don't believe such acts of brutality depict feelings of love. Viewing brutality (of any kind) as an act of love likely stems from emotional damage due to earlier violent or sexualized trauma and the subsequent development of a twisted sense of what love is. Many individuals who have been abused as children feel that the abuse is somehow an expression of love from the abuser (especially if the abuser is a parent or relative). It may have been the only time they were touched and held by their parent.

Degradation of both men and women seemed to have been part of Kinsey's protocol. Kinsey's wife was often on duty during these filmings, changing soiled sheets but also engaging in varied forms of sex at her husband's command. Apparently, Kinsey wasn't just an observer, but an active, enthusiastic participant.

---

[43] Resiman & Fink (1990)
[44] Reisman (2013 p. 74)
[45] Reisman (2013 p. 71, 77)

Other areas of interest to Kinsey included

• Bestiality
• Pedophilia
• Group sex

He promoted these as natural sexual "outlets," a word Kinsey used regularly. Remarkably Kinsey excluded 31 females from his study who had copulated with animals, as he deemed them unrepresentative of society. Kinsey's associate, Pomeroy, in his sex education text called *Boys and Sex*, recommends many forms of sexual deviation for children, including bestiality:

Having sex with a male animal, whether it is a dog, horse, bull, or some other species, may provide considerable erotic excitement for the boy or adult…enhanced by the fact that the male animal response to the point of orgasm…animal reactions may become of considerable significance… in no point basically different from those that are involved in erotic responses to human situations.[46]

One needs to remember that these studies were compiled in the 1940s and early 50s, when societal norms were vastly different from those we experience today. This was an era largely devoted to upholding the ideal of the nuclear family. The values of morality rooted in the Judeo-Christian tradition began to give way to rising sexual permissiveness, largely a result of Kinsey's sex research. Bestiality, apart from the Kinsey research, had been largely unheard of by the majority of "ordinary folk." This of course doesn't mean it wasn't practised in rare instances; still, societal perception was that this kind of behaviour was a total deviation from natural sexual behaviour. For Pomeroy it was applauded as simply another way to experience sexual pleasure!

Clarence Tripp (research photographer) declares that Kinsey hired him to film 2000 orgasms – heterosexual copulation; masturbation; and significant masochism. Kinsey warned the photographer that filming sex every day would cause him to lose his normal sensitivities. In fact, Kinsey's own sexual obsessions were driving him to deeper depravations to the point where he circumcised himself with a pocket knife without sedation![47]

[46] Reisman (2003)
[47] Reisman & Fink (1990)

YORKSHIRE TELEVISION INVESTIGATION

Yorkshire Television, a British television service, produced a 1998 documentary called "Secret History: Kinsey's Paedophiles"[48] (available on YouTube). This disturbing documentary provides a strong case against Kinsey, suggesting that he and his colleagues courted pedophiles and it was their crimes he presented as scientific data! Yet to this date little has been done to rectify the results of his study. In fact, Kinsey's perceptions have gained ever-increasing momentum in the new millennium.

The documentary features Jonathan Gathorne-Hardy, James Jones (Kinsey biographers); critic Judith Reisman; Kinsey colleagues Vincent Nowlis, Paul Gebhard and Clarence Tripp; and John Bancroft, Kinsey Institute director. Kinsey's colleagues believed his anger toward Christianity (and an apparently strict father) fueled his research. It is definitely worth listening to this entire documentary, but perhaps Vincent Nowlis's admission, partway through the documentary, that Kinsey groomed children for homosexual sex solidifies much of what I have stated about Kinsey's homosexual obsessions.

Much of Kinsey's research material seems to have come from "Mr. Green," a U.S. federal government land surveyor whose real name was Rex King. The Kinsey Institute continues to refuse to release Green's diaries, filled with extreme child sexual abuse, declaring that they are confidential. According to Pomeroy in his book, *Dr. Kinsey and the Institute for Sex Research,*[49] King raped at least 800 infants, children, kin and strangers.

Clarence Tripp, writer and researcher for Alfred Kinsey, offers this supposed justification for the experiences of girls (and boys) being abused by a man named King from whom Kinsey received "research" data:

> The children thought he was wonderful… There was no force, no damage, no harm, no pain… Well there were two instances in which a young boy or girl—I think it was a girl—agreed to sexual contact, but then they found it very painful and yelled out when it actually took place. This was because they were very young and had small genitalia and [King] was a grown man with enormous genitalia and there was a fit problem. (emphasis mine)

According to another Kinsey associate, Paul Gebhard:

---

[48] Tate (1998)
[49] Pomeroy (1972)

King had sex with men, women, children and animals… nursery school people… parents… couldn't give us the extraordinary detail that [King] did. It was illegal and we knew it was illegal and that's why a lot of people are furious… they say we should have turned him in instantly… if we had turned him in it would have been the end of our research project.

When interviewed in the Yorkshire documentary (1998), Tripp describes Kinsey as wanting to see everything; he wanted to validate it. This included personally observing King's sex with children! This was again validated by Gathorne-Hardy on the Yorkshire Television interview.

In the Yorkshire documentary, Gebhard stated that the Kinsey team asked prisons for lists of those with a "pedophilia charge and we'd go after him." There was also a pedophile organization that cooperated.[50] Further on is a description of a German man who offered Kinsey his own history of pedophilia. This man was Dr. Fritz von Balluseck, a former senior Nazi party official who during the war commanded a ghetto in a Nazi-occupied Polish town. During this time and the years that followed, he sexually abused hundreds of pre-adolescent girls and boys, recording his experiences in diaries. He claimed to have "masturbated and penetrated the children to assist their sexual development—much the same theory as Kinsey himself adhered to."[51] As a Nazi commander, he had complete access and absolute authority to abuse and torture Jewish children. Von Balluseck's diaries had been sent to Kinsey. After the murder of one of von Balluseck's victims, Interpol and the FBI became interested in the diaries upon finding von Balluseck's correspondence with Kinsey. Although these agencies put an enormous amount of pressure on Kinsey to disclose the diaries, he refused, stating he would destroy it before he would let them have it! At von Balluseck's trial, even the judge criticized Kinsey's lack of cooperation.

Kinsey claimed, as I previously mentioned, that pedophilia was an almost non-existent crime and the thing he hated the most was the paranoia surrounding child molestation. He claimed that this paranoia does the child more damage for life than all the pedophiles in the world would do[52]! His claim doesn't change the fact that while some boys who are groomed to willingly participate in sexual activities may seem to somewhat adjust to sexual abuse, the vast majority face lifelong complications from childhood sexual abuse,[53] such as reduced quality

---

[50] Tate (1998, at 31 min.)

[51] Ibid (at 32:30 min.)

[52] Ibid (at 47:10 min)

[53] Fergusson, Lynskey & Horwood (1996)

of life, impaired social relationships, less than optimal daily functioning and tremendous grief over the loss of childhood, leading to self-destructive behaviours such as cutting and attempted suicide. [54]

As noted previously, children who have been sexually abused can wrestle with a distorted sense of love that may seem like "adjustment to the abuse." The reality is that their childhood confusion can lead to a lifetime of self-punishment through addictive behaviours, primarily with drugs, alcohol, sexual deviance and sexual addictions. This "adjustment" to sexual abuse is what groups like NAMBLA have

> "Sex before 8 or else it's too late."
> NABMLA

sought to achieve through their support of the Rene Guyon Society (a national association promoting legislation permitting adults to have sex with children), whose motto is "sex before 8 or it's too late."[55] This group (and others like it) acknowledges the significant impact Kinsey's research had in furthering their movement. They admonish members to hold Kinsey's work dear and see it implicit to the struggle they fight.[56]

Moira Greyland, sexually abused daughter of LGBT parents, believes that what sets the gay culture apart from straight culture is the belief that early sex is good and beneficial, and the sure knowledge that the only way to produce another homosexual is to provide a boy with sexual experiences before he can be "ruined" by attraction to a girl.[57]

This chapter has concentrated on the work of Alfred Kinsey and his associates in order to expose his research bias; his skewed and unsubstantiated research; and his chief purpose: to redirect cultural thought on sexuality. Kinsey's personal life of obvious adultery, bi-sexual promiscuity and sadomasochistic tendencies became the catalyst for his biased research.

Kinsey's manipulation and coercion of people is unprecedented in his field; his sexual abuse of children unimaginable; his uncensored findings, and the blind acceptance of his work by academia and the media, are astonishing.

The data and the emotional reactions of the children Kinsey used as proverbial "guinea pigs" are repulsive, and yet they remain largely unquestioned. His declaration that infants and young children derived definite pleasure from the masturbation and rape they were subjected to, while at the same time documenting their deep distress and pain, is beyond comprehension.

---

[54] Valente (2005)
[55] Plummer (1991 p. 234)
[56] Reisman, McAlister, & Gallagher (2016)
[57] Greyland (2018 p. 5581)

The material in this chapter is profoundly disturbing for parents and other members of the public alike, but it has remained undisclosed to the very people it affects in the greatest way. Kinsey's goal of ripping apart long-held beliefs has been accomplished. In doing so, he has opened the door to his interests of bestiality, pedophilia, and group sex. Kinsey's research, and the subsequent media propaganda, have been consumed by the masses.

I will be discussing more on how this sexual revolution has become a rushing river, affecting government, law, media and education, and plunging us further into cultural chaos.

CHAPTER 2

The Widening Stream: Childhood Sexual Abuse

WHAT IS CHILD SEXUAL ABUSE?

CHILD SEXUAL ABUSE OCCURS WHEN AN ADULT USES A CHILD FOR HIS OR her own sexual pleasure and gratification. Under the Age of Majority and Accountability Act, the Children's Law Reform Act, and the Divorce Act, one is considered an adult at the age of eighteen. In limited situations a sixteen-year-old may be considered an adult.[58] A child may also be sexually abused by another child or adolescent. Both boys and girls can be abused from a young age, although it would seem that the sexual abuse of boys is even more under-reported than that of girls.[59]

Sexual abuse of children includes:
- Sexual touching – including penetration with object
- Masturbation between adults and children
- Vaginal or anal intercourse
- Oral/genital contact or sex
- Indecent exposure/flashing
- Use of children in pornographic films or photographs
- Showing children pornographic films or photographs
- Encouraging or forcing children to prostitute themselves
- Encouraging or forcing children to witness sexual acts

---

[58] Feldstein (2015)
[59] Lab, Feigenbaum, & De Silva (2000)

As we are looking at definitions let me continue with a few more. One aspect of sexual abuse is conditioning by the act of *grooming*. This is a relatively new term which has been defined as the following:

> A course of conduct enacted by a suspected pedophile; which would give a reasonable person cause for concern that any meeting with a child arising from the conduct would be for unlawful purposes.[60]

PEDOPHILIA

It should come as no surprise that there has been a pattern of gradual normalization of adult/child sexual relations over the past several decades. Central to the sexualization of children has been the current obsession to alter societal attitudes toward adult/child sexual relationships. I believe the rise in child sexual abuse over the last decades and current explosion of young girls being sold as sex slaves may be the tip of the iceberg in exposing the buried aquifer of pedophilia.

The Merriam-Webster[61] dictionary describes pedophilia as a "sexual perversion in which children are the preferred sexual object"; *specifically* it is "a **psychiatric disorder** in which an adult has sexual fantasies about or engages in sexual acts with a prepubescent child."

According to *Psychology Today*,[62] pedophilia is considered a type of paraphilia: a condition in which a person's sexual arousal and gratification depend on fantasizing about and engaging in sexual behaviour that is atypical and extreme. Pedophilia is defined as fantasized or actual sexual activity with children who are **generally thirteen years or younger**. Pedophiles are usually men, and can be attracted to either or both sexes.

Pedophilic Disorder is a DSM-5 (Diagnostic and Statistical Manual of Mental Disorders, fifth edition) diagnosis assigned to adults (defined as age sixteen and up) who have sexual desire for prepubescent children.[63]

Symptoms
For pedophilic disorder to be diagnosed, the following criteria must be met:

- Recurrent, intense sexual fantasies, urges or behaviours involving sexual activity with a prepubescent child (generally thirteen years or younger) for a period of at least six months.

---

[60] Craven, Brown, & Gilchrist (2007)
[61] https://www.merriam-webster.com/dictionary/pedophilia
[62] Psychology Today, 2018
[63] American Psychiatric Association (2013)

• These sexual urges have been acted on or cause clinically significant distress or impairment in social, occupational or other important areas of functioning.

• The person is at least age sixteen and at least five years older than the child in the first category. However, this does not include an individual in late adolescence involved in an ongoing sexual relationship with a twelve- or thirteen-year-old.[64]

An individual must either act on their sexual urges or experience significant distress as a result of their urges or fantasies. Without these two criteria, a person maybe considered to have a *pedophilic sexual orientation* but not pedophilic disorder.

The prevalence of pedophilic disorder is unknown, but is estimated at 3–5%.[65] The prevalence in the female population is thought to be a small fraction of the prevalence among males. An estimated twenty percent of American children have been sexually molested, making pedophilia a common paraphilia, even though the prevalence rate of pedophilia is supposedly only 3–5%.[66] Between 2009 and 2014, there were 19,292 police-reported incidents of sexual offences against children in Canada. The majority (70%) of sexual offences were against children and youth.[67]

Child victims thirteen years of age and younger were three times more likely than victims aged fourteen and older to have been sexually assaulted by a family member (52% versus 15%). Also, children were less likely to have been sexually assaulted by a stranger than older victims (5% versus 16%). This was true whether the child victim was male or female.[68]

Of sexual assaults involving a charged accused who met the age-based criteria for pedophilia, over half (55%) of child victims were sexually assaulted by a family member. By comparison, less than one in five (17%) sexual assaults in the non-pedophile group were perpetrated by a family member of the victim. Sexual assaults involving child victims who were victimized by a family member that met the age-based criteria for pedophilia included extended family like uncles, cousins, or grandparents (21%), parents (13%), step-parents (9%), and other immediate family members (9%). Male victims accounted for a larger proportion

[64] Ibid
[65] Ibid
[66] Ibid
[67] Rotenberg (2017)
[68] Ibid

of children sexually assaulted by a pedophile. Male children sexually assaulted by a pedophile were more likely than female children to have been victimized by someone in a position of authority (14% versus 7%).[69]

A pedophile is a person who sexually abuses children. There are no typical pedophiles. They do not look different from other people. They don't carry signs declaring their deviance. They can be found in all professions at all levels of society and can sometimes hold respected and powerful positions in the community – you'll read more about this further along. They can come from any racial or religious background, and more commonly than not are related to or known by the victim or their family. Pedophiles may act alone or organize themselves into groups which may operate within a local community, nationally or internationally. In such groups, children and child pornography are passed between members. These associations have gained momentum in recent years with the easy access of internet and the relative safety from exposure it brings.

Pedophiles are often very good at making friends with children quickly and can appear warm and approachable. They often come across as "nice men." This enables them to get close to children, something they will go to great lengths to do. They are manipulative and sophisticated in how they attach themselves to families. Women pedophiles up to this point have been considered to be a rarity.

Although the terms grooming and pedophile may be relatively new to some, the behaviour is not. Let me share again the statement of Pomeroy (Kinsey's associate) that I highlighted in chapter one. Pomeroy has the mindset of a pedophile!

> Incest between adults and younger children can also prove satisfying and enriching experience. Incestuous relationships can – and do work out well – we find many beautiful and mutually satisfying relationships between fathers and daughters. These may be transient or ongoing, but they have no harmful effects (!)[70]

As can be expected, the consequence of such a belief has become a raging river. Dr. T. Sandfort, formerly of the Gay and Lesbian Studies department, University of Utrecht, was also former president of the Dutch Society of Sexology and the International Academy of Sex. He is currently Professor of Clinical Sociomedical Sciences (in Psychiatry) at Columbia University.

---

[69] Ibid
[70] Pomeroy (1976 p. 10)

Sandfort stresses that:

Sexual contacts between pedophiles and young males did not have a negative influence on boys' wellbeing and that the problems arose because of the reactions of parents and legal authorities![71]

Let me continue with Sandfort: "It can be expected that when the boundaries around the nuclear family disappear, children will more readily accept emotional ties with adults other than their parents."[72] This statement sounds very similar to Kinsey's mindset.

In a 1980 article in the Sex Information and Education Council of the US (SIECUS) Report, R. Hawkins states: "most pedophiles (people who are sexually interested in minor children) ...are *gentle and affectionate* and are not dangerous in the way child molesters are stereotypically considered to be"[73] (emphasis added). "Nice men" is the term used above to describe these pedophiles. These people come across as "gentle, affectionate, nice men" in order to groom vulnerable children for sexual exploits that are totally focused on the man achieving his desire for sexual pleasure, and initiating the child into the world of sex so that they can become easily manipulated.

> "It can be expected that when the boundaries around the nuclear family disappear, children will more readily accept emotional ties with adults other than their parents." Sandfort

In the early 1990s, Dutch law advocate Edward Brongersma assured a student body that it was only a matter of time before legislation would be passed in the Netherlands – and throughout the world – which would be more liberal toward pedophilic relationships[74]. Brongersma went on to write a book entitled *Intergenerational Intimacy.*[75] [More on this in chapter eight.]

Sexual abuse in all its forms has been around for centuries. Children have been victims without a voice throughout history. Certainly no one was listening to the children of the Kinsey sex research study. After all, who would listen to a child? It's time we listen!

---

[71] Masters, Johnson, & Kolodny (1995 p. 84)
[72] Ibid
[73] Reisman & Eichel (1990 p. 134)
[74] Reisman & Eichel (1990 p. 133)
[75] Sandford, Brongersma, & van Naerssem (1991)

HOW VULNERABLE ARE OUR CHILDREN?

In the U.S. over 45 million children ages 10-17 use the internet. Of these:

- One in 4 has encountered unwanted pornography
- One in 5 has been sexually solicited
- One in 17 was threatened or harassed in the past year
- One in 33 received an aggressive sexual solicitation (was asked to meet someone in person, called on the phone, and/or sent correspondence or gifts) in the past year
- Nearly 60 percent have received an e-mail or instant message from a stranger and half responded to the stranger's message[76]

TARGETING CHILDREN

Abusers rarely pick children at random. They are skilled at identifying children who may be vulnerable. They may choose a child who is:

- Too trusting
- Seeking love or affection
- Lonely or bereaved
- Lacking in confidence
- Bullied
- Disabled or unable to communicate well
- In care or away from home
- Already a victim of abuse
- Eager to succeed in activities such as sport, school, or other interests

GROOMING CHILDREN

Pedophiles will often carefully introduce or "groom" children through a progression of activities, including introducing children to pornography. "Innocent" cuddling may turn into sexual touching or masturbation, which then can lead to sexual intercourse.

Abusers may groom a child by:

- Forming a friendly relationship with the child and his/her parents or caregivers
- Taking a strong interest in the child or his/her activities

---

[76] San Diego District Attorney (n.d.)

- Offering the child gifts, money or favours such as sweets, video games, day trips and holidays; illicit gifts may also be offered, including alcohol, cigarettes or drugs
- Telling the child that what is happening is not wrong

MAKING SURE CHILDREN KEEP THE ABUSE A SECRET

Sexual abusers will use many methods to ensure a child does not disclose the abuse. They use a child's natural fear, embarrassment, guilt, and shame, as well as threats of punishment, injury or death to the child or someone the child loves. Many threaten to kill the child or their parent(s) in order to keep them silent. It is often a parent or step-parent who is the abuser, so these threats are taken very seriously by the child, attempting to protect the other parent who in many situations is often unaware of what is happening to their child.

CYBER SEXPLOITATION

Communication technologies have the ability to alter restrictions on victims on three levels: accessibility, opportunity and vulnerability. The internet affords greater opportunity for adults or adolescents with a sexual interest in children to gain access to children even while the child is at home with his/her parents.

Mobile devices enable abusers to schedule contact with children; the limited amount of control that may be afforded by parents keeping a computer in the living room is essentially removed if children are accessing the internet via mobile devices. This in turn makes the child increasingly vulnerable.

Let's look at the patterns for Internet exploitation:

- Friendship-forming stage; relationship-forming stage
- Risk assessment stage; exclusivity stage
- Sexual stage; child erotica and child pornographic image creation and exchange
- Fantasy enactment; damage limitation (to reduce risk of child telling others)[77]

Gentle pressure is applied, and a sense of mutuality is maintained by the adult acting "repentant" if the child begins to feel uncomfortable, which in turn promotes greater trust of the child for a period, until the abuser determines he/she has enough "hold" on the child to proceed to their desired end.[78]

---

[77] Batty (2003)
[78] Craven, Brown, & Gilchrist (2007)

INDICATORS OF CHILD ABUSE

It is important that parents and educators be aware of the indicators of child abuse.[79] Although they may never encounter it, being prepared will ensure quick assistance for the child. The following tables contain many symptoms. A child suffering from sexual abuse usually shows several of the following.

Physiological Indicators of Sexual Abuse

Gastrointestinal disturbance	Difficulty in walking or sitting
Torn, stained or bloody underclothing	Unexplained bruises, lacerations, redness, swelling or bleeding in the genital, vaginal or anal areas.
Blood in urine or stools	Pain or itching in genital areas
Complaints of genital or rectal pain	Pain experienced in elimination
Sexually transmitted disease	Pregnancy

Emotional and Behavioural Indicators of Sexual Abuse in the Young Child

Becomes frantic when diaper is changed	Is hyperactive	Is disruptive and/or demanding	Shows unhappiness by crying or being unduly anxious
Displays regressive behaviour – returning to younger, more babyish behaviour, i.e.: thumb sucking, bed wetting, soiling, baby talk, etc.	Protests suddenly or continuously when left with someone he/she knows	Has sleep disturbances – fear of the dark, fear of going to bed, screaming, phobias, hysteria	Attempts sexual behaviour with other children, toys, or animals, and may act in an angry, aggressive, or controlling fashion
Has a short attention span or displays lack of attention	Is clinging or excessively dependent	Is preoccupied "in a dream world"	Inserts objects into the vagina or rectum
Behaves in an overly compliant manner	Has a change or loss of appetite	Shows unusual and exaggerated interest in people's bodies	Is inappropriately affectionate toward strangers
Suddenly resistant to going to a specific place, i.e.: school, babysitter	Unable to concentrate at school	Has a fear of a particular area of the house or a particular family member	Poor peer relationships
At play, explicitly mimics sexual activities	Draws sexualized pictures	Has non-specific physical complaints	Hints or states he/she has been abused
Afraid to remove clothing for gym class; refuses to use toilet facilities away from home May act out with sexual approaches that appear to be sexually provocative behaviour with adults	Displays unusual interest in or preoccupation with sexual acts or language beyond developmentally appropriate level	Girls may show seductive behaviour with males Wears excessive amounts of clothing	Poor self-image and lacks self-esteem Does not trust significant others

---

[79] Finkelhor (1993)

Psychosocial Indicators for the Older Child

Loses friends	Has academic problems	Is unable to concentrate	Is truant
Withdraws, both from activities and others	Has recurrent physical complaints that are without physiological basis: headaches, sore throat, abdominal pain, nausea	Does not trust people, particularly those in close relationships	Engages in self-destructive behaviour: drug/alcohol abuse, cutting/burning, suicide attempts
Is unable to "have fun"	Suffers from clinical depression	Has suicidal feelings or behaviour	Unable to sleep
Unable to eat or overeats excessively	Acts out or behaves aggressively	Makes unusual statements that only make sense in a sexual context	Sudden loss of interest in self: change in personal hygiene
Hints or states he/she has been abused	Sudden interest in sexual activity, pregnancy, or sexually transmitted diseases	Acts out sexually or engages in prostitution	

Childhood traumas—such as neglect, physical and sexual abuse—have more long-lasting psychological effects than other traumatic experiences. Such traumatic experiences also tend to leave children more vulnerable to further victimization in their teen and adult years. In these cases, not only is the individual dealing with past childhood abuse, but often continuing to be abused throughout life (i.e. rape/domestic abuse). Survivors frequently lack the ability to set appropriate boundaries, since saying "no" was often not an option in childhood. Unless they are able to connect with secure, confident individuals who can mentor them, they are unlikely to develop healthy boundaries on their own.[80]

Among young women participating in a 2008 study, those describing themselves as "mostly heterosexual" reported higher rates of childhood sexual abuse (nearly half) than did those describing themselves as a heterosexual.[81] These are adolescents and young women who do not want to identify as bisexual but seem to "dabble" in same-sex encounters.

The prevalence of police-reported sexual offences against children and youth varies across the country.[82] Like crime in general,[83] rates of sexual offences

---

[80] Polusny & Follette (1995)
[81] Austin et al (2008)
[82] Cotter & Beaupré (2012)
[83] Perreault (2013)

against children and youth were highest in the territories in 2012. The following statistics are derived from the Canadian Incidence Study of Reported Child Sexual Abuse and Neglect.[84] The Northwest Territories (895 per 100,000 children and youth) and Nunavut (878 per 100,000) recorded the highest rates in Canada in 2008, followed by Yukon (514 per 100,000).

Child and youth victims of sexual offences by province

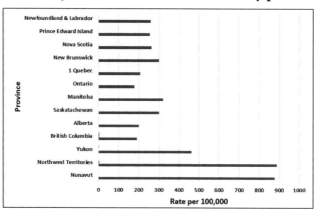

Based on police-reported data, very young children were usually victimized by a family member, while older children were most frequently victimized by an acquaintance or stranger. For those aged 0 to 3 years, a family member was the accused person for two-thirds (66%) of victims. Incest is more common when there are pre-adolescent children in the home.[85]

The involvement of family members as accused persons decreased with age, reaching 19% for victims aged 16 to 17 years. For a larger proportion of male victims than female victims, the offence is delayed in coming to the attention of police. Of the sexual offences that came to the attention of police in 2012, two-thirds (67%) of those involving a male child or youth victim occurred during 2012, while three-quarters (76%) of those involving a female child or youth victim occurred in that year. When children and youth were the victims of a sexual offence, the accused was frequently someone close to their age.

As I read the description of charges, two items stood out to me: corrupting children, and making sexually explicit material available to children. How will such charges play out in the future as our elementary schools become

---

[84] Trocmé et al (2008)
[85] Cotter & Beaupré (2012)

more open to depicting graphic images and sex toys to younger and younger children?[86]

SEXUAL ABUSE STATISTICS:

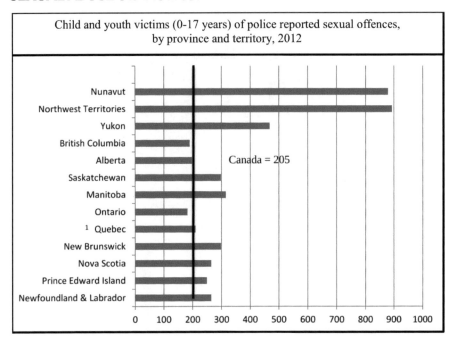

Child and youth victims (0-17 years) of police reported sexual offences, by province and territory, 2012

This chart excludes a small number of victims whose age was unknown but miscoded as 0[1]. The sexual offen this chart include aggravated sexual assault, sexual assault with a weapon or causing bodily harm, sexual assa sexual interference, invitation to sexual touching, sexual exploitation, sexual exploitation of a person with a disability, incest, corrupting children, making sexually explicit material available to children, luring a child via a computer, anal intercourse, bestiality (commit/compel/incite), and voyeurism.
(Statistics Canada, 2012)

- 1 in 4 girls and 1 in 6 boys is sexually abused in some way by the age of 18[87]
- 10% of those children are preschoolers
- 85-90% involve a perpetrator known to the child
- 35% involve a family member
- 50% of all assaults take place in the home of the child or the offender
- The average offender is involved with over 70 children in his or her "career" of offending[88]

---

[86] Cotter & Beaupré (2012)
[87] Finkelhor (1979)
[88] HALT (2012)

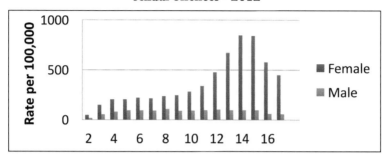

Canadian child and youth victims (0-17) of police-reported sexual offences - 2012

Offenses include aggravated sexual assault, sexual assault with a weapon or causing bodily harm, sexual assault, sexual interference, invitation to sexual touching, sexual exploitation, corrupting children, making sexually explicit material available to children, luring a child via computer, anal intercourse, bestiality (committing/compelling/inciting), and voyeurism

(Statistics Canada, 2012)

LONG-LASTING EFFECTS

Another psychological effect suffered by the individual who is abused is dissociation. I discuss this at length in my book on complex trauma[89], but will briefly recount the facts that are pertinent to our discussion on abuse.

Continuum of Dissociation

Normal Consciousness	Dissociative Episode	Acute Stress / PTSD, CTSD Disorder (under 4 wks) (4 wks +)	Dissociative Disorder	Dissociative Identity Disorder (DID)
Highway Hypnosis	Religious Experiences	Flashbacks Numbness, Detachment	Dissociative Amnesia	DID
Ego States	(e.g., Meditation, Ecstatic Experiences)	Absence of Emotional Response	Dissociative Fugue	Poly-Fragmented DID
Automatisms		Reduced Awareness of Surroundings	Dissociative Trance Disorder	
Childhood Imagery		De-realization	Possession Trance Disorder	
Absorption/ Daydreaming		De-personalization Amnesia for Aspects of Trauma		

[89] Gillies (2016)

The Diagnostic and Statistical Manual of Mental Disorders, 5th Edition,[90] describes dissociation as "a disruption of and/or discontinuity in the normal integration of consciousness, memory, identity, emotion, perception, body representation, motor control and behaviour."

Most dissociative symptoms are linked to a history of trauma. Some dissociative responses seem to be connected with childhood neglect experiences and/or insecure attachment with primary caregivers.[91] As you can see by the chart "Continuum of Dissociation" below, we all experience mild levels of dissociation from time to time. What children (and adults) who have experienced chronic sexual abuse exhibit are the symptoms found under the CTSD, Dissociative Disorder and DID sections.

This can become a debilitating condition in the lives of those who already have so many hurdles to jump. Successful therapy is that which helps the individual identify triggers that touch off a dissociative experience. Exposure therapy then allows the person to process the experience and emotion connected to the memories. Much time will need to be invested by abuse survivors to grieve the losses of childhood.

WHAT SHOULD I DO IF MY CHILD TELLS ME HE/SHE HAS BEEN ABUSED?

Although you may feel shock, it is important to try to put your feelings aside for the moment (you'll have much to process later!). The following suggestions are guidelines.

- Listen
- You will be upset by what your child has told you, but try not to react in a way which may add to your child's distress
- Your child needs to know that he/she is not to blame and you should make it clear that you do not doubt what he/she says
- Allow your child the opportunity to talk about what has happened, but do not put any pressure on him/her to do so
- Tell your child that he/she was right to talk to you. Don't tell him/her off if the abuse occurred because he/she disobeyed you – for example, your child was walking in a place which you had told him/her to avoid.
- You will need to contact authorities: either the police or CAS immediately

---

[90] American Psychiatric Association (2013 p. 291)
[91] Harari, Bakermans-Kranenburg, & Van Ijzendoorn (2007); Ogawa et al (1977)

It will be important that you seek emotional and spiritual support during this time. Processing your own emotions surrounding the event(s) will help the child. It's likely that police will press charges, at which point you could become embedded in the justice system. One thing I learned from my own experience: never take the outcome for granted even if the crown attorney says it's a slam dunk! Also in the case of abuse, I believe it's wise to have a jury, rather than just a judge.

HOW CAN I KEEP MY CHILD SAFE?

The very best safeguard is creating a secure attachment from birth forward. There will be more regarding this aspect in the chapter on Attachment. Basically, secure attachment involves building a safe relationship where your child knows they are loved unconditionally. Here are some suggestions:

- Make time for your children
- Build an open and trusting relationship
- Always listen carefully to their fears and concerns and let them know they should not be worried about telling you anything
- Remember the three W-s: know
  - *where* your children are
  - *who* they are with
  - and agree on a time *when* they should return.
- Ensure that your children always know where you are, as well as how and where you can be contacted
- Be alert to any adult who is paying an unusual amount of attention to your children or buying them sweets, expensive gifts, video or computer games, etc.
- Be cautious about anyone who has unsupervised contact with your children and find out as much as possible about anyone who is looking after them
- Your children need to know what is and what is not "appropriate" touching. Do not be too embarrassed to talk about this; you must help them to understand what unacceptable behaviour is and that they must always tell you if anyone, including a relative or friend, is behaving in a way which worries them.
- Teach your children to feel confident to refuse to do anything which they feel is wrong or frightens them.

- Explain to your children the difference between "good" and "bad" secrets. Tell them, for example, that it is OK to have a secret about a surprise birthday party, but not about anything which makes them feel unhappy or uncomfortable.

As we look at the subject of childhood sexual abuse, it becomes clear that there is an underlying insidious agenda. Stemming from the records of Alfred Kinsey's research, this agenda has treacherously left its mark in the lives of children, who have simply become avenues of pleasure to those consumed with the concept of infant and childhood sexuality.

I have scarcely touched on the tremendous effect of sexual abuse on a child. To do so would require another book. Suffice it to say, the immediate and long-term consequences to the psyche are in many cases irreparable, and they predispose children and adolescents to long-term mental health concerns, relationship issues, and sexual promiscuity.

Childhood sexual abuse, instead of dissipating in the past decades as we have learned more about its long-term effects, has instead continued to rise. I suggest that unless there is a quick, dramatic change in our cultural mind-set we will see an explosion of the sexual abuse of our children. Given the immense increase of mental health issues in children and adolescents over the past decade, it makes me wonder if this is not already happening. As we have embraced a culture that encourages sexual activity with children, how much easier it will now be for parents, relatives, and friends to cross this generational line. Are we now reaping the consequences of what has been sown for the past several decades?

CHAPTER 3

Rushing Rivers:
The Indoctrination of Our Children

IN 2016 THE OXFORD DICTIONARY WORD OF THE YEAR WAS…

Post Truth: relating to or denoting circumstances in which objective facts are less influential in shaping public opinion than appeals to emotion and personal belief.[92]

This has become an era of the denial of truth, denial of science, and denial of reason.

Truth has become subservient and subject to how a person feels.

ONCE UPON A TIME…sex education was a simple biology lesson. It was non-confusing. You are a boy—I am a girl! Children were taught the facts of life. Sex was part of something bigger – far grander – called marriage. For the millennial generation, marriage is a strange word, and unmarried but committed couples seem as solid as married couples. I am far from alone in asserting that marriage is a moral and healthy way to live, and it is a fact that heterosexual marriage is still by far the healthiest lifestyle.[93] A good marriage produces safety, security, intimacy, and increased physical and mental health.[94] It also even

[92] Oxford Dictionaries (2016)
[93] Harvard Health Publications (2010)
[94] Marshall (2004)

provides a place to grow in secure attachment. Many individuals who have been raised in an insecure home environment will find healing and wholeness in a healthy marriage. I am a testament to that.

Once upon a time, not so long ago, certain behaviours were not considered normal and people who practiced them were in need of psychological care and compassion. Most of all, a child's innocence was precious. Now society considers children to be sexual from birth – and that's what we're teaching them. We now have a comprehensive sex education program in our schools that discusses identity, gender, and sexual and reproductive rights.[95]

The American Academy of Child and Adolescent Psychiatry lays out principles for the sex education of children and is clear on what is the healthy way to educate them about sex:

> Parents should respond to the needs and curiosity level of their individual child, offering no more or no less information than their child is asking for and able to understand.[96]

The blatant disregard of the new sex-ed curriculum for well-established principles of respect for a child's personal boundaries when discussing such sensitive issues is shocking. Children as young as eight are being taught in co-ed classes that they have a right to sexual pleasure, birth control and abortion, returning home distraught and confused.

Fifty years ago there were only two sexually transmitted diseases; today there are over two dozen. One doctor states on YouTube: "Expect to have HPV once you become sexually intimate. All of us get it." Do you and/or your friends have HPV? Perhaps if you're under 40 and promiscuous, but for the majority of the population the answer is "no!" But because a doctor said it, it must be true! Materials given to children today would make most adults blush – nothing is taboo. Behaviours once considered "deviant" are now called good and normal!

The terms husband and wife, parent, mom or dad are no longer being used. In fact, last week when my son went to register his daughter for school, he was given several options – none of which said parent, mother or father! He struck them all out and wrote *parent*. That's who I am, he told the administrator.

There may not be much about biology in the current sex-ed, but there are volumes about all kinds of varieties of sexual expression and the great harm of portraying gender stereotypes: i.e. man and woman. Gender is now a very

[95] Grossman (2009, 2013a)
[96] American Academy of Child & Adolescent Psychiatry (2013)

complicated concept. A boy might turn into man, a woman or something else. Girls want their breasts removed. And just this week a CNN headline read "Trans Man and Partner Expecting First Child"[97] (more about this in chapter 8).

Although what I have shared up to this point is definitely unpleasant and in my estimation evil, this chapter brings it home. Kinsey's unsubstantiated research is now affecting the ones we love the most—our children, our future, our inheritance. What I discuss in this chapter is necessarily graphic. We, as a nation, need a reality check in our education system. As parents you need to be aware of what your children are being exposed to in the name of education. It is our job as parents to protect our children from atrocities such as these, and it is long past time to speak out in protest!

A person sexualized from childhood is taught:

> …it is right to live out all of your instincts without reflection. It is wrong for you to set boundaries for them. He or she uses his own body and the bodies of other people for satisfying the sex drive, instead of expressing love.[98]

Well, let's start down the raging river. This trip will resemble riding a rubber raft over Niagara Falls.

LESSON #1: THE GENDERBREAD PERSON

The Genderbread Person is a graphic designed to teach young people about sexual and gender fluidity, and can be found on the website www. itspronouncedmetrosexual.com. According to this site,

> Gender is one of those things everyone thinks they understand, but don't. This tasty little guide is meant to be an appetizer for understanding. It's okay if you're hungry for more.[99]

The website goes on to state:

> …we know that most people aren't 100% straight or gay. A continuum of gay to straight (think Kinsey) leaves us with bi– in the middle. What about folks who are pansexual? Asexual? Mostly asexual? Hypersexual?

---

[97] Hassan & Andone (2017)
[98] Ruby (2015 p. 9)
[99] It's Pronounced Metrosexual (2015)

None of those identities can be mapped on our old model. Ditto goes for folks who are agendered, pangendered, two-spirited, and the list goes on. The amount of –ness is, in many cases, as crucial to one's identity as which –ness they possess. (emphasis in original)[100]

So on a continuum of 1 – 10, how confused are you right now? I actually describe these, and many other terms, in chapter six.

The article states, "We know most people aren't 100% straight or gay," directly relating this statement back to Kinsey. Hear again the choice of words thrown out there by media…inclusivity, diversity, affirming…if the LGBT culture and their advocates can get our children on this path, they will be led into a well-camouflaged pit. Once fallen into, it will be extremely difficult to get out.

The site continues:

Just as adorable

…while we upped the ante on accuracy and inclusivity, we did our best not to compromise what was arguably the most effective aspect of the old Genderbread Person: he is freaking adorable! The original genderbread I baked a few months ago has been gobbled up (googled) well over 3 million times and I attribute the wealth of that interest to the fact that it was easy to understand and visually appealing. While this one is a bit harder to understand at first glance — mostly due to the fact that we're using a method we created, instead of a standard graph — most people in our test group *got* it (even "non-mathy" people). So that's good. It's an introduction, after all, and we know how important introductions are.[101]

LESSON #2: GENDERBREAD TO GENDERUNICORN

The Trans Student Educational Resource group states that biological sex is an ambiguous term with no scale and no meaning, other than that it is related to some sexual characteristics. The concept is deemed to be harmful to trans people.[102] Biology actually sounds like a great reference point from which to begin, but the reason biology is now harmful is because it directly repudiates the trans identity.

This is an interesting theory and one that is being continually referenced in media platforms that declare that trans people aren't safe if the rest of the

---

[100] Ibid
[101] Ibid
[102] Trans Student Educational Resources (2017)

population (99%) doesn't agree with their assumptions and their identity designations. The continual barrage against Canadians stating that it is our fault that trans people are not safe and healthy has beaten us down. We all want people to feel safe, don't we? Of course—but what does "safety" really mean to the trans community? Total acceptance, and now, the indoctrination of our children. The saddest thing is that trans individuals really often have been targeted. But we need to realize that the vast majority of people just ignored them and went about their business as usual. The greater reality is that trans people are not safe from themselves, as you will see in chapter 9.

As for the Gender Unicorn, this is a graphic that expands on the Genderbread Person and tries to be even less "gender binary." Trans educators prefer referring to "sex assigned at birth" instead of male or female, as they maintain this provides a more accurate description than "biological sex." It's kind of an "I want it my way" attitude!

The adorable creature can be viewed at www.transstudent.org/gender. I'm wondering what age this graphic is targeting? Not the teens particularly. This is now published as a colouring page for children. I don't know about you, but in my memories colouring used to be a big thing from kindergarten to grade 5. From what I can tell with my grandchildren, it still is.

The site continues with an example of how to fill out your own Gender Unicorn:

Sex Assigned at Birth: It is important we don't simply use "sex" because of the vagueness of the definition of sex and its place in transphobia.

Is biological sex really vague? It seems pretty obvious—baby boy; baby girl.

Sexually Attracted To: Sexual Orientation. It is important to note that sexual and romantic/emotional attraction can be from a variety of factors including but not limited to gender identity, gender expression/presentation, and sex assigned at birth.

Romantically/Emotionally Attracted To: Romantic/emotional orientation. It is important to note that sexual and romantic/emotional attraction can be from a variety of factors including but not limited to gender identity, gender expression/presentation, and sex assigned at birth.

The Gender Unicorn is definitely meant to be attractive to children. How much a six-year-old would understand is questionable, but I don't think that's really the point. The objective here is to get them on this sexualized path quickly and as young as possible. The objective here is to deconstruct gender and the foundation of marriage and family.

LESSON #3: TONI THE TAMPON

In a campaign designed to continue to blur differences between men and women, create a genderless society, and further confuse children and parents everywhere, a new colouring book came on the market in 2016 called *The Adventures of Toni the Tampon*.[103] While at first glance this book might look like we are finally coming out the dark ages and speaking frankly about human biology and women, it is anything but that. I shared earlier about the trans man and partner expecting their first child. Check out the "Toni the Tampon" cartoon online. It teaches kids that men can menstruate, thereby introducing the concept of men giving birth.

CHILDREN'S SEXUAL RIGHTS!

Moving right along, I want to introduce you to the next level in education—junior high style. Let's turn our attention to information I recently acquired from a medical doctor. She had been appalled as she read it, and I certainly had strong feelings of repulsion. The following material may be disturbing, but it is readily available for our children and adolescents. EXCLAIM! Young People's Guide to Sexual Rights[104] is a 40 page declaration, or more aptly, a manifesto, published by the International Planned Parenthood Federation (IPPF). In fact EXCLAIM! is distributed worldwide via the United Nations. Planned Parenthood was also a key player in creating the US National Sexuality Educational Standards. Part of their proclamation is that there really is *no such thing as right or wrong childhood sexuality*. Let me share their motto:

> All young people should be able to explore experience and express their sexualities in healthy, positive, pleasurable and safe ways. This can only happen when young people's sexual rights are understood, recognized and guaranteed. Exclaim! seeks to increase awareness and understanding about young people's sexual rights. This youth guide explores what sexual rights are and how they relate to young people. It also examines

---

[103] Clemmer (2016)
[104] International Planned Parenthood Federation (2011)

strategies to translate sexual rights into actions for and by young people around the world.

Perhaps you're thinking, well what's wrong with this? We were all young once, and increasing awareness sounds pretty good. As parents, we need all the help we can get, right? After all, we really don't understand sexual rights for our children! Let me fill you in on some of the information that is being disseminated to your children from the Planned Parenthood (PP) organization.

ANAL PLAY 101 - ACCORDING TO PLANNED PARENTHOOD AND TEEN HEALTH SOURCE[105]

The following information may seem too repugnant to include in this book, but I want to remind you that this material is openly available and being distributed to our children in elementary schools. This information is from Teen Health Source. I am simply reporting what is being spread to our children.

Backdoor sex. Anal. Rimming. No matter what you call it, according to Planned Parenthood anal play is healthy and normal and "It's a good way to share pleasure and avoid pregnancy, but not everyone is into it."

According to Planned Parenthood, anal play is healthy and normal. It has become a "good" way experience sexual pleasure while at the same time avoiding pregnancy.

They define anal play as any kind of sexual activity that involves your anus, including:

- Putting fingers around/inside someone's butt
- Putting a tongue around/inside someone's butt (rimming)
- Putting a penis inside someone's butt
- Putting a dildo or other sex toy inside someone's butt
- Putting a hand inside someone's butt (fisting)

Heterosexual, homosexual, and bi-sexual alike can all become participants in this pattern of sexual behaviour, which Planned Parenthood and Teen Health Source describe as healthy and normal. While promoting anal play, they neglect to accept the reality of pain, incontinence, hemorrhoids, and infection caused by this behaviour. In fact, with regards to pain, their stance is that if you take it slow, and use lots of lubrication it shouldn't hurt and won't be messy.

---

[105] Teen Health Source (n.d.)

Cleanliness is not necessary prior to anal intercourse, although it is recommended that the bed be covered with a towel or plastic sheet before one begins. Having wipes nearby "just in case" is also recommended.

Instructions for getting the most out of anal play include the following:

- Start on the outside: relax the area by touching near and around the outside of the anus with toys or fingers for at least 15 minutes before going inside the butt.
- If and when you are ready to try something inside, start with small toys or body parts until you and your partner feel ready moving on to something bigger.
- Take your time. Relax, breathe and be patient. If you are short on time or feeling stressed out, you may want to save anal play for another time.
- Your anus doesn't naturally get wet, so have lots of water-based lubricants on hand (oil-based lubricants can break down latex condoms and silicone-based lubricants don't work well with silicone toys). Use lots of lube and re-apply often.
- Some people like to use sex toys for anal play. Make sure anything you put in your butt or someone else's is: smooth, unbreakable, flexible, clean, comfortable in size and has a flared base so that it can be gripped and removed easily. Putting condoms on toys can help keep them clean.

Anal play seems like a great way to avoid pregnancy—but this can still result if sperm is ejaculated in or near the vagina. Not only is pregnancy a possibility, but anal play exposes one to Sexually Transmitted Diseases. Protection is important and the following examples are recommended:

- Yes, you could be exposed to STDs during anal sex.
- Protect yourself by using condoms on sex toys and penises, gloves on hands and dental dams (or condoms cut up one side) for oral sex.
- If you have an outbreak of herpes or warts around the anus, you may want to avoid anal play until the outbreaks have healed and/or been treated. This will reduce the risk of passing an STD on and make anal play more comfortable.

The anus is a body part designed for excrement, yet it is being lauded as an object for sexual penetration.

Upon my first read through this material, I was repulsed! The culture has taken something naturally disgusting and tried to make it seem normal and healthy, for sexual fulfillment, in an attempt to convince our children to practise something that is abnormal, unhealthy and repulsive.

So, I have some questions which I've listed here. What do you think?

1. How is inserting fingers, tongue, penis, hand or toys in the anus healthy? I was of the understanding that the anus was designed for waste elimination and now parents are instructed to teach their children that the anus is healthy to use for sex!
2. What is meant by "done safely"? I've never heard that phrase used to describe vaginal sex.
3. It's normal? Understand that the anus doesn't naturally get wet, like the vagina does naturally in preparation for sex. Many women do not like anal intercourse. Why not? Because it's painful.
4. Is the anus really designed for sex?

The handbook even declares that it is not necessary to clean the area before anal play! I can't get my head around that one, given the number of germs and diseases encountered. My goodness, we are hypervigilant in teaching our young children the basics of hygiene and live in a society that has become so paranoid about keeping our children out of the dirt, yet here we are allowing our children to be taught that it's OK not to wash your butt, it's OK to let someone else use it, and it's OK to "get your fingers dirty" with excrement no less. How does giving in to this behaviour make one feel valued, loved and wanted?

This reminds me of a story I heard about 35 years ago from a friend who was an emergency nurse. Here's the story. A man came into ER with a watermelon in his anus. Apparently neither he nor his gay friend could remove it. What are we teaching our children when we tell them to insert toys or anything else into their butt? Imagine how stretched the walls of his anus had become to even think to do this.

A child groomed and conditioned to accept anal sex may begin to associate it with love and excitement even in the midst of the pain. It's called masochistic behaviour. Remember again Stewart's assertion (see chapter two) that *brutality to the genitals can be loving and sexually exciting*! These behaviours don't constitute loving kindness.

Anal intercourse does not come highly recommended by doctors. It would seem there are legitimate risks that Planned Parenthood either downplays or blatantly lies about. Here are some of the most identifiable:

- passing on of infection (if one of you has one)
- damage to the anus – it lacks natural lubrication and the interior tissue is not well protected
- spread of germs from anus to vagina (if you have vaginal sex immediately afterwards)
- possible urinary infection in the man (very uncommon).
- possible transfer of HPV (human papilloma virus), which may be a cause of rectal cancers[106]

HPV is exploding exponentially amongst our youth. The anus does indeed become looser. Muscular widening of the anus can lead to problems with "soiling" of underwear. Also, there are some hygiene risks in having anal sex—particularly the fact that the rectum does contain germs. Very often, it's the man who is keen on anal intercourse and the woman who is much less enthusiastic. Anal intercourse is a favourite of gay men; in fact, 90% of men who have sex with men engage in receptive anal intercourse.[107]

Not mentioned in the above list are STDs which can easily be passed along through anal sex play. In short, anal sex brings pain, possible infections or STDs, and incontinence, yet parents are being expected to go along with the idea that anal sex is healthy. Regular anal intercourse does make the opening of the anus more slack. This change is clearly visible in anyone (male or female) who has often been on the receiving end of rectal penetration.

The anus was designed to hold in feces. The anus is surrounded with a ring-like muscle that tightens after we defecate. When the muscle is tight, anal penetration can be painful and difficult. Repetitive anal sex can lead to weakening of the anal muscle, making it difficult to hold in feces until you get to the toilet.[108] A 2016 study of 4,170 adult men and woman published in the American Journal of Gastroenterology indicates that receiving anal sex results in a 34% increased risk of fecal incontinence in woman and a ***119% increased risk*** of fecal incontinence (defined as leakage of liquid, solid stool, or mucus at least monthly) in men! Anal sex significantly raises the risk of having

---

[106] Net Doctor (2012)
[107] Web MD (n.d.)
[108] Ibid

fecal incontinence.[109] If this is a problem for younger people, can you imagine the incontinence of senior gay men who have experienced a lifetime of anal intercourse?

PHYSICAL RISKS OF ANAL INTERCOURSE

An Ontario medical doctor and psychiatrist[110] reiterates the above issues and is alarmed at the lack of information in the recent Ontario sex education curriculum, where teens are not being provided medical facts. Here are some of her concerns.

- The skin of the cervix is more vulnerable to infection in teens
- HPV is the main cause of cervical cancer
- HPV vaccine only protects against four types of HPV (30% of cancers are not protected against!)
- You can contract HPV at your first experience of intercourse (anal or vaginal), even while using a condom (see the "Sexual Exposure Chart" in the next chapter—the risk increases exponentially)
- Anal intercourse carries the greatest risk of STIs (sexually transmitted infections – also known as STDs). More teens are engaging in anal intercourse which is promoted as a way to avoid pregnancy[111]
- Chlamydia infection can cause infertility, and the infection rate is climbing
- STIs are steadily rising
- The number of new diagnoses of sexually transmitted infections is on the rise
- Planned Parenthood grievously distorts medical facts and scientific research

This MD goes on to explain what the curriculum is silent and negligent about:

- Misleading about HIV—the curriculum states that with treatment, the damage that HIV does to the body's immune system can be slowed or prevented, and that people with HIV who are treated early have the opportunity to live a *near-to-normal* life span.

She notes that if a student is infected with HIV:

---

[109] Gandolfo (2016)
[110] Nyhus (personal communication, 2015)
[111] Teen Health Source (n.d.)

- They should never have sex without a condom for the rest of their lives
- They may have to adopt children
- If female, they will never be able to breast feed
- Their ability to live in other countries will be limited
- They will be required to take strong medications (2 – 4 at a time) for the rest of their lives
- Missed doses can result in treatment failure (viral resistant), so their life will be regimented
- The medication may damage their organs

PSYCHOLOGICAL RISK

Psychological risks of early sexual experimentation are high: depression and suicide are three times higher for teens who are sexually active. The idea that everyone is doing it is a fabrication, although 2013 stats show that nearly half (46.8%) of students in grades 9-12 report having had sex.[112]

Ignoring the risks and dangers while encouraging the pleasure and "right" of sexual freedom for children and adolescents is creating an atmosphere of indulgence, while minimizing life-threatening medical and psychological perils. This doesn't paint a pretty picture for the future of our children as they explore their "sexual rights."

There was a time when our culture was committed to the protection of children. The collapse of family structure has left children immensely vulnerable and unprotected. Personal boundaries, age, and the maturity of the child, once considered the norm when discussing sensitive sexual issues with children, are now ignored under the guise of so-called sexual rights and childhood sex education. In the next chapter, I expand on the overwhelming effects of early childhood sexualization.

THE CULTURAL MANDATE

The cultural mandate to educate young children about sexual practices that just a few years ago would not even have been spoken of among mature adults is inconceivable. Current sex education—encouraging sexual exploration, anal intercourse, and non-binary genders—is hardly conducive to the future health of our children. The expectation that children and youth should be able to explore, experience, and express their sexuality in a healthy manner after such training is improbable.

---

[112] ReCAPP (2013)

Attempting to convince young girls that anal intercourse is a safe and painless way to experience sex glorifies the idea that sex and pain are synonymous. It also pressures children into sexual experiences long before they are physically or mentally equipped for them. Grooming our children in public school to accept all sexual behaviour is introducing them to a life of promiscuous behaviour, depression, anxiety, abandonment, rejection, and disease.

Dr. Miriam Grossman is a renowned practicing physician, writer and speaker. Dr. Grossman's professional focus is on sex education and reproductive health: sexually transmitted infections, high risk behaviours, contraception, fertility, and abortion. She argues strongly in favour of protecting children's innocence against activists, governments and powerful lobby groups that are pushing for a misguided sexual "freedom" instead of the safety, health and wellbeing of students. She speaks out of her experience:

> It is difficult for me to convey how it feels to witness not a few, not dozens, but hundreds and hundreds of young people in distress due to medical issues, only to discover how esteemed health authorities give an enthusiastic thumbs up to the very behaviours that fuel those problems.[113]

In 2015, Dr. Grossman spoke in Ontario, Canada at an event sponsored by a number of parent groups regarding the latest Health and Physical Education document. The document does effectively cover many topics, including the importance of physical exercise, proper diet and hygiene, the risks of smoking and the responsible use of alcohol. On these issues, parents should support the curriculum. After all, they want to make sure that their children have a healthy and sound lifestyle.

However, Dr. Grossman pointed out that the new curriculum contents fail badly in the area of human development and sexual health. Why? Because the sex education curriculum makes it a priority to shape student thinking rather than teach them the science of sexual and reproductive health.[114] Grossman is the author of two books; *Unprotected* and *You're Teaching My Children What?*

---

[113] Laurence (2015)
[114] Ibid

CHAPTER 4
The Watershed Effect: The Consequences of
Early Adolescent Sexuality

The brain can be molded positively by structure and guidance.
It can also be molded negatively by poor input.
What is certain is that the brain will be molded by one or the other.
McIlhaney & McKissic Bush (2006)

SEXUAL DEVELOPMENT
COMPLEX AND RICH, THE PROCESS OF HUMAN DEVELOPMENT IS A PRODUCT
of many elements—the mixing of biological and the cultural, with the interlinking
of thought and feeling. Sexuality is so much more than just sex—it's our values,
attitudes, feelings, interactions, and behaviours.[115] It's emotional, cultural, social
and physical.[116] Credible education on the topic is rare, which leaves the media
and pop culture to inform and fill in the gaps according to their values and
hyper-sexualize our children.

Puberty usually begins for children around the age of 10, although some girls
may begin to experience body changes as young as seven years old. Family and
community values and beliefs become a foundation for development, where a
child's knowledge of sex and sexual behaviour are shaped. It is in this environment
that they understand body changes, public and private behaviour, pregnancy,

---

[115] DeLamater & Friedrich (2002)
[116] Society of Obstetricians and Gynecologists of Canada (n.d.)

birth, intimacy and relationships. Unfortunately, family hour television and current sex education in our public school system that promotes sexual activity are rampantly affecting the minds of children.

Explicitly sexual images from media sources have a big impact on childhood behaviour. It is paramount that parents "set the tone" in their homes, answering questions at age-appropriate levels. Parents also need to understand what is being taught to their children in the school system so that they can respond accurately.

> **The latest teen trends... ambisexuality, the heteroflexible and cuddle groups. Gay is in and especially fun are two females hooking up with one male.**

Although our culture believes it has made great strides in creating a sexually free atmosphere, I suggest that this "freedom" comes at great cost. Sexual liberation seems to have reached a pinnacle in Western societies, where any expression of sexuality is considered to be a healthy, normal expression of human behaviour. Finally, we have obtained true sexual freedom—or have we? In fact, as Kinsey proposed, perhaps the prevailing thought amongst many of our youth might just be that *the only unnatural sex act is that which you cannot perform*.

In creating a sexually free atmosphere of liberation, have we created another social experiment? I would suggest that the sexualization of society has created a downward spiral in terms of the age of first sexual experiences, now including preadolescent children—which of course is what Kinsey proposed, as we saw in chapter two.

There is probably no other time in history when sexuality has so pervasively permeated society to such an extent. Open a magazine, turn on the TV, or watch a movie and you'll find them all full of sexual innuendo and explicit sexual activity. New York Magazine (2006)[117] touted the latest teen fad labelled ambisexuality, the heteroflexible or pansexual teen: teens who partake in "cuddle groups" of hugging, kissing and more, while piled in a group. Gay is "in" for both young men and women, and especially "fun" are two females "hooking up" with one male. I recently read of a new designation of sexual attraction, GSA (genetic sexual attraction), being espoused by teenagers in sexual relationships with their biological cousins.[118] Are we approaching a time when there are no sexual experiences considered off limits in our culture?

Youth are very skilled at bypassing electronic blocks placed by parents. The Internet, smart phones, tablets, social media and the like, provide instant access

---

[117] Morris (2006)
[118] Butterfield (2015 p. 4)

to sociality and sexuality as our youth explore without the necessary boundaries and/or filters created through face-to-face communication. Most parents have believed that education is empowerment, and many have talked to their children about sex at an appropriate age. The problem lies in the fact that parents don't understand that they are not the only or likely even the first to "educate" their children regarding sex; therefore, they have the mistaken belief that their children won't do it, or if they do, that they'll be responsible and sensible.

Marketers have documented that 13 is the age that many life-long buying habits are set. It's called the "branding age."[119] What other decisions are being made at such a young age, and how will a young teen's decisions affect his/her life? The Rand Corporation says that children exposed to sexual lyrics and media programming are two times more likely to get involved sexually than those not exposed to it.[120]

The data consistently show that young people are entering into sexual behaviour at an increasingly younger age. In the U.S., 7.4% of students nationwide reported that they had sexual intercourse before the age of 13. There is very little information on this age group, but there are some indicators that the number will increase.[121]

Parents, doctors, psychologists, family therapists and teachers are beginning to shrug their shoulders in frustration. "We know our kids are having sex all the time, and we know they may get sick, but what can we do?"[122]

Let's arm ourselves with information, so that, on behalf of our children, we can become proactive rather than inactive in truthfully educating our children about sexuality.

EFFECTS OF EARLY ADOLESCENT SEXUALITY

Pre-adolescent children are now experimenting with a variety of sexual behaviour. Early sexual experience will shape or mold the brain. There is a critical period for human development in adolescence when sexual behaviour is organized either successfully or unsuccessfully.[123] Contemporary neuroscientists and psychologists are just now experimentally confirming and appreciating the influential role of pubertal hormones in adolescent brain organization and sexual behaviour.[124]

---

[119] Luce (2008 p. 20)
[120] Ibid (p. 28)
[121] Attwood (2006)
[122] Meeker (2007)
[123] Scott, Stewart, & De Ghett (1974)
[124] Sisk (2006)

THE FLEXIBLE BRAIN

One recently-understood aspect of this remarkable remodeling of the human adolescent brain is the overhaul of cortical and limbic circuits, which leads to the acquirement of adult-typical cognitive skills, decision-making strategies and social behaviours. Adolescent brain development is dynamic and protracted, occurring over the course of a decade or more, with individual variation in the developmental course.[125] Several limbic structures mature during human adolescence in sex-specific ways.[126] Limbic bonding is the reason casual sex doesn't really work on a whole mind and body level.[127]

Let me explain. Your brain creates your world! It perceives and experiences life.

"Every experience begins and ends in your brain. The actual physical patterns of the brain have a dramatic impact on how we think, feel and behave from moment to moment."[128] There is a competitive nature of brain plasticity that affects each of us. This is the "use it or lose it" quality. Without getting too technical, a synaptic pruning of neurological connections occurs.[129] The thoughts and emotions we "feed" as we mature become strengthened, while those we ignore diminish—some to the point of annihilation. The more we practice an activity the more ingrained it becomes in our brain, mapping our brains for future similar experiences.[130] The saying goes, *neurons that fire together, wire together.*

Because the brain is designed for one partner, confusion will arise when sexual and emotional bonds are formed with multiple partners.[131] Breaking of the limbic bond produces both physical and emotional distress. It takes time for the chemical bond to dissolve, and as a result the teen may experience deep levels of depression. We see the emotional impact of depression and anxiety exploding in our youth culture as sexual activity becomes more and more an expected social norm for young adolescents who are not ready for such deep relational pain.[132]

As our culture becomes more accepting of all forms of sexual expression and behaviour, our children's brains are being affected. Sex enhances an emotional bond between partners, whether they want it or not. Often it is the girl who forms a quick attachment and will be deeply wounded when the casual affair

---

[125] Sisk & Zehr (2005)
[126] Pinos et al (2001)
[127] Amen (1998)
[128] Ibid (p. 36)
[129] Zukerman & Purcell (2011)
[130] Doidge (2007)
[131] Leaf (2011)
[132] Amen (1998)

is over. The reason for this is that the female limbic system is larger than the male's. Deep limbic translation of emotion is powerful. When the limbic system is switched on, emotions tend to take over.[133] The rate of promiscuity among our children is increasing, leading to serious mental, emotional and physical health issues and increasing the prevalence of STDs in our youth.[134]

The earlier an individual initiates sexual intercourse, the more likely they will be to have multiple partners. A study for the Center for Disease Control and Prevention[135] showed that if girls were younger than 16 at their first sexual experience, 58 percent of them would report more than five sexual partners by their late 20s. Another study of adolescent females who begin sexual activity at 15-19 years of age shows them, on average, having more than seven voluntary sexual partners during their lives. Data for males also shows that delay of sexual intercourse significantly reduces the number of lifetime partners.[136] These are powerful arguments for delaying sexual activity, yet our education system is encouraging early childhood sexual experimentation and experience.

Psychological stress, such as depression and suicidal ideation, has been indicated with early sexual involvement.[137] Exactly how much is unclear, though some is thought to be due to the short-term nature of such relationships. Not only is psychological stress a factor of early sexual involvement, physical health is impacted as well. One in four sexually active adolescents is newly infected with an STD each year, and more than 70 million Americans are living with some form of sexually transmitted infection, with a whopping 19 million new cases each year.[138]

VERY EARLY AGE SEXUAL ACTIVITY

In a large 2008 Canadian study,[139] "very early age" of first sexual intercourse (FSI) was defined as 11 years or less for males and 12 years or less for females. FSI was associated with having experienced pressure to have unwanted sex, having used drugs other than marijuana, and believing that popularity at school is dependent on rebelling and rule-breaking. This same study indicated non-biological factors of FSI are associated with four broad conceptual categories: family relationships, psychological factors, peers and risk-taking, and partner-related factors.

[133] Amen (1998)
[134] Institute of Medicine (2011)
[135] Chandra et al (2005)
[136] Rector, Johnson, & Noyes (2003)
[137] Manning et al (2014)
[138] Centers for Disease Control and Prevention (1999, 2004, 2009, 2015)
[139] Boyce, Gallupe, & Fergus (2008)

Early First Sexual Intercourse has been associated with *dysfunctional family history, family turbulence* and *not living with both parents*. This is a definite result of our divorce and co-habitation culture. Secure attachment with parents in early childhood will build positive emotional family ties and will reduce the likelihood of early FSI.[140]

PSYCHOLOGICAL FACTORS

In a study of 6500 adolescents, sexually active teenage girls were more than three times as likely to be depressed, and nearly three times as likely to have had a suicide attempt, as girls who were not sexually active.[141]

We are not only affected biologically (by STDs including HIV and many other diseases) but we are affected psychologically, emotionally, and physiologically (as we understand how powerfully the chemicals and hormones affect an adult brain) every time we have sex with someone. Sexual exposure encompassing all areas of our soul is multiplied by the number of partners you have had in your lifetime. Each person exponentially increases the possibility of transmission of disease—physically, emotionally and spiritually.

Number of Sexual Partners	SEXUAL EXPOSURE CHART (if every person has only the same number of partners as you)	Number of People Exposed to
1		1
2		3
3		7
4		15
5		31
6		63
7		127
8		255
9		511
10		1023
11		2047
12		4095

"When you have sex with someone, you are having sex with everyone they have had sex with for the last ten years, and everyone they and their partners have had sex with for the last ten years."
C. Everett Koop, M.D., Former U.S. Surgeon General

"Many teenagers, as well as adults, are indirectly exposed to more than one sexual partner each year because their partner has had sex with someone else."
Alan Guttmacher Institute, 1994

---

[140] Resnick et al (1997)
[141] Rector, Johnson, & Noyes (2003)

If you have had sexual intercourse with 12 people, each of whom has had sexual intercourse with 12 people, you have been exposed physically and spiritually to over 4000 individuals.

Greater family connectedness with both parents/family and being part of an emotionally and verbally expressive family have been found to be related to later first intercourse.[142] The increased absence of fathers in the home is having devastating effects on children being raised by single mothers. Chapter 13 explains the benefits of secure childhood attachment, one of which is an increased ability for the child to express discomfort and fear. Securely-attached children are more likely to talk with their parent(s) about inappropriate sexual advances or behaviours by other children and/or adults.

Some will scoff at these ideas, seeing it as just another strategy to limit sexual expression. The implications of direct and indirect sexual exposures are unnerving. The greater the number of indirect sexual exposures, the greater one's risk of contracting a sexually transmitted infection. The Sexual Exposure Chart is especially useful in bringing awareness of the consequences of having multiple sexual partners. The sexual histories of indirect partners are imparted to and carried with you. The true level of risk—physically, emotionally, socially and spiritually—seen here will hopefully encourage you as parents and grandparents to think again about the precarious results of early adolescent sexuality and commit to speaking out against it.

The multiplied effect of indirect sexual exposure is life-threatening and soul-wounding. As Louie Giglio[143] says,

They don't make a condom that can fit over your soul.

Pre-teens are especially vulnerable to sex talk on the computer as they are at a stage when sexual attitudes and beliefs are still forming. We know that what we see, hear and do affects the developing brain. This being the case, it makes sense that the longer children can forestall sexual experience, the safer it will be for them. We issue warnings to our culture with regard to all other things that can potentially harm our children: drugs, chemicals, certain foods, etc., yet instead of offering warnings about early childhood sexuality, our education systems are intent on exposing them to varied sexual behaviour as early as possible.

We are seeing phenomenal physical, mental and social health concerns. Teaching abstinence is neglected since we can no longer discuss such subjects without

[142] Resnick et al (1997)
[143] Lusko (2017 p 40)

being dubbed insensitive, non-tolerant and moralistic. We've become so fearful of offending someone's sexual preference that we are allowing our children to be indoctrinated by a social sexual agenda while doing nothing about it.

Higher self-esteem is found to be associated with less likelihood of early intercourse for both genders.[144] This relates as well to greater school connectedness and greater academic participation.[145] Having secure childhood attachment to caregivers creates a safe place for the child to experience healthy relationships, educational pursuits, and increasing independence. Factors such as greater religiosity, more frequent church attendance, and greater prayer frequency have also been found to be associated with a lower likelihood of early First Sexual Intercourse.[146]

> 70% of girls under 10 who were involved with sexual experience were involved in incest with their father, uncle, brother, caretaker, stepfather, grandfather, mom's boyfriend, step brother or babysitter.

PEERS AND RISK TAKING

Associations have been found between early First Sexual Intercourse (FSI) and a perception that friends are sexually active, greater peer support for sex, and attitudes that engaging in sexual activity leads to gains in popularity.[147] Early age FSI may be related to coercive or forced sex, but it may also be associated with other personality-based and/or social variables. A 2006 study[148] of 1300 pre-teen girls over a five-year period found that their young lives were filled with sexual behaviour of one sort or another. In some cases, the girls were forced into sexuality by a relative; in other cases they appear to have engaged freely with their boyfriends, and in other cases they were forced by an older male. In this study, 70% of girls under 10 with sexual experience were involved in incest with their father, uncle, brother, caretaker, stepfather, grandfather, mom's boyfriend, step brother or babysitter.

Same sex sexual "playing" is becoming common at this age and is unrelated to a child's sexual orientation. For many young teens, their first exploration into partnered sex is oral or anal sex, a relatively recent historical phenomenon. Many

---

[144] Laflin, Wang, & Barry (2008)
[145] Resnick et al (1997)
[146] Ibid
[147] Kinsman et al (1998)
[148] Attwood (2006)

young people see oral sex as "not really having sex" and as protection against pregnancy and STDs. The data indicate that parents did not have a clue that their children were engaging in sexual activity and were unaware of their internet chatting, and that the girls themselves did not think about the consequences of their sexual behaviour.[149]

Adolescent and young adult women who are attracted to both genders without describing themselves as bisexual are estimated to represent 6-10% of female youth.[150] This is a much larger group than those who identify as lesbian or bisexual, who remain steady at 1 – 2% of the population. This newly identified subgroup of adolescent girls who describe themselves as "mostly heterosexual" is at higher risk for tobacco use, binge drinking, eating disorder symptoms, and sexual risk behaviours compared with those who describe themselves as heterosexual.[151]

Another meta-analysis (synthesizing the results of several studies) of the relationship between childhood sexual abuse and HIV risk behaviour among women found that across 46 studies, there was an increased risk of unprotected sexual activity; having multiple partners; engaging in sexual intercourse in exchange for money, drugs, or shelter; and sexual revictimization in adulthood.[152]

As the prevalence of greater and greater experimentation with sexuality continues to increase, I believe we are going to witness a mental health crisis on a scale we could never have imagined. Young people, indoctrinated since elementary school with the motto that "all sex is good," that sex is a right rather than a privilege, and that pleasure trumps love and commitment, are likely to embark down this sexual river earlier and earlier, without any idea of the devastation to come.

THE EPIDEMIC IS REAL

Nearly one out of four sexually active teens is living with a sexually transmitted disease. Public health offices call this explosion of STDs among our children a "hidden epidemic."[153] This silence comes from a lack of public outrage, media and magazine coverage. It is threatening the lives of our children and the future health of our county, yet few are crusading for change. The prevalence of sexually transmitted diseases has also increased exponentially. Forty years ago, there were two sexually transmitted infections, now there are 25.[154] A 2015 US data

[149] Attwood (2006)
[150] Austin et al (2008)
[151] Ibid
[152] Arriola et al (2005)
[153] Centers for Disease Control and Prevention (n.d.)
[154] Grossman (2013b)

study shows that both the numbers and rates of reported cases of chlamydia and gonorrhea continue to be highest among young people aged 15-24.[155] Both young men and young women are heavily affected by STDs, but young women face the most serious long-term health consequences. It is estimated that undiagnosed STDs cause infertility in more than 20,000 women each year.

The Journal of American Medical Association reported in 2002 that the number of people with asymptomatic STDs (no outward signs) probably exceeds those whose diseases have been diagnosed.[156]

BRAIN DEVELOPMENT DURING PUBERTY: THE MOLDABLE BRAIN

In the last several years, scientists have developed new technologies such as Magnetic Resonance Imaging (MRI), functional MRI (fMRI) and positron emission tomography scans (PET). Primarily with the aid of the MRI, scientists have made important discoveries about the brain's growth and maturation. The part of the brain controlling the ability to make fully mature decisions is not physically mature until the individual reaches their mid-twenties. In the two periods of explosive proliferation of connections between brain cells (neonatal and pre-pubescence), the brain manufactures more of these connections, called synapses, than are necessary. Some of these synapses are meant to be strengthened and some are meant to die. It just depends on what we experience. The synapses that are not used weaken or die—kind of a "use it or lose it" scenario.

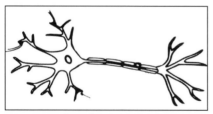
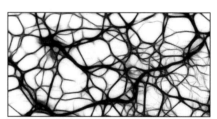

Single neuron   **Multiple neurons**[157]

Neurons are joined and strengthened through repetitive thought and action as a result of synaptic plasticity. What we think about repeatedly strengthens our connectivity to those thoughts. When the brain forms memories it encodes new information by tuning the connections between neurons. It is the synapse that strengthens these new connections by sending chemical signals to the receiving

[155] Centers for Disease Control and Prevention (2015)
[156] Fortenberry (2002)
[157] Source for both images: Creative Commons

cells.[158] This explains the role of the synapse and gives understanding to how the synapse can change, hence the term plasticity (meaning the flexible brain).

From birth to death the brain is moldable and adaptable. The things we do, see and experience actually cause certain parts of our brains to flourish. Neurochemicals are essential to brain functioning, and some of these chemicals are very involved in sexual interest. Discussing all of these chemicals is beyond the scope of this chapter, but I want to touch on a few of the major chemicals involved in sexuality.

CHEMICALS IN THE BRAIN

Dopamine

This is a messenger chemical which makes a person feel good. It has great influence over human behaviour and is the official "reward signal." Dopamine rewards us by flooding our brains with a feeling of excitement or wellbeing. It is value-neutral, meaning that it rewards all kinds of behaviour without distinction, and it plays a powerful role in the lives and brains of adolescents.

Dopamine levels peak in late childhood, and continue to increase in one area of the brain: the prefrontal cortex, which is the part responsible for mature decision-making. The desire for this "good feeling" can overwhelm an adolescent's accurate calculation of risk behaviour. Good feelings from dangerous behaviours such as driving too fast, smoking, drugs, and sex impel the teen to increase that behaviour to achieve the same good feeling again.[159] Sex is one of the strongest generators of the dopamine reward,[160] and for this reason our youth are particularly vulnerable.

Oxytocin

Oxytocin is another neurochemical essential to healthy sex and bonding, primarily in females. It is important not to confuse Oxytocin, the naturally occurring chemical in your body, with more commonly-known, similar words like Oxycontin or Oxycodone, which are opioid pain medications. According to recent research[161] the female body generates oxytocin at four different times, which have to do with reproduction and the nourishment of and provision for a supportive and protective environment for a child.

---

[158] Trafton (2015)
[159] McIlhaney & McKissic Bush (2006)
[160] Brizendine (2006)
[161] McIlhaney & McKissic Bush (2006)

When two people touch each other in a warm, meaningful and intimate way, oxytocin is released into the woman's brain. It then does two things: increases the woman's desire for more touch and causes bonding of the woman to the man.[162]

Oxytocin is also value-neutral (or impartial) and can cause a woman to bond to a man even during what was expected to be a short-term sexual relationship, with the result that it becomes difficult to break the attachment. For young women and pre-pubescent girls, being physically close to and hugging a man can trigger the bonding process, creating a desire to trust. Oxytocin is naturally released from the brain after a twenty-second hug from a partner.[163] Each short-term relationship and break-up creates and then breaks the oxytocin bond, designed to allow them in the future to have a healthy bonded marriage.

Vasopressin

Oxytocin is only half of the story. Women are not the only ones who bond during intimate physical contact. The neurochemical responsible for male brain response is vasopressin, which has two primary functions related to relationships: bonding of the man to his mate and attachment to his offspring. Vasopressin has been referred to as the "monogamy molecule" and it has a powerful impact on human behaviour. A man may question why he would return to a woman who treats him poorly or may wonder why he is unable to feel committed to a woman after having multiple sex partners. Vasopressin floods the brain during sexual intercourse and creates a partial bond with each woman a man has sex with.

The individual who goes from sex partner to sex partner causes his brain to mold so that the brain begins to accept this sexual pattern as normal. This pattern seems to interfere with the development of neurological circuits necessary for long-term relationships and damages the ability to bond in a committed relationship. Brains molded for promiscuity lose the natural bonding effect, in much the same way as adhesive tape that is pulled from an envelope will lose its stickiness and no longer be able to adhere to the paper.[164]

Pheromones

Pheromones are chemicals secreted by the skin and sweat glands, which when inhaled can stimulate surprising and unexpected thoughts, feelings, and

---

[162] Eiensberger & Lieberman (2004)
[163] Brizendine (2006)
[164] McIlhaney & McKissic Bush (2006)

behavioural responses, and have a strong psychological and behavioural impact.[165] Although pheromones do not overwhelm the other factors that preclude sexual behaviour, they are a powerful influence.

THE DEVELOPING BRAIN

A 1999 study[166] found that brain centers that produce feelings of romance and love are different and separate from brain centers for lust. Brain activity differentiates between lust and love. The brain is far more involved in our decisions about sex, and the actions that follow, than we may give it credit for. Each person changes the structure of his/her brain with the choices he/she makes and the subsequent behaviour. This is a complicated process, designed to lead toward and strengthen long-term monogamous relationships.

Thoughts are measurable and occupy mental "real estate." Thoughts are active; they group and change. Thoughts influence every decision, word, action and physical reaction we make. Thoughts are basically electrical impulses, chemicals and neurons. They look like a tree with branches. As the thoughts grow and become more permanent, more branches group and the connections become stronger. As we change our thinking, some branches go away, new ones form, the strength of the connections changes, and the memories network other thoughts.[167]

Emotions are involved in every thought we form, have formed, and ever will form. For every memory, you have a corresponding emotion. What you think about expands and grows, taking on a life of its own. Your thoughts create changes even down to genetic levels, restructuring the cell's makeup.[168] This is an interesting concept when we consider the LGBT culture and causation.

It's not a huge stretch to conceptualize the findings of recent research on the flexible brain into the field of adolescent sexuality. What is seen, heard, or experienced is taken into the mind and then pondered upon. The more a child focuses on sexual messages, the more likely they are to begin to embed neural pathways in the brain and the more likely they are to continue activating these thoughts and pathways. When this is done, they are changing the physical structure (neuroplasticity) of the brain. This is not only relevant to children, but to each adult as well.

For as [a man] thinks in his heart, so is he. (Proverbs 23:7, NKJV)

---

[165] McClintock et al (2005)
[166] Stoleru et al (1999 p. 1-21)
[167] Leaf (2009)
[168] Ibid

All this could be good news for us and our children. We can change our thoughts by limiting or eliminating what we put in our minds. Is this difficult in a modern age of internet pornography, the wholesale media exploitation of healthy sexuality, and mockery of moral values? Yes. Impossible? No! It is up to each of us as parents to provide safe places for our children to learn, grow, and become the healthy adults we desire them to be.

This raises the question: what about our current sex education? Is what we are teaching our children within the school system promoting disease prevention and ensuring healthy sexuality in the future, or does our teaching tend to inculcate and maintain a value system which elevates sexual freedom? Teachers and parents alike can feel trapped, believing in personal and sexual freedom, yet facing deadly diseases spawned by unrestrained and premature sexual activity.

Sex is more complicated than just the physical act of pleasure, and it almost always carries long-term psychological consequences. To elicit tolerance, our postmodern view has normalized individuals involved in sexual activity at younger and younger ages.

HEALTHY SEXUAL DEVELOPMENT

Studies[169] show that adolescents who were strong enough to avoid sexual involvement had three primary things in common:

1. High levels of family connectedness
2. Parental disapproval of the adolescent becoming sexually active
3. Parental disapproval of the adolescent using contraceptives

A healthy progression of relationships strengthens the brain cells associated with the attachment of one person to another and permanence within relationships. Infatuation (the incredibly exciting awakening of sexual awareness) can "hit" any person at any age! It is the great imitator of true love. Although brain scans cannot tell whether infatuation will become true love or not, they can show the difference between the early, passionate stage of romantic love and that of long-term, comfortable, relaxed loving attachment. Healthy human behaviour demands the integration of all of who we are—body, mind, will, emotions and spirit.

EFFECT OF PARENTAL RELATIONSHIPS

Neuroscientists have discovered specific brain cells and chemicals involved in attachment. If you recall the earlier discussion on oxytocin, this chemical

[169] Resnick et al (1997)

is initially released in the mother/infant dyad. Secure attachment bonding in infancy to both parents promotes emotional and physical health. A secure attachment to parents can safeguard an adolescent from early sexual activity, and be a safe-haven to run to in life's storms. It provides a trustworthy person to whom you can turn, knowing that person will be emotionally available and will respond to you in a caring manner. As parents, this is the ultimate provision we can give our children. We are all happiest and able to use our talents to their best when we are confident that standing behind us are trusted people, who will be there should difficulties arise.

Parental Responsibilities

Our job as parents is to teach our children how to see through the shallowness of our culture and the motives of those who shape it. Even parents with an imperfect sexual past are not disqualified from playing an important role in healthy sexual training for their children. Our real defense is to build a culture in our family that is so strong and foundational that it pulls the hearts of our children toward us and keeps them looking to us to shape their values.[170]

- Do you have rules about how much TV your children watch each day?
- Do you know what songs are on your children's smart phones or tablets?
- Is there a computer in your child's bedroom? *Never* allow this!
- Do you know what sites your child visits?
- Do you have internet protection on every device?
- Do you know the video games your children are playing?
- What about cellphones: if you allow your teen to have one, do you install limiting options?[171]

For more information, look up "Strength to Fight" online (https://strengthtofight.ca).

Another parental control device I recently discovered is called Circle®. This device is a 3-inch white cube that connects to your Wi-Fi network. The device allows you to filter content, add time restrictions, and see activity reports for every device on your network. It's like *God Mode* for your household's Wi-Fi devices!

The days of mindlessly allowing our children to be transfixed with the media of their choice are over if we hope to raise this generation with any kind of real

---

[170] Luce (2008)
[171] Luce (2008)

moral conscience and propensity for wholesome living.[172] The average parent spends 3.5 minutes in meaningful conversation with his/her child compared to 72 hours of media consumption per week.[173] The bottom line is that parenting means sacrifice! You can choose to sacrifice up front—time, sleep, career, hobbies while your children are young—or you will sacrifice later. Parenting requires emotional and mental engagement, starting at an early age.

If your children are older, be on the lookout for moments that contain a vulnerability to engage your child's heart, those moments of openness which usually come at inconvenient times! It's tragic when a child blogs his/her pain for all the world to see because Mom or Dad sitting 10 feet away from where the child types is too busy to listen.[174]

Parents Need to Parent

Parents are deferring to their children's whims because they have relinquished parental authority and lost confidence in themselves. Their intentions might be good and certainly their efforts are impressive, but they are also trying to please the child in order to avoid conflict. Many of the problems within the modern family come from a problem of role reversal. Watch what happens at meal time and one quickly sees that children have often taken over as decider of the family—the boss, the one in charge.[175] Children are now overpowering their parents from infancy onward.

The family actually functions well under the concept of hierarchy. The parent has to be the final authority or else the child actually loses their ability to trust and depend on them. When this happens, respect for authority goes out the window.

Children still need to learn right from wrong. Studies show that children left to discover right from wrong on their own are more likely to have negative future outcomes. They are more likely to be anxious, less likely to be healthy, and more likely to be addicted to drugs or alcohol. Parents who are authoritative raise children with better outcomes.[176] *The Collapse of Parenting: How We Hurt Our Kids when We Treat Them Like Grown-ups* by Dr. Leonard Sax[177] is one for your bookshelf.

---

[172] Ibid
[173] Borchgrave (2007)
[174] Luce (2008)
[175] Gulli (2016)
[176] Ibid
[177] Sax (2015)

Factors in a Healthy Family

1. Good parental couple relationship.
   a. Handling of power.
   b. Power securely in parents' hands, but children are respected and listened to.
   c. Easy leadership.
2. Closeness.
   a. Family shares consistently, feels strongly connected, yet each is an individual.
   b. Communication patterns: clear, self-responsible, spontaneous.
   c. Problem-solving. Every family faces problems; healthy families are no exception. The way in which a family solves problems is crucial.
      i. Identify problems early.
      ii. No denying of problems.
      iii. Accepting of mistakes.
      iv. Very little blaming of individuals.
      v. Negotiation skills.
   d. Dealing with feelings.
      i. Family members remain expressive.
      ii. Practice the use of empathy, general tone of warmth, humour, and concern for one another
   e. Adaptability. Ability to deal with change and loss in a healthy way.
      i. Openness to input from outside, new experiences.
      ii. Values and shared beliefs around the nature of humankind and the meaning of life.
   f. Balance. Family's capacity for intimacy while respecting autonomy.[178]

RELIGIOUS PRACTICES

Research suggests that sincere devotion and frequent participation in a religious community benefits mental health.[179] Religious commitment encourages healthy behaviours such as avoidance of smoking, alcohol and drug use and sex outside of marriage, and protects against early sexual activity and suicide. Prayer and other rituals are associated with positive emotions like empowerment and contentment.[180]

---

[178] Source unknown
[179] Grossman (2007)
[180] Tix & Frazier (1998)

A FINAL WORD

What researchers are discovering about the moldable brain and attachment is at once thrilling and sobering. Hopefully this information propels us to deeper understanding of our children and youth and causes us to pause as we consider the implications for our children in our highly-sexualized society. There is an increased vigilance needed by parents as they encounter the truth of early adolescent sexuality and the dangers therein.

There is a move afloat to extinguish family and community values in the area of sexuality. Explicit sexual images, pornography, and the explicit nature of new sex education materials are affecting the minds of our children. The training of our children has been handed over to the public square, and it will come at great cost.

There is a downward spiral in regard to the age of first sexual experience and an expectation of experimentation in risky sexual practice, all of which affect the developing brain of the child. Promoting casual sex minimizes the love and intimacy enjoyed in marriage. Children are creating new neural pathways that will impact their future experience, and when it comes to sex, many are experiencing the deep emotional pain of rejection and abandonment—repeatedly. The earlier they begin having sex, the more likely they are to have multiple partners. They also increase their risk of disease exponentially.

Young lives, filled with sexual behaviour, lose the innocence and liveliness of childhood. They are filled with cares and concerns far above their years. Those who are strong enough to avoid sexual involvement in their youth typically have strong family attachment and often experience religious participation.

CHAPTER 5

The Flood of the Century: Sexual Addiction

For our struggle is not against flesh and blood...
(Ephesians 6:12, NIV)

LET'S BEGIN ROWING THROUGH THE SWAMP OF SEXUAL ADDICTION.

THE FACE OF SEXUAL ADDICTION

A sexual addiction is sexual behaviour that in some way is out of control.

Sex addiction is a condition characterized by persistent and escalating patterns of sexual behaviour amid negative consequences to oneself and others.[181] Although there are no distinct sexual addiction categories, this designation comes in different forms, including addiction to:

- Pornography
- Prostitution
- Masturbation or fantasy
- Sadistic or masochistic behaviour
- Exhibition/Voyeurism
- Other excessive sexual pursuits

---

[181] Herkov (n.d.)

Several signs can serve to indicate whether someone is addicted to sex. These can be emotional or physical. Furthermore, it's important to know the debilitating effects of sexual addiction. Sex addicts are more likely to choose new or novel images than familiar sexual images.

The Diagnostic Criteria for Sexual Addiction[182] indicates that three or more of the following symptoms must be present:

1. Recurrent failure to resist impulses to engage in specific sexual behaviour
2. Frequent engaging in sexual behaviours to a greater extent or over a longer period of time than intended
3. Persistent desire or unsuccessful efforts to stop, reduce, or control sexual behaviours
4. Inordinate amount of time spent in obtaining sex, being sexual, or recovering from sexual experience
5. Preoccupation with sexual behaviour or preparatory activities
6. Frequent engaging in sexual behaviour when expected to fulfill occupational, academic, domestic, or social obligations
7. Continuation of sexual behaviour despite knowledge of having a persistent or recurrent social, financial, psychological, or physical problem that is caused or exacerbated by the behaviour
8. Need to increase the intensity, frequency, number, or risk of sexual behaviours to achieve the desired effect, or diminished effect with continued sexual behaviours at the same level of intensity, frequency, number, or risk
9. Giving up or limiting social, occupational, or recreational activities because of sexual behaviour
10. Distress, anxiety, restlessness, or irritability if unable to engage in sexual behaviour

EMOTIONAL SYMPTOMS OF SEX ADDICTION

According to Sex and Love Addicts Anonymous,[183] if you are addicted to sex, you might become easily involved with people sexually or emotionally regardless of how well you know them. Because most sex addicts fear being abandoned, they might stay in relationships that aren't healthy, or they may jump from relationship to relationship. When alone, they might feel empty or incomplete. They might also sexualize feelings like guilt, loneliness or fear.

---

[182] Hatch (n.d.)
[183] Sex and Love Addicts Anonymous (n.d.)

EFFECTS OF SEX ADDICTION

The effects of sex addiction can be severe, both for the addict and for his or her loved ones. According to the Departmental Management of the USDA,[184] about 38% of men and 45% of women with sex addictions have a venereal disease as a result of their behaviour.

Pregnancy is also a common side effect that can occur due to risky behaviour. In one survey, nearly 70% of women with sex addictions reported they'd experienced at least one unwanted pregnancy as a result of their addiction. Additionally, sex addiction likely has a negative impact on several areas of one's life. It can lead to a decline in personal relationships, social, and family engagement as well as decreased concentration and productivity at work.

Physical consequences like sexual dysfunction or sexually transmitted diseases (STDs) are frequent and there are also profound psychological effects, like feelings of shame, inadequacy, and emotional distress, that often lead to comorbid psychological disorders such as

- Anxiety
- Depression
- Substance abuse
- Problems related to impulse control and emotional dysregulation
- Obsessive-Compulsive type symptom

Emotional dysregulation is a common side effect of childhood traumatization. It is defined as a poorly-modulated response that doesn't fit within acceptable ranges of emotional reactions, such as angry outbursts, threats toward self or others, and suicidal ideation. Experiencing increased sexual interest and responsiveness during times of depression and anxiety is more common in men and women with out of control sexual behaviour. Dissociation was evident in a 2004 study, where 45% of the sex addicts described their state of mind during their acting out as a form of dissociation from reality.[185]

Nearly 12 million people suffer from sexual addiction in the United States, according to the American Association for Marriage and Family Therapy.[186] With the accessibility of sexual material available on the internet, the number of people with sexual addiction is increasing.

---

[184] Voon et al (2014)
[185] Ibid
[186] Carnes and Carnes (2010)

In the chapter on childhood sexual abuse, I briefly touched on dissociation as a common theme for those who had experienced sexual abuse, extreme neglect, or trauma as children. The sex addict, then, may simply be acting out much of the buried pain of earlier abuse, with no thought to their self-punishing behaviours.

PORNOGRAPHY

How accustomed we've now become to seeing lots of skin on TV (Victoria`s Secret is now blasé). Over the last four decades our TV shows, movies, magazines and ads have become increasingly lewd. We're like the proverbial frog in the pot of cold water. The water begins to heat, but because it's gradual the frog doesn't realize the danger he's in until it's too late to do anything about it—he's immobilized. If we don't wake up from our stupor, folks, we are going to be cooked!

> "You can't have a healthy soul
> And mainline toxic substances."
> Lusko, 2017

Pornography. Let me give you a rundown of some of the effects. Due to the reality that sexual thoughts, behaviours and experiences track faster than drugs in the brain, viewing pornography becomes highly addictive. The addictive effect on the brain may be amplified by the accelerated novelty and the "supranormal stimulus" factor afforded by internet pornography,[187] which is now readily available—anywhere, anytime.

Our brains naturally seek novelty, and sex can condition the reward center of the brain. According to D.L. Hilton, Jr., MD, pornography is the perfect laboratory for novel learning and is fused with a powerful pleasure incentive;[188] Wolf states that for the first time in human history the power and allure of images have supplanted that of real naked women.[189]

Is pornography addiction actually harmful to the individual? The American Society of Addiction Medicine defines addiction as a chronic disease of the brain that affects the reward, motivation and memory systems.[190] The facts speak for themselves. Over 75% of sex addicts report cybersex[191] as the beginning or catalyst to their sexual acting out, and sex addicts are shown to be more likely to

---

[187] Hilton (2013)
[188] Ibid
[189] Struthers & Wolf (2016)
[190] American Society of Addiction (n.d.)
[191] Carnes & Carnes (2010)

choose new or novel images than familiar sexual images.[192] Popular pornography overwhelmingly portrays aggression toward women.[193] Porn has become the "wallpaper" of our lives now. It has deadened male libido in relation to real women, leading them to see fewer and fewer women as "porn-worthy."[194]

Brain activity in sex addiction mirrors that of drug addiction, according to Voon and associates.[195] Sex addicts were discovered to have a marked reduction in the dorsal anterior cingulate cortex (the reward-based decision-making mediator) when the same sexual image was shown over and over again. Hence, the authors conclude that in the same sense, sex addicts may be less interested in familiar photos and might search for new images to feed their addiction.[196] In the US it is estimated that one in 25 adults is a sex addict.[197] I failed to find a Canadian statistic on sex addiction, but would assume that the statistics are similar in Canada. Use of pornography is one of the main features identified in many people with compulsive sexual behaviour.[198]

A correlation between brain activity and age has also been identified. The younger the person, the greater the level of activity in the ventral striatum (a key component of rational decision-making; the reward circuit, central to assessing likely outcomes from choices) in response to pornography. The frontal regions of the brain (the brakes on compulsivity) continue to develop into the mid-twenties,[199] therefore the propensity for addictive behaviour is greater when a child is introduced in early years to pornography.

As with other addictions, sex-addicted individuals often long for emotional attachment, connection, relationship, security and a sense of community. In their quest for community they often chose associations that will facilitate their addictions.

There is a good reason to resist the temptation of pornography and sexual activity—individuals who don't have a background of pornography or multiple partners tend to have a higher level of sexual pleasure in marriage than those who do. Sexually active singles have the most sexual problems, get the least pleasure out of sex and are more likely to experience depression.[200] It is never too late to deal with addictions and retrain the brain for a life of purity.

---

[192] Ibid
[193] Struthers & Wolf (2016)
[194] Wolf (2003)
[195] Voon et al (2014)
[196] Laguipo (2015)
[197] Voon et al (2014)
[198] Ibid
[199] Ibid
[200] Lusko (2017 p. 70)

Sexual addiction affects the individual and the people they love. Many of the sexually addicted are inflicted with venereal diseases as a result of their behaviour. Unwanted pregnancies and abortions plague this population. Deep feelings of shame, inadequacy and intense loneliness contribute to psychological disorders such as anxiety, depression and increased substance abuse.

Sexual addictions have increased with the availability of easily accessible pornography. Kinsey literally opened a "Pandora's box" that has liberated sex from love and paved the way for pornography to seep into every media market, literally changing the brains of our youth. Men who have prolonged exposure to pornography experience sexual insensitivity toward women, placing expectations on women that they should never have to deal with. Pornography has socialized women to accept sexual abuse.

Sexual thoughts, behaviours, and experiences are as addictive as drugs, perhaps more so. As our brains seek novelty, those who are sexually addicted are often driven to pursue more excitement. The very thing that they desire most—emotional attachment—increasingly diminishes the longer the addiction remains untreated.

We are a culture enslaved by our own pursuit of pleasure. Pornography has contributed enormously to the collapse of marriages. Porn changes the way we look at each other. The impact of pornography diminishes trust in relationships and causes people to abandon hope of sexual monogamy, creating an internal disbelief about the need for affection. Hopes are dashed, dreams denied. The marriages of our grandparents are viewed as a small reflection of what may have been.

We have sown to the wind and are reaping the whirlwind.

CHAPTER 6

Confluence of Choices: Gay, Lesbian, or Bi-Sexual

There is a generation that is pure in its own eyes
Yet is not washed from its filthiness.
There is a generation – oh, how lofty are their eyes!
And their eyelids are lifted up
There is a generation whose teeth are like swords,
And whose fangs are like knives.
Proverbs 30:12-14 (NKJV)

AUTHOR AND LESBIAN ACTIVIST CAMILLE PAGLIA,[201] PROFESSOR OF Humanities & Media Studies at the University of the Arts in Philadelphia, writes:

In nature, procreation is the single relentless rule. That is the norm. Our sexual bodies were designed for reproduction: Penis fits vagina. No fancy, linguistic game-playing can change that biological fact. Homosexuality, in my view, is an adaptation, not an inborn trait.

As mentioned previously, the past several decades have seen fundamental changes in viewpoints of what is normal sexual behaviour. Sexual behaviour has

---

[201] Paglia (1994 p. 71)

now become who you *are* rather than something you *do*. Sexual identification has become self-identification rather than biological recognition.

Sexual identity is a broad construct that has emerged as an increasingly important concept in the study of human sexuality and sexual behaviour.[202] Sexual identity development is now considered to be a complex, multidimensional and often fluid process. The impact of cognitive, social, emotional, cultural, and familial complexities, as well as other aspects of the individual's experiences, are considered integral to this process. It is currently claimed that no singular sexual identity model can represent the diverse trajectories of male and female sexual identity development.[203] The topic of homosexuality and sexual fluidity in whatever form they manifest are important, because they affect the lives of human beings who experience same-sex attraction and impacts family and friends.

> What was at one time, in the not too distant past, considered a deviation from male/female design, is now being recognized as a different class of personhood. This is often based on scientific studies which show substantial change of sexual preferences, depending on the immediate situation the individual is in. These thoughts were largely unheard of 20 years ago, yet now they are being propagated and even taught to our young people.[204]

Homosexuality is considered to be a human condition that develops, as do most other complex behavioural phenomena, through a complicated and quite distinctly human intermingling of many factors—psychological, social and perhaps biological.[205] From a scientific perspective, no one knows what causes homosexuality, but historically we know that homosexual behaviours have been practiced for thousands of years, according to ancient texts such as the Bible and other historical documents. It has been found in many societies, although Ford & Beach found that homosexuality is rare or absent in 29 out of 79 cultures they surveyed.[206] Whitehead and Whitehead indicate the prevalence of homosexuality has varied considerably in different cultures; in some it has been unknown, while in others it has been obligatory for all males: "Anthropologists have found huge variations in

---

[202] Yarhouse & Tan (2004)
[203] Ehrensaft (2016); Goldberg (1992 pp. 53, 63); Greenberg (1988 pp. 74-77); LeVay (1996)
[204] Monimore (1996 p. xii)
[205] Ibid
[206] Ford & Beach (1952)

heterosexual and homosexual practice from culture to culture and sudden changes in sexual practice and orientation, even over a single generation."[207]

If sexuality is highly fluid as current culture suggests, then it would stand to reason that reversals from homosexual to heterosexual sexual behaviours are very possible. Of course, such a line of thinking is counter-cultural and highly refuted by LGBT activists. Habit is stubborn, especially once sensory pathways have been blazed and deepened by repetition. Nevertheless, sexual preferences sometimes change.[208] For homosexuals wishing to function heterosexually, change is a perfectly worthwhile aim.[209]

Paglia goes on to say:

> We should be honest enough to consider whether or not homosexuality may not indeed be a pausing at the prepubescent stage. There is an element of choice in all behaviour, sexual or otherwise. It takes an effort to deal with the opposite sex; it is safer with your own kind. The issue is one of challenge vs comfort.[210]

Challenge versus comfort is certainly something to consider as we maneuver through this difficult topic.

TERMINOLOGY

Homosexual orientation normally refers to the consistent preference of a person for same-sex attractions and experiences.[211] Sexual orientation is generally characterized by whether an individual is erotically attracted to males, females, or both. Some researchers use the terms same-sex attraction and homosexuality interchangeably. Researchers[212] describe sexual orientation as one's degree of sexual attraction to men or women, which should be closely related to sexual experience with one sex or the other. A more recent descriptor of same-sex attracted individuals is the term "non-heterosexual."[213]

There are suggestions that homosexuality and heterosexuality are best conceptualized as being on a continuum. I clarify this idea further on. Some modern-day researchers suggest that sexuality is flexible, rather than static,

---

[207] Whitehead & Whitehead (1999 p. 116)
[208] Mock & Eibach (2016)
[209] Paglia (1994 p. 77)
[210] Ibid
[211] Jones & Yarhouse (2007)
[212] Bailey, Dunne, & Martin (2000)
[213] Savin-Williams & Ream (2007); Busseri et al (2008)

especially for women.[214] Perhaps the following is the most succinct description of same-sex attraction.

> Same-sex attraction (SSA) includes any desire toward another individual of the same gender, in reality or fantasy, that may involve erotic feelings, sexually charged sensations or a strong preoccupation with nonsexual physical affection such as being held, hugged, casually touched or cuddled. The presence of SSA does not preclude the presence of opposite sex attraction or behaviours.[215]

As one can imagine, just identifying and describing the phenomenon of same-sex attraction itself has required a process of reformation and adaptation in order to adequately capture the essence of same-sex attraction development. The term same-sex attraction is currently used in lieu of homosexuality, especially among people who are now uncomfortable applying the term homosexual to themselves.

As the concept of sexual fluidity was further developed during the 1990s,[216] terms such as sexual orientation, same-sex attraction, and most recently non-heterosexual became common. These terms allegedly have arisen in an attempt to more accurately capture the essence of male to male and/or female to female sexual attraction.

Let me take a moment and expand on the idea of fluidity. According to Wikipedia, sexual fluidity is one or more changes in sexual identity (or orientation) over the course of the lifespan.[217] This reflects the position that sexuality is fluid or malleable throughout life.

While any one of us has the capacity to pursue any form of sexual expression and/or gender we decide that we want, it is not essential nor even moral to act on these assumptions. The issue at stake for our children is: do we encourage and affirm such behaviours, or is it time to shake the fog out of our brains and begin to once again teach our children sexual morals?

Here's an example. One homosexual man had successive relations with men from one race or ethnic group, then with those from another, and in each period he could be attracted only to men in the group that was currently "hot." The plasticity of this man's sexual tastes depicts a general truth: the human libido is

---

[214] Hallman (2008); Savin-Williams & Ream (2007); Vrangalova & Savin-Williams (2010)
[215] Hallman (2008 p. 12)
[216] Diamond (2012); Sandfort (1997)
[217] Sexual Fluidity (n.d.)

not hardwired, but can be curiously fickle, easily altered by psychology and the history of our sexual encounters.[218]

The sixth edition of the Publication Manual of the American Psychological Association describes sexual orientation as: "an enduring pattern of attraction, behaviour, emotion, identity and social contacts."[219] Terms such as lesbian, gay men, bisexual men and bisexual women are preferred by members of the LGBT culture. All these terms refer primarily to "identities" and *to the culture that has been developed among people who share those identities.*

UNDERSTANDING CONCEPTS AND TERMINOLOGY BEHIND OTHER EXPRESSIONS OF SEXUALITY

Before proceeding further, an explanation of current sexual terminology is in order. The following descriptors are obtained from the University of Michigan's Lesbian, Bisexual, Gay, and Trans Resource Center.[220]

Asexual	A person who generally does not feel sexual attraction or desire to any group of people. Asexuality is not the same as celibacy.
Ally	Typically, any non-LGBT person who supports and stands up for the rights of LGBT people, though LGBT people can be allies, such as a lesbian who is an ally to a transgender person.
Biphobia	Aversion toward bisexuality and bisexual people as a social group or as individuals. People of any sexual orientation can experience such feelings of aversion. Biphobia is a source of discrimination against bisexuals, and may be based on negative bisexual stereotypes or irrational fear.
Cisgender	Types of gender identity where an individual's experience of their own gender matches the sex they were assigned at birth.

---

[218] Doidge (2007 p. 95)

[219] American Psychological Association (2010 p. 74)

[220] University of Michigan Lesbian, Bisexual, Gay, and Transgender Resource Center (n.d.)

Gender expression	A term which refers to the ways in which we each manifest masculinity or femininity. It is usually an extension of our "gender identity," our innate sense of being male, female, etc. Each of us expresses a particular gender every day – by the way we style our hair, select our clothing, or even the way we stand. Our appearance, speech, behaviour, movement, and other factors signal that we feel – and wish to be understood – as masculine or feminine, or as a man or a woman.
Gender identity	The sense of "being" male, female, genderqueer, a gender, etc. For some people, gender identity is in accord with physical anatomy. For transgender people, gender identity may differ from physical anatomy or expected social roles. It is important to note that gender identity, biological sex, and sexual orientation are separate and that you cannot assume how someone identifies in one category based on how they identify in another category.
Genderqueer	A term which refers to individuals or groups who "queer" or problematize the hegemonic (ruling/dominant social context - heterosexual) notions of sex, gender and desire in a given society. Genderqueer people possess identities which fall outside of the widely accepted sexual binary (i.e. "men" and "women"). Genderqueer may also refer to people who identify as both transgendered *and* queer, i.e. individuals who challenge both gender and sexuality regimes and see gender identity and sexual orientation as overlapping and interconnected.
Homophobia	A range of negative attitudes and feelings toward homosexuality or people who are identified or perceived as being lesbian, gay, bisexual or transgender (LGBT). It can be expressed as antipathy, contempt, prejudice, aversion, or hatred, may be based on irrational fear, and is sometimes related to religious beliefs.
Intersex	A person whose sexual anatomy or chromosomes do not fit with the traditional markers of "female" and "male." For example: people born with both "female" and "male" anatomy (penis, testicles, vagina, and uterus); people born with XXY.

Polyamorous	This is the practice of, or desire for, intimate relationships where individuals may have more than one partner, with the knowledge and consent of all partners. It has been *described as "consensual, ethical, and responsible* non-monogamy." The term should not be confused with polysexuality (attraction towards multiple genders or sexes), although the two may overlap in some individuals
Queer	1) An umbrella term sometimes used by LGBTQA people to refer to the entire LGBT community. 2) An alternative that some people use to "queer" the idea of the labels and categories such as lesbian, gay, bisexual, etc. Similar to the concept of genderqueer. It is important to note that the word queer is an *in-group* term, and a word that can be considered offensive to some people, depending on their generation, geographic location, and relationship with the word.
Questioning	For some, the process of exploring and discovering one's own sexual orientation, gender identity, or gender expression
Pansexual	A person who experiences sexual, romantic, physical, and/ or spiritual attraction for members of all gender identities/ expressions, not just people who fit into the standard gender binary (i.e. men and women).
Transgender	This term has many definitions. It is frequently used as an umbrella term to refer to all people who *do not identify with their assigned gender at birth or the binary gender system.* This includes transsexuals, cross-dressers, genderqueer, drag kings, drag queens, two-spirit people, and others. Some transgender people feel they exist not within one of the two standard gender categories, but rather somewhere between, beyond, or outside of those two genders.
Transphobia	The fear or hatred of transgender people or gender non-conforming behaviour. Like biphobia, transphobia can also exist among lesbian, gay, and bisexual people as well as among heterosexual people.

Transsexual	A person whose gender identity is different from their biological sex, who may undergo medical treatments to change their biological sex, often times to align it with their gender identity, or they may live their lives as another sex.

Acronyms such as LGBT, LGBTQ, or LGBTQA refer to Lesbian, Gay, Bisexual, Transgender, Queer or Questioning, and Asexual or Ally. These are just some of the current 25 LGBT-preferred abbreviations. The different identities within "LGBT" are often lumped together, yet there seem to be specific needs and concerns related to each individual identity.

A further note regarding identity "labelling." It is now considered important to respect each individual's desired sexual self-identifications and not assume another person's identity based on that person's appearance. Non-discrimination legislation relating to sexual identity was recently passed in the Canadian Senate. In the interpretation of some activists and universities, this law means that Canadians of all stripes will be required to ask LGBT individuals *how they identify*, including whatever names (pronouns) they prefer, and to respect their wishes. However, it is unlikely that the Supreme Court would uphold this extreme position. The following table gives some examples of possible pronouns. Is your head spinning yet?

1	2	3	4	5
[f]ae	[f]aer	[f]aer	[f]aers	[f]aerself
e/ey	em	Eir	eirs	eirself
he	him	His	his	himself
per	per	pers	pers	perself
she	her	her	hers	herself
they	them	their	theirs	themselves
ve	ver	Vis	vis	verself
xe	xem	xyr	xyrs	xemself
ze/zie	zir	zir	zirs	zirself

How is one even to know who is gay, lesbian, bi- or transsexual, let alone remember one pronoun? Facebook recognizes 71 different gender identities (in

2017—I can't imagine how many there will be by 2020). Here is a summary of this list of gender identities:

> Agender, Androgyne, Androgynous,
> Bigender,
> Cis, Cisgender, Cis Female, Cis Male, Cis Man, Cis Woman, Cisgender Female, Cisgender Male, Cisgender Man, Cisgender Woman,
> Female to Male, FTM,
> Gender Fluid, Gender Nonconforming, Gender Questioning, Gender Variant, Genderqueer,
> Intersex,
> Male to Female, MTF,
> Neither, Neutrois, Non-binary,
> Other
> Pangender,
> Trans, Trans Female, Trans Male, Trans Man, Trans Person, Trans Woman, Transfeminine, Transgender, Transgender Female, Transgender Male, Transgender Man, Transgender Person, Transgender Woman, Transmasculine, Transsexual, Transsexual Female, Transsexual Male, Transsexual Man, Transsexual Person, Transsexual Woman, Two-Spirit

Pursing the passion of sexual identification (or even non-identification, as we will see later) has become an obsession of our culture, more important than relationships themselves, and definitely more important than sustaining a family or commitment to children. For many, sexual identification and the ability to be recognized by society as "normative" have become a mission, with the media espousing such belief and society swallowing it—hook, line and sinker!

Dr. Jordan Peterson, Professor of Psychology and Clinical Psychologist at the University of Toronto, is one man who refuses to cave to pressure from within the university to refer to people by these identities! He has chosen to take a politically incorrect stand.

PREVALENCE

Our culture has been clouded for generations with many misrepresentations regarding the causation and prevalence of homosexuality. Perhaps the most widespread has been the oft-presented 10% prevalence rate, primarily based on the erroneous representation of the 1948 Kinsey report.

As described in chapter two, the Kinsey research on human sexuality is foundational to the field of sexology and has influenced social and cultural values throughout the world. Although Kinsey married in 1921, monogamy was not in his plans. Both he and his wife agreed they could sleep with other people, including

> Kinsey advocated for the idea that all sexual behaviours previously considered deviant were normal.

those of the same sex. His biographer James H. Jones points out that Kinsey was not only a scientist; he was a reformer who sought to rid himself of his personal sexual demons, while at the same time revolutionizing what he saw as the repressive society in which he had grown up.[221] Kinsey's ideas were radical, introducing the philosophy of a new world of sexual opportunities that has brought us to the chaotic place we are now at in our nation.

No man in modern times has shaped attitudes and perceptions of human sexuality more than Alfred Kinsey. *He advocated for the idea that all sexual behaviours previously considered deviant were normal,* while maintaining that exclusive heterosexuality (experienced by over 95% of the population) was abnormal—simply a product of cultural inhibitions and societal conditioning. He and his team of researchers attempted to present the American people with "statistical data" showing that what they were supposedly already doing sexually was more liberal, and more consistent with his own ideology, than anyone had thought. As you've already discovered, it was his ideology that was twisted, and his statistical verification equally so.

It was Kinsey who emphasized the continuum between exclusively homosexual and exclusively heterosexual histories, and proposed his heterosexual-homosexual rating scale, based on both overt and psychological experiences.[222]

Kinsey summarized his findings[223] on the incidence of homosexual behaviour among white males in the U.S. population, then reinforced it by suggesting that it depends on how you define "homosexual."

Kinsey stated:

I think that much of human sexual behaviour is no more complicated than a person's likes or dislikes for particular foods, books, amusements, or anything else. Through it all, association is a very important factor.

[221] Brown & Fee (2003)
[222] Kinsey et al (1948 p. 638-41)
[223] Ibid (p. 650-651)

This means that what a person happens to do one time is avoided or repeated another time, depending upon the pleasure derived from the first experience.[224]

Kinsey painted a portrait of human sexuality quite different from the rigid categories of gay and straight, initiating the current LGBT gender revolution. Although his data were not representative of societal norms, Kinsey's conclusions are largely accepted today as scientific fact.

CURRENT UNDERSTANDINGS OF THE PREVALENCE OF LGBT PEOPLE

But what does *empirical research* say about the prevalence of the gay and lesbian population?[225] Lauman and colleagues presented a study of 5,000 respondents, and found that 2% of men and 0.9% of women identified themselves as homosexual; 0.8 of men and 0.5% of women identified themselves as bisexual; and 6.5% of men and 4.4% of women reported having felt attracted to the same sex, independently of their heterosexual involvement.

Homosexuality was also found to be clearly distributed within categories of the social and demographic variables, with the majority of the gay and lesbian population living in large cities.[226]

Percentage of Adults who report Same-sex Attraction and Behaviour

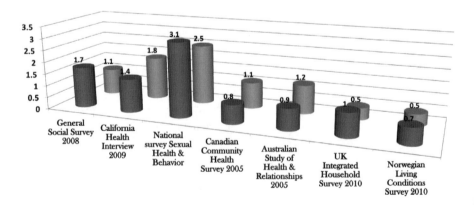

■ Gay/Lesbian   ■ Bi-sexual

---

[224] Pomeroy (1972 p. 324)
[225] Laumann et al (1994 p. 283)
[226] Ibid (p. 307)

A 2005 study of over 8000 U.S. and Canadian college students found that although only 2% to 3% identified as homosexual, bisexual or uncertain, 6% to 8% indicated some same-sex attraction, although many never acted on these attractions. Sexual attitudes and experiences become more liberal as the degree of same-sex interests increase.[227]

As women's same-sex interests increased they manifested lower religiosity, greater interest in non-monogamy and marginally greater acceptance of casual sex. The degree of same-sex desires among heterosexually identified men was not

> The average person now thinks that 25% of the population is gay!

significantly correlated with any outcome variables, although as they became less exclusive in their desires, they showed trends toward more liberal political attitudes and acceptance of non-monogamy.[228]

A forum research poll, commissioned by the National Post[229] and taken twice in June of 2015, found that 5% of Canadians identify as lesbian, gay, bisexual or transgender (LGBT), which is a significant increase since Statistics Canada asked this question in 2009. At that time only 2% of Canadians aged 18-59 said they were gay, lesbian, or bisexual. Of course, even the 2015 rate of 5% is still only ½ of the "one in 10" cliché that has circulated in the media since the Kinsey report of 1948.

In a 2003 Canadian enumeration of the LGBT population completed in a British Columbia Health survey, only 1.5 percent of all boys identified themselves as bisexual, mostly homosexual or 100% homosexual, while 3.5 percent of sexually active boys said they had had sex with someone of the same gender in the past year. Girls had a higher percentage of same gender sex, with 6.4 percent of sexually active girls reportedly having sex with someone of the same gender in the past year.[230]

These statistics are a far cry from a 2010 Gallup[231] poll that asked Americans, in an open-ended format, to estimate the percentage of men and women who were homosexual. The average estimates were that 21% of men were gay and 22% of women were lesbians. So much for getting the facts correct! Our society

[227] Diamond (2008)
[228] Vrangalova and Savin-Williams (2010 p. 98)
[229] Carlson (2012)
[230] Ibid
[231] Newport (2015)

has been so inundated with misleading information, mostly media produced, that the average person now thinks that approximately 25% of our society is gay! It may seem that way in some places, but that doesn't change the reality of 3% overall in the population.

And what about the *hottest news item of 2017—the transgender*. According to the Williams institute,[232] only .03% identify as transgender. Analyses suggest that there are more than 8 million adults in the US who are LGB, comprising 3.5% of the adult population. This is split nearly evenly between lesbian/gay and bisexual identified individuals—1.7% and 1.8%, respectively. There are also nearly 700,000 transgender individuals in the US. It should be noted that some transgender individuals may identify as lesbian, gay, or bisexual. Therefore, it is not possible to make a precise combined LGBT estimate. In reviewing homosexual compared to heterosexual behaviour;

- 97.2 % of males and 98.6% women identify heterosexually
- Average lifetime partners of heterosexuals is 4, while the average for homosexuals is 50
- 83% of heterosexuals are faithful in their relationship, whereas only 1.6% of the small percentage of LGBT people claim monogamy

Dr. Harold Lief, of the Center for Sex Education in Medicine at the University of Pennsylvania, made an observation about the extremely large numbers of sex partners of the majority of homosexual men and the frequency with which partners are complete strangers.[233] He made the distinction that casual sex in the heterosexual life does not have the overwhelming intensity, compulsivity and sex-only orientation of so much of homosexual behaviour.

A 1978 study indicated far higher rates of sexual partners throughout the lifetime of homosexual males. Almost half of white homosexual men (WHM) and one-third of black homosexual males admitted to having sex with more than 500 different males in their lifetime, while 28% indicated having had sex with 1000 or more partners. One-quarter of the WHM said they had sex with youth sixteen or younger (when the respondents were at least 21 years old).[234] Most of the WHM said that more than half of their partners were persons they only had sex with once.[235]

---

[232] Gates (2011)
[233] Reisman & Eichel (1990)
[234] Bell & Weinberg (1979 p. 85)
[235] Ibid

In 1985, Pollack[236] found that gay men on average had several dozen partners a year and some hundreds in a lifetime. While Pollack's research was conducted before the onset of HIV/AIDS, a 1997[237] study of older homosexually active men further supports his findings. These men had as many male and female sexual partners in the past six months as did younger men; the modal range for the number of sex partners was 101-500, with over 15% having had between 501 and 1000 lifetime sexual partners. Monogamy among gay couples is considered to be a homophobic stage that some gays pass through in an attempt to avert discrimination, while promiscuity is considered to be definitional to male homosexuality.[238]

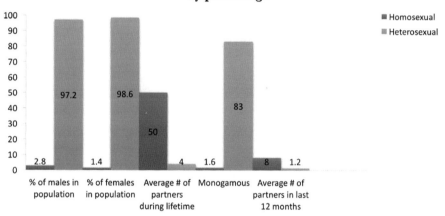

Homosexual vs Heterosexual Behaviour by percentage

These statistics are sobering when you consider the health concerns plaguing members of the LGBT culture. Promiscuity among lesbian women is much less extreme, but as noted, it's still higher than that of heterosexual women.

A 2004 study of young homosexual men in Amsterdam indicated that gays within a "committed" gay relationship have an average of eight sexual partners outside of the "committed" relationship.[239]

It was Freud who stated that the "sexual instincts are noticeable to us for their plasticity, their capacity for altering their aims," thereby laying the foundation for an understanding of sexual and romantic plasticity.[240] This speaks to the whole

[236] Pollack (1985)
[237] Van de Ven et al (1997)
[238] McWhirter & Mattison (1984)
[239] Xiridou et al (2004)
[240] Freud (1965 p. 97)

subject of choice in sexual behaviour. An understanding of the plasticity of sexual instincts indicates that sexuality is highly culturally adaptive.

While we wish to teach respect for all, are we at the same time minimizing sexual indoctrination's hazardous effects on our children? Just as the brain has been discovered to be highly flexible, allowing for the restructuring of thoughts, so is sexuality, the expression of which is initiated in the mind. This understanding flies in the face of media presentation in the late 20th century, which claimed that homosexuality is unchangeable, an idea which is still widely accepted by the public.

SCIENTIFICALLY SUPPORTED SAME-SEX ATTRACTION THEMES

Several themes in same-sex development identified since the 1950s have been supported in subsequent empirical research:

- exposure to violence
- child sexual abuse
- gender nonconformity and social polarization
- parental influence
- genetics
- generational transmission

GENDER NONCONFORMITY AND SOCIAL POLARIZATION

Gender nonconformity refers to a gender expression by an individual that does not match the masculine and feminine societal norm (or at least what was until recently the acknowledged societal norm). Scientific evidence also supports an association between childhood gender nonconformity and sexual orientation; some homosexual men recall having feminine traits as boys. The association between gender nonconformity and adult sexual orientation has been well documented and is so strong that

> It is difficult to think of other individual differences that so reliably and so strongly predict socially significant outcomes across the lifespan.[241]

A large study[242] of Australian twins found consistent evidence that family factors influenced sexual orientation and two related traits: childhood gender nonconformity and continuous gender identity. It is difficult in general to unravel genetic and shared environmental contributions to familial influences.

---

[241] Bailey, Dunne, & Martin (2000 p. 526)
[242] Ibid

A study[243] on gender nonconformity, childhood rejection, and adult attachment with homosexual men suggests that gender nonconformity is one of several childhood factors associated with homosexual orientation. Gender nonconformity has been identified as a risk indicator for childhood abuse and posttraumatic stress in youth. Exposure to childhood physical, psychological and sexual abuse were higher in youth in the top percentile of gender nonconformity.[244] Parents reinforcing or accepting childhood nonconformity (e.g. dressing a boy as a girl, even for entertainment value) are likely to encourage such patterns. Dissecting this chicken and egg conundrum, although difficult, is what may actually help us to understand this population of people. One difficulty is that the trauma of abuse (male or female) creates vulnerability, relational isolation and social polarization, which can be perpetually reinforced throughout childhood and adolescence by gender nonconformity.

My observation is that most studies on gender nonconformity assume that it results in childhood abuse. We should be looking at early childhood attachment injuries and trauma. It could well be that childhood sexual abuse has precipitated gender nonconformity—not the other way around. It is acknowledged that subsequent abuse and posttraumatic stress usually continue throughout the lifespan of members of sexual minority groups. In fact, gender nonconformity predicts an increased risk of the lifetime probability of PTSD, although such studies have not determined the causal relationship between abuse and gender nonconformity.

VIOLENCE & ABUSE

Exposure to violence, such as physical and sexual abuse during childhood, is associated with long-term psychological effects.[245] A 2009 study found that *most homosexual men surveyed* described that aspects of their sexuality were influenced in some way by their childhood sexual abuse experiences.[246] Many men have indicated that the sexual abuse they experienced influenced how they came to view themselves as sexual beings, causing them to experience shame, confusion and low self-esteem regarding their sexuality, and they questioned whether the abuse accounted for their sexual problems, contributed to their sexual orientation, or caused them to question their relationship and intimacy issues. An important but largely swept under the rug statistic is that:

---

[243] Landolt et al (2004)
[244] Roberts et al (2012)
[245] Finkelhor (1979)
[246] Roller et al (2009)

The experience of child sexual abuse triples the likelihood of later homosexual orientation.[247]

Childhood Sexual Abuse (CSA) is not only associated with same-sex orientation, but also with mental health problems;[248] it is a major risk factor in suicidal ideation. Sexual abuse by someone of one's own sex was found to be related to a same-sex orientation and sexual orientation was associated with different levels of perceived parental closeness.[249] Sexual abuse in childhood has been found to damage self-esteem, self-concept, relationships and the ability to trust. It can also leave psychological trauma that compromises a child's confidence in adults. As Valente puts it, "While some boys groomed to willingly participate may seem to somewhat adjust to sexual abuse, many others face life long complications from childhood sexual abuse such as reduced quality of life, impaired social relationships, less than optimal daily functioning and self-destructive behaviour."[250]

As noted previously, children who have been sexually abused can develop a distorted sense of love that may seem like "adjustment to the abuse." The reality is that their childhood confusion can lead to a lifetime of self-punishment through addictive behaviours, primarily with drugs, alcohol, sexual deviance and sexual addictions.

"Adjustment" to sexual abuse is what groups like NAMBLA have sought to achieve.[251] Kinsey's experiments with children and his misguided representation of their experiences was totally out of touch with the reality of sexual abuse and the damage flooding from one generation to another. Yet Kinsey's research has successfully fueled the pornography industry as well as the acceptance of homosexual and bisexual behaviour and the current impetus toward accepting pedophilia.

Another study[252] contained data on the life stories of 24-year-old males, finding that sexual abuse prompted the boys to question who they were and why this happened to them. *Normal development of gender identity, self-esteem and self-concept was disrupted.* The boys felt they must be flawed and that their behaviour signaled they were less masculine, more vulnerable and more inadequate. Some feared that sexual abuse would make them homosexual, or

[247] Laumann et al (1994)
[248] Mullen et al (1993)
[249] Eskin, Kaynak-Denir, & Demir (2005 p. 186)
[250] Valente (2005)
[251] Plummer (1991 p. 234)
[252] Valente (2005)

that they must have been homosexual and that's why they attracted the abuse in the first place.

Research examining the sexuality of Childhood Sexual Abuse survivors found that most participants described aspects of their sexuality that were influenced in some way by their CSA experiences. "Many indicated that their abuse caused them to engage in high-risk sexual behaviours, such as having sex at an early age, having many sexual partners, having frequent or unprotected sex and having sex while using drugs or alcohol to excess. CSA influenced how they came to view themselves as sexual beings. They talked about experiencing shame, confusion and low self-esteem about their sexuality."[253]

Previous studies have found elevated rates of Post-Traumatic Stress Disorder—a mental disorder that develops in response to exposure to a potentially traumatic event, including violence (e.g. childhood abuse, sexual assault, effects of war)—among sexual minorities in comparison with heterosexuals.[254] And a 2010 study found:[255]

Individuals with minority sexual orientation (e.g., gay, lesbian, bisexual) reported elevated frequency, severity, and persistence of physical and sexual abuse in childhood. Intimate partner violence and sexual assault in adulthood are also disproportionately prevalent among sexual orientation minorities.

A 2013 study[256] explored adult attachment and same-sex attraction and found that all the same-sex attracted men had suffered from loss, abandonment and/ or childhood sexual abuse. Despite evidence supporting these multidimensional correlations between same-sex attraction and high levels of child sexual abuse, the American Psychiatric Association[257] stated:

No specific psychosocial or family dy-namic cause for homosexuality has been identified, including histories of child-hood sexual abuse. Sexual abuse does not

> Is it possible that "born that way" impressions stem from unrecognized pre-language infant abuse?

---

[253] Roller et al (2009 p. 53)
[254] D'Augelli, Grossman, & Starks (2006)
[255] Brown & Herman (2015)
[256] Gillies (2013)
[257] American Psychiatric Association (2011)

appear to be more prevalent in children who grow up to identify as gay, lesbian, or bisexual, than in children who identify as heterosexual.

How does this statement align with empirical research? The child abuse of infants by Alfred Kinsey and team has illuminated something many have long speculated about when considering causation of homosexual behaviour. There are a number of homosexual men and women who believe they were "born that way," yet this has never been proven. Wouldn't infant abuse that the individual is unable to remember support their concept of "born that way"? It would seem to some that they had been born that way, as their body would remember the abuse they could never put words to. In all likelihood, their bodies would manifest their early abuse "story" in acting out the sexual storyline imposed on them!

PARENTAL RELATIONSHIPS

Early research in homosexuality primarily focused on interactions and relationships between parents of homosexual males in their early childhood years. Numerous significant replicated studies[258] indicate the following paths in the development of same-sex attraction.

- mother/son enmeshment
- father/son distant, detached[259]
- findings of vast family dysfunction in the childhood of homosexuals[260]

A 1974 study that compared 307 homosexuals with a control group of 138 heterosexuals, both from clinical and nonclinical samples, confirmed Bieber's study, indicating, "Homosexuals, in contrast to the heterosexuals, reported their fathers and mothers to be more rejecting and less loving."[261] Thirty years after the Bieber study, the Archives of General Psychiatry found that the literature suggests that many homosexual men report family constellations like those suggested by Bieber to be causally associated with the development of homosexuality. This association has been observed in nonclinical, as well as clinical, samples.[262]

---

[258] Bailey, Dunne, & Martin (2000); Bieber et al (1962); Brown (1963); Byne & Parsons (1993); Evans (1969); Siegelman (1974); Sprigg & Dailey (2004 p. 20); van den Aarweg (1984)
[259] Evans (1969)
[260] Ridge & Feeney (1998)
[261] Siegelman (1974 p. 10)
[262] Byne & Parsons (1993)

Throwing away such facts because they seem inconvenient won't lessen the effect on individuals and subsequently on our society. Research concluded what we intrinsically already know:

> that a constructive, supportive, warmly-related father precludes the possibility of a homosexual son since he acts as a neutralizing, protective agent should the mother make seductive or close-binding attempts.[263]

GENETICS

Some research indicates that male homosexuality may run in families. I have experienced this in my own family, although I do not see this as genetically inherited. Rather, it appears to be an outcome of generational same-sex sexual abuse. Research on a biological basis for homosexuality since the 1980s has produced several genetic theories including:

- *prenatal hormonal hypothesis*: sexual orientation hypothesized to be affected by hormonal changes before birth[264]
- *genetic theory*: homosexuality is determined the moment of conception[265]
- *maternal stress* during pregnancy[266]

The first major study linking male homosexuality to family inheritance was published in 1986. Researchers[267] found that straight men had far fewer gay brothers than the gay men had. Their observation was that *there is a significant family component* to male homosexuality. Is it possible that this could be a result of sexual abuse within the family of origin?

Evidence suggests that family factors influence sexual orientation, as well as childhood gender nonconformity and continuous gender identity, although these factors were again difficult to disentangle.

As early as 1974, a study concluded: "On the basis of present knowledge there is no basis on which to justify a hypothesis that homosexuals or bisexuals of any degree or type are chromosomally discrepant from heterosexuals."[268] In 1985, Masters, Johnson & Kolodny stated that, "The *genetic theory of homosexuality has*

---

[263] Bieber et al (1962)
[264] Ellis & Ames (1987); Garcia-Falgueras & Swaab (2010); Loche et al (2010)
[265] Bailey & Pillard (1991)
[266] Ellis & Ames (1987)
[267] Weinrich & Pillard (1986)
[268] Money (1974 p. 67)

generally been discarded today" and that "no serious scientist suggests that a simple cause-effect relationship applies."[269]

Despite these findings, North American society is still consumed with the idea that gays and lesbians are "born that way."

MATERNAL STRESS

Additional research indicates that homosexuality may be related to maternal stress. A study[270] of male babies born during WWII in Germany to mothers who had experienced horrific (traumatic) conditions found that the fetus was exposed to unusually high hormonal fluctuations. This longitudinal study also found an unusual number of male homosexuals born to these mothers. In a follow-up study[271] of 285 women with offspring 19 years of age and older, retrospective accounts of stressful experiences were provided, beginning 12 months prior to pregnancy up to the point of giving birth. When weighted to severity, stressful experiences helped predict the sexual orientation of male offspring. The data suggest that "the most critical time in gestation for influencing human sexual orientation of male offspring is during the second trimester."

There have been suggestions of hormonal disruptions that could affect the development of sexual orientation.

EQUIFINALITY OR *MULTIFINALITY*

I introduced the concepts of Equifinality and Multifinality in *Deep Impact: The Integration of Theology and Psychology in the Treatment of Complex Traumatic Stress.*[272] These principles hold true for many variances in human behaviour. Equifinality means that a diversity of pathways can lead to one outcome.[273]

Many scientists, especially neurologists, maintain that thoughts and emotions affect our functioning even to the cellular and biochemical level. As well, changes at biological levels could influence thinking and feeling. There is a growing recognition of the role of the developing person as a processor of experience.[274] Reality then, to a large degree, is constructed subjectively (personally/individually) through the processes of the mind. This does not diminish the fact that objective, absolute truth exists, but it is important to

---

[269] Masters, Johnson & Kolodny (1985 p. 319-320)
[270] Dörner et al (1983)
[271] Ellis et al (1988 p. 152)
[272] Gillies (2016)
[273] Mayr (1964, 1988)
[274] Cicchetti & Rogosch, 1999

recognize that the process of perception, interpretation, and the conclusions we come to has a significant impact on the way we experience life.

Multifinality means that different outcomes may stem from similar beginnings. Two people may begin on the same major pathway, but, as a result of subsequent choices, exhibit very different patterns of behaviour. "An understanding of equifinality and multifinality in development encourages individuals to 'look outside the box and perceive underlying elements that could be directing behaviour.'"[275]

To explain this more clearly, early physical abuse might lead to a conduct disorder or to a personality disorder, depending on the person's preferences and environmental supports. Or take another example: poverty predisposes one toward conduct disorder but also toward substance abuse disorder.

No one actually knows what causes homosexuality; current theory holds that there are probably many different developmental paths. Sexual orientation is currently assumed to be *shaped and reshaped by a cascade of choices* made in the context of changing environments, circumstances, enormous social and cultural pressures and considerable predispositions toward certain types of preferences.[276]

Same-sex attraction development is a complex constellation of events, giving rise to the possibility of the equifinality of same-sex attraction. The same is true for Gender Dysphoria. The chart below may help conceptualize this in a visual manner.

Equifinality –
Multiple Risk Factors and One Outcome

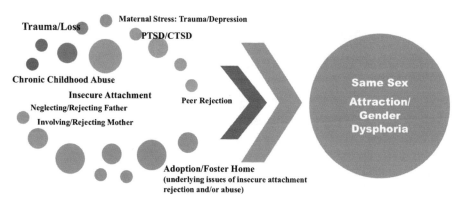

Maternal Stress: Trauma/Depression

Trauma/Loss

PTSD/CTSD

Chronic Childhood Abuse

Insecure Attachment

Neglecting/Rejecting Father

Involving/Rejecting Mother

Peer Rejection

Same Sex Attraction/ Gender Dysphoria

Adoption/Foster Home
(underlying issues of insecure attachment rejection and/or abuse)

---

[275] Cicchetti & Cohen (2006 p. 13)
[276] Jones & Yarhouse (2000); Landolt et al (2004)

Heredity, Temperament… (source: Cohen 1999, p. 29)

Heredity	Temperament	Hetero/Homo-emotional Wounds	Sibling Wounds/Family Dynamic	Body Image Wounds	Sexual Abuse	Social or Peer Wounds	Cultural Wounds	Other
Inherited Wounds	Hyper Sensitive	Enmeshment	Putdowns	Late Bloomer	Homosexual Imprinting	Name Calling	Media	Divorce
Unresolved Family Issues Misperceptions	High Maintenance	Neglect	Abuse	Physical Disabilities	Learned & Reinforced Behaviours	Putdowns	Educational System	Death
Mental Filters	Artistic Nature	Abuse	Name Calling	Shorter	Substitute for Affection	Goody-Goody	Entertainment Industry	Inter-uterine Experience
		Abandonment		Skinnier		Teacher's Pet	Internet	Adoption
Predilection for Rejection		Addictions				Nonathletic	Pornography	Religion
	Gender Non-conforming Behaviors; Male more Feminine	Imitation of Behaviors		Larger		Too Rough/Tumble (boy)		
	Female more Masculine	Wrong Sex		Lack of Coordination		Too Rough/Tumble (girl)		

Cohen (1999) developed a detailed chart (see preceding page) explaining his concept of the development of same-sex attraction, which expands on much of the above research in environmental causation and states that, "The severity of wounding in each category will have a direct impact on the amount of time and effort it will take to heal."[277] Further, according to Cohen, "Homosexuality is not about sex; rather it is ultimately about rejection of and detachment from self, from others and from one's own gender identity."[278] Although we cannot separate same-sex attraction from the complexities of human development, this approach illuminates a new concept *called same-sex attachment disorder.*

1. Homosexuality can be a symptom of:

   • Unhealed wounds of the past
   • Unmet needs for love
   • Reparative drive to fulfill homo-emotional and/or homosocial love needs

2. Homosexuality can be an emotion-based condition:

   • Need for same-sex parent's/same-sex peers' love
   • Need for gender identification
   • Fear of intimacy with members of the opposite sex

3. Homosexuality can be a same-sex attachment disorder (or SSAD, a term coined by Cohen) caused by any of the following:

   • Detachment from same-sex parent
   • Detachment from same-sex peers
   • Detachment from one's body
   • Detachment from one's own gender[279]

A 2013 research project,[280] based on a phenomenological (life experience narratives) study of a small sample of Christian men experiencing same-sex attraction, substantiates much of what has been expressed herein. This research

---

[277] Cohen (2006 p. 29)
[278] Ibid (p. 18)
[279] Ibid (p. 44-49)
[280] Gillies (2013)

focused on how adult attachment injury influenced same-sex attraction, as it assessed not only attachment to primary caregivers but also illuminated significant losses and traumas. The development of SSA, as indicated above, is complex, seemingly stemming from numerous environmental and possibly biological interactions.

HEALTH CONCERNS FOR MEMBERS OF THE LGBT CULTURE

Health concerns for this small minority of the population are vast.[281] Relationships have been demonstrated between anal intercourse and anal cancer in gay men.[282] Lesbian and bisexual women seem more likely than heterosexual women to report a diagnosis of heart disease.[283] Use of tobacco products was significantly more frequent among gay and bisexual men and women in several population-based studies.[284] Differences were also found for rates of alcohol use.[285] Studies suggest that substance abuse in gay and lesbian populations is higher than in heterosexual populations.[286] Finally, there is evidence suggesting that obesity is more likely among lesbian women (though to be fair, it is also less likely among gay men) in comparison to their heterosexual counterparts.[287]

Sexually transmitted diseases (STDs) are on the rise. Men who have sex with men (MSM) have increased rates of HIV infection and sexually transmitted diseases compared to heterosexual men. One of the major factors is the increased risk-taking behaviour by MSM that comes with the use of prohibited drugs and alcohol.[288]

The U.S Center for Disease Control and Prevention[289] indicates that MSM account for the majority of primary and secondary syphilis cases.

HIV/AIDS and Other Sexually Transmitted Infections

A 2003 British study indicates that the majority of homosexual men (60%) engage in anal sex, frequently without a condom and even when they know they are HIV positive![290] In 2014 gay, bisexual and other men who have sex with men (MSM) accounted for 83% of syphilis cases where the sex of partner was known.

[281] Institute of Medicine (2011)
[282] Frisch, Smith, & Johansen (2003)
[283] Diamant et al (2000)
[284] Tang et al (2004)
[285] Valanis et al (2000); Stall et al (2001)
[286] Clutterbuck et al (2001)
[287] Carpenter (2003)
[288] Mayer (2011); Orenstein (2001)
[289] Centers for Disease Control and Prevention (2004)
[290] Mercer et al (2003)

Gay, bisexual and other MSM are *17 times* more likely to get anal cancer than heterosexual men and HIV positive men are at even greater risk than those who don't have HIV to get anal cancer.

Young men who have sex with men account for almost 60 percent of HIV diagnoses among all young people, and represent twice as many diagnoses as young women across all risk categories.[291] The Center for Disease Control showed for 2001–2006 that young men who have sex with men were the only risk group with an increasing number of HIV/AIDS diagnoses; the increase was an *alarming 93 percent among young black men.*[292]

Bisexual young men were more likely to report having unprotected penetrative anal intercourse during their last sexual encounter with a non-primary male partner, as well as using drugs or alcohol during their last sexual encounter with either a primary or non-primary male partner.[293] Increases in unsafe sex have also been associated with an increase in rectal gonorrhea among MSM, and those diagnosed with rectal gonorrhea are more likely to be HIV-infected.[294] Young homosexual men aged 15-22 who have ever had anal sex had a five-fold increased risk of contracting HIV over those who had never engaged in anal intercourse.[295]

According to a 2015 US national STDs study,[296] most reported chlamydia and gonorrhea infections occur among 15–24-year-olds. Data trends show that rates of syphilis are increasing at an alarming rate (19 percent in 2015).

Primary and secondary syphilis are the most infectious stages of the disease, and if not adequately treated, they can lead to long-term infection, which can cause visual impairment and stroke. Syphilis infection can also place a person at increased risk for acquiring or transmitting HIV infection. *Gay and bisexual men face the highest number of syphilis infections—and the number is rising.* Homosexual behaviour comes with inconceivable physical & mental health risks. The cost to our health care system is astronomical.

According to a Canadian study[297] the documented life span of the average homosexual male is about 20 years shorter than that of the general public. The study found that life expectancy at age 20 for gay and bisexual men ranged from 34 to 46 years and estimated that nearly half of gay and bisexual men would not reach their 65th birthday. The 1997 study has been widely disputed by LGBT

---

[291] Centers for Disease Control and Prevention (2010)
[292] Ibid
[293] IOM (2011)
[294] Centers for Disease Control and Prevention (1999)
[295] Valleroy et al (2000)
[296] Centers for Disease Control and Prevention (2015)
[297] Hogg et al (1997)

activists, but two more recent studies show significantly higher rates of mortality for gays and lesbians than the general population.[298]

Mental Health

Acute mental health problems as measured with the General Health Questionnaire were more frequently reported by gay/lesbian than heterosexual people as a percentage of the respective populations.[299] The association between sexual orientation and mental health has been recognised for certain conditions including:

- suicide attempts
- eating disorders
- substance-use disorders
- panic attacks
- depression
- anxiety disorders[300]

High rates of mental illness in the LGBT culture have been well documented for years and are currently more attributed to "homophobia." It is not disputed that the stigma resulting from this lifestyle has caused a vulnerability to discrimination in past decades, but that stigma has been lessening. Even so, the mental health issues are rising.

An important fact continues to present itself: lesbians and gay men, bisexuals of both sexes, and heterosexuals who reported having had any same-sex sexual partners over their lifetime all had a greater experience of childhood maltreatment, interpersonal violence, trauma to a close friend or relative, and unexpected death of someone close than did heterosexuals who have not had same-sex partners. Profound sexual orientation disparities exist in risk of PTSD and in violence exposure, beginning in childhood.[301] As noted earlier, individuals with a minority sexual orientation (e.g., gay, lesbian, bisexual) report elevated frequency, severity, and persistence of physical and sexual abuse in childhood.[302]

Despite suggestions that the rates are not significantly different from the heterosexual population, a large, 2004 UK-based comprehensive survey[303] of

[298] Cochran & Mays (2011)
[299] Sandfort et al (2006)
[300] Meyer (2003); Sandfort et al (2001)
[301] Roberts et al (2010)
[302] Ibid
[303] Warner et al (2004)

psychological well-being among gay men, lesbians, and bisexual men and women found high rates of planned and actual deliberate self-harm and high levels of psychiatric illness:

- 42% among gay men
- 43% among lesbians
- 49% among bisexual men and women

Psychiatric disorders among gays and lesbians are in many cases double that of the heterosexual population. The exception to this is anxiety among lesbian and straight women, which is almost equal.

Younger gay and bisexual men are more open about their sexuality with family, friends and colleagues than their older counterparts; however, this openness does not appear to be associated with better mental health outcomes. Gay and bisexual men and women under 40 years old were at higher risk of mental disorders, harmful drinking and deliberate self-harm than older men.[304] Thirty-one percent of LGBT youth make a suicide attempt at some point in their life.

SUICIDAL IDEATION

While reports point to seemingly higher rates of suicide among LGBT youth, there are discrepancies between what they report and what they're actually doing. There seems to be a high level of catastrophizing among this group. Reports on two studies concluded that even though gay, lesbian and trans teens are more likely than heterosexual youth to report suicide attempts, *half of those reports represent thoughts of suicide without acting on them.* This report also found that many of the true attempts the young people reported weren't life-threatening.[305]

There's a script we have in our culture—a "suffering suicidal" script—that these kids have picked up on[306]

PARTNER VIOLENCE AND ABUSE

Partner violence in gay, lesbian and bisexual relationships is substantial. There has been little research on violence in non-heterosexual relationships, yet partner

---

[304] Ibid
[305] Savin-Williams (2001)
[306] Savin-Williams (2001)

violence is a problem in the gay community. The Williams Institute completed a review of 42 studies from 1989 to 2015 and found that the lifetime prevalence of interpersonal violence among lesbian and bisexual women, gay and bisexual men and transgender people is higher than that of the heterosexual population.[307] Sexual coercion is also reported as a type of intimate partner violence. A 2013 study[308] found the highest prevalence of intimate partner violence—40.4% among lesbians and 56.9% among bisexual women. Other studies range from 25% among lesbians to 50% among bisexual women.[309]

A similar variation in percentages is found in studies of gay men, ranging from 13.9% to 44% in lifetime prevalence of interpersonal violence,[310] and findings for interpersonal violence with transgender individuals have been found to range from 31.1% to 50% throughout their lifetime.[311]

A study of 214 gay men experiencing *abuse by a partner*[312] showed results broken down into categories:

- 13% experienced sexual abuse
- 44% experienced physical abuse
- 41% experienced coercion
- 45% experienced threats
- 17% experienced stalking
- 63% experienced shaming
- 37% experienced financial abuse
- 83% experienced emotional abuse

A study of 52 gay men who identified themselves as victims of intimate partner abuse reported that 73% had experienced some form of sexual abuse from partners.[313]

The results of these studies suggest a very high incidence of victimization, as well as the complex and varied nature of violence experienced by gay men within partner relationships. The high rates of abuse do not provide a positive picture of healthy relationships within the gay culture.

---

[307] Brown & Herman (2015)
[308] Walters et al (2013)
[309] Goldberg & Meyer (2013); Walters et al (2013)
[310] Brown & Herman (2015)
[311] Ibid
[312] Turrell (2000)
[313] Merrill and Wolfe (2000)

LGBT PARENTING

In the confluence of choices, how do the children raised by gay, lesbian and bisexual parents fare? Do children who are raised by homosexual parents or caregivers incur disadvantages in comparison to children raised in other family structures—particularly children raised by a married mother and father? Many LGBT studies suggest that there is no difference in parenting results.[314] However these studies most often compare gay and lesbian families with heterosexual single-parent families.

A meta-analysis of 59 previous studies[315] on homosexual parenting debunks the idea that children of lesbian or gay parents have the same parenting advantages as children of heterosexual parents. Amidst shouts of "hatred" and "fake science" uttered by LGBT activists whenever a study comes to light indicating concerns for children parented in these relationships, the facts keep popping up! The analysis showed that only four of the 59 studies cited met the APA's own standard of empirical evidence.[316]

A 2016 survey of a large, random sample of American young adults (ages 18–39) who were raised in different types of family arrangements asked about their experiences growing up. This survey compared how the young-adult children of parents who had a same-sex romantic relationship fared on 40 different social, emotional, and relational outcome variables when compared with six other family-of-origin types. The study drew attention to the presence of delayed onset depression for children with same-sex parents. At age 28, the adults raised by same-sex parents were at over double the risk of depression as persons raised by man-woman parents. This elevated risk was associated with imbalanced parental closeness (enmeshment or neglect) and parental child abuse in family of origin; depression, suicidality, and anxiety at age 15; and stigma and obesity.[317]

The high prevalence of obesity in the adult children of lesbian parents also reflects known characteristics of this parent population. Obesity among lesbians was associated with a lower quality of life in terms of health, something that predicts higher mental distress among both lesbian and (nonobese) heterosexual women.[318]

The prevalence of intimate violence present in same-sex relationships was extremely high! A large, well-balanced same-sex parenting study found that,

[314] Golombok & Tasker (1996)
[315] Marks (2012)
[316] Ibid
[317] Regnerus (2012, 2016)
[318] Fredriksen-Goldsen et al (2010)

compared with offspring from married, intact mother/father homes, children raised in same sex homes are much more likely to:

- experience poor educational attainment
- have impulsive behaviour
- report lower levels of happiness, mental and physical health
- be in counselling
- suffer depression (by large margins)
- have recently thought of suicide
- identify as bisexual, lesbian or gay
- have a dramatically higher number of same-sex partners
- co-habit as adults
- be unfaithful in marriage or cohabiting relationships
- have an STD
- be sexually molested
- be unemployed
- be on public assistance
- drink with the intention of getting drunk
- smoke tobacco and marijuana
- spend more time watching TV
- have frequency of arrests[319]

All other same-sex parenting studies were based solely on lesbian parents. Regnerus's study is the first to use a large, nationally representation population sample, and primarily addresses the "no-difference" thesis presented by existing gay family literature.

Same-sex relationships are much more likely to break up than those in heterosexual homes, which has a dramatic negative effect on children.[320]

The response by pro-LGBT media: "*Mark Regnerus finds a new bullshit study!*"[321] There is no concern to fix what might be wrong, but only to discredit scientific research that might shed light on the problem!

An attempt to locate statistics on the cost of homosexual behaviour to society was futile. I was shocked to find such little data available, given the extremely high rates of disease, abuse and psychological issues affecting this population. What was showing up was the *cost of homophobia to society*! My sense is that there

[319] Regnerus (2012)
[320] Regnerus (2012, 2016)
[321] Hart (2016)

is little current data on the effects of homosexual behaviour because it would be politically incorrect to do such a study.

It saddens me to think that we are indoctrinating our children about the normalcy of the LGBT culture while refusing as a society to address the very real life and death issues of this group simply because this is considered "homophobic." Scientific fact, reason and rational thought have been swept away in the flood of "political correctness."

Sexual identity and human sexual behaviour are considered to be complex, and all the more so with the coming of the sexual revolution. Sexual development, something that had clear norms a generation ago, has now become confused, with no simple identity model to follow. It is now considered to be multidimensional and fluid, suggesting that changing your sexual desire is akin to changing your hat.

Same-sex experience, once considered a deviation of biology, is now considered normal and defines a distinct class of personhood. Acknowledging homosexuality as a complex psycho-social-biological development perhaps paves the way to understanding. The vast range of identities now being developed and espoused by the LGBT culture identify a sense of sexual confusion and the desperate need to fit into some criteria.

Despite the fact that gay men, in particular, have extremely large numbers of sex partners, and the reality that monogamy among gay couples is a contradiction of terms, this very small percentage of the population have gained media acclaim and social acceptance.

Childhood sexual abuse remains closely associated with same-sex attraction in the development of homosexuality. Low self-esteem and the inability to maintain close relationships, along with the psychological problems that haunt abuse survivors, mirror the mental health issues of many in the LGBT culture. Partner violence is high amongst LGBT people. This fact alone should increase the awareness of subsequent instabilities in their family dynamic.

Along with psychological disorders, there is a heightened risk of sexually transmitted disease within this population. In fact, rates of syphilis increased nearly 20% in this group in 2015, which speaks to the levels of unprotected sex amongst young people.

Physical and mental health amongst LGBT individuals is far more compromised that many are prone to acknowledge.[322] Minimizing these statistics puts this group of people at further risk, and increases the overall cost to society.

---

[322] Frisch & Brønnum-Hansen (2009)

CHILD ABUSE IN THE LGBT COMMUNITY

In an autobiographical account, Moria Greyland, the daughter of a famous science fiction author, reveals the horrors of growing up with LGBT parents who repeatedly sexually abused her and her brothers. She's been challenged by suggestions that "Your parents were evil because they were evil, not because they were gay," but she disagrees, and goes on to say:

> The **underlying problem is a philosophical one** that is based on beliefs that are not only **common to gay culture but to popular culture.** This is the central belief: **All Sex is Always Right No Matter What.**[323]

She was expected not to want them to love her and protect her, or to act like normal parents. She was supposed to be happy that they were doing their own thing, no matter what they did to their children. She claims they were both pedophiles, and her surviving brother agrees.

In her e-book,[324] Greyland reveals that her parents' sympathetic views of pedophilia and pederasty had been a public fact for decades, known particularly among science fiction and fantasy fans who attended fan conferences. Science fiction fans documented her father's molestation of at least ten children by 1963, but this was never reported to the police, and only resulted in his temporary exclusion from the largest science fiction fan convention, Worldcon!

But it wasn't just her father who abused her. Her mother began sexually molesting Moria when she was just three years old. Her mother's lesbian lover also abused Moira.

Family secrets began to unravel in the 1980s, when Moira, now an adult, saw her father abusing a boy and reported him to police. Upon his arrest, police uncovered a previous abuse conviction in the 1950s and other accusations of sexual assault against him. Her father saw himself as a victim of an ignorant and backward society.[325]

> "Every single child of gay parents with whom I spoke had certain things in common," she writes in *The Last Closet*. "Those with only same-sex parents in the home ached for their missing parent and longed for a real father, and nearly all of us had been sexualized far too young."[326]

---

[323] Hoffman (2018), emphasis added
[324] Greyland (2017)
[325] Hoffman (2018)
[326] Greyland (2017)

The trauma suffered by Moira and her brother Patrick was so great that both of them chose a new last name, "Greyland," to repudiate their parents' last names. The abuse was not only sexual, but also physical and psychological, and was so savage that both siblings continue to suffer from powerful symptoms of post-traumatic stress disorder.[327]

Moira's story does not stand alone. I believe we are going to see an ever increasing flood of such horror stories as children raised by LGBT parents grow into adulthood, and finally feel safe enough to share the stories of their childhood.

---

[327] Hoffman (2018)

CHAPTER 7
Muddied Tributaries: Gender Dysphoria & Transgenderism

DR. WILLIAM BRENNAN, IN HIS BOOK *DEHUMANIZING THE VULNERABLE*, wrote:

> *the power of language to color one's view of reality is profound.*[328]

Linguistic engineering, the like of which we are flooded with today, precedes social engineering—even in medicine. Prior to the 1950s, gender applied only to grammar, not to persons.[329] The scientific definition of biological sex is, for almost all humans (the extremely small number born intersex being the exception), clear, binary and stable, reflecting an underlying biological reality that is not contradicted by exceptions of sexual behaviour and cannot be altered by surgery or social conditioning.[330] No one is born with a gender. Everyone is born with a biological sex. Gender—an awareness and sense of oneself as male or female—is a sociological and psychological concept; not an objective biological one.[331]

Deception that leads people to misery is not love. It is indeed kind to be honest and truthful.

---

[328] Brennan (1995)
[329] Jefferys (2014 p. 27)
[330] Mayer & McHugh (2016 p. 92)
[331] American College of Pediatricians (2016)

The Gay, Lesbian, Bisexual and now Transgender culture have established allies—those who are not LGBT, but who support the LGBT agenda. Many from this group are now the primary engine behind the acceptance train, and instrumental in changing how we, as a society, look at sex and gender.

WHAT IS GENDER DYSPHORIA?

Gender Dysphoria is described as the *distress a person experiences because of the sex and gender they were assigned at birth.*[332] Gender Dysphoria (GD) is indeed a complex topic; it is also classified as a mental illness in the DSM-5.[333] The stories are heartbreaking, both at the onset of these thoughts and feelings, but also for those who have chosen hormone therapies or followed through with gender reassignment surgery. So, it is with humility and respect for the pain endured that I approach this subject.

The experience of Gender Dysphoria has gained public prominence through sensationalism in popular media. Wading into the discussion on Gender Dysphoria and transgendered individuals is a social minefield—it doesn't matter where you step, someone is going to get wounded.

According to the American Psychiatric Association,[334] individuals with Gender Dysphoria often experience significant distress and/or problems of functioning, associated with the conflict between the way they feel and think of themselves (referred to as experienced or expressed gender) and their physical or assigned gender.

Gender dysphoria is a *subjective (personal) experience*, much like that experienced by anorexics who feel they are obese and have an overwhelming need to rid themselves of all those (imagined) unnecessary pounds. For anorexics, this compulsion can become so intense that in some cases it will lead to death. The individual literally becomes so delusional that they refuse to eat. For those who suffer with Gender Dysphoria (and suffer they do), the goal is different, but in a fundamental way it's the same—they long to become someone they are not.

In layman's terms, Gender Dysphoria shows up when a child (or adult) exhibits a gender identity that does not match their biological identity. For example, a biological girl may identify herself as a boy and show a preference for playing with boy's toys and wearing boy's clothes, while a biological boy may identify himself as a girl and choose to play with girl's toys and wear

---

[332] What is Gender Dysphoria? (n.d.)
[333] APA (2013)
[334] American Psychiatric Association (2013)

girl's clothing. Most adults who self-define as gender-variant considered themselves different before the age of 13.[335] Behaviours such as wearing opposite-sex clothes or playing with toys can be viewed as benign, but may escalate quickly, with children threatening to cut off their genitals or even attempting suicide.[336]

As we move into the actual diagnostic criteria for Gender Dysphoria, I want to first identify the difference between this and the biological condition of intersex children.

INTERSEX

Occasionally a child is born with genitalia which cannot be classified as female or male. The name for this condition is Intersex. A genetically female child (i.e., with XX chromosomes) may be born with external genitalia which appear to be those of a normal male. Or, a genetically male child (XY chromosomes) may be born with female-appearing external genitalia. In very rare cases, a child may be born with both female and male genitalia. Because these conditions are in some sense "in-between" the two sexes, they are collectively referred to as intersex.[337] Such individuals account for 0.02% of the general population, affecting fewer than 2 out of every 10,000 live births.

Fausto-Sterling maintains that the percentage is higher (1.7%) and affirms her belief that all possible combinations of sexual anatomy must be considered normal.[338] While a cow might have a two-headed calf (which happened on my cousin's farm), this "natural process," produced by nature as it is, is *nevertheless an abnormal condition.*

Further, Gender Dysphoria is a mental illness, unlike the intersex diagnosis, which is a medical diagnosis accounting for 0.02% of the general population, affecting fewer than 2 out of every 10,000 live births.[339] The waters are muddy, though, as there is a move afoot to expand the definition of intersex beyond classic intersex conditions to include individuals who deviate from the "Platonic ideal" of physical dimorphism (differences of male and female).[340]

Scientific data supports the conclusion that human sex is a dichotomy; it is binary—male and female—not a continuum. More than 99.98% of humans are born either male or female. Therefore, the term *intersex* is accurately used to

---

[335] Kennedy & Hellen (2010)

[336] Grossman & D'Augelli (2007)

[337] Sax (2002)

[338] Fausto-Sterling (2000)

[339] Sax (2002)

[340] Blackless et al. (2000)

describe a group of medical conditions where there is a *discrepancy between the external genitals and the internal genitals (the testes and ovaries).* The older term for this condition is hermaphroditism.

DIAGNOSTIC CRITERIA FOR GENDER DYSPHORIA

Gender identity issues are a classifiable mental disorder under the Diagnostic and Statistical Manual.[341]

> Children or adolescents must exhibit strong, persistent cross-gender identification for at least 6 months, (not merely a desire for any perceived cultural advantages of being the other sex). In children, the disturbance is manifested by four (or more) of the following:
>
> 1. Repeatedly stated desire to be, or insistence that he or she is, the other sex
> 2. In boys, preference for cross-dressing or simulating female attire; in girls, insistence on wearing only stereotypical masculine clothing
> 3. Strong and persistent preferences for cross-sex roles in make-believe play or persistent fantasies of being the other sex
> 4. Intense desire to participate in the stereotypical games and pastimes of the other sex
> 5. Strong preference for playmates of the other sex
>   - In adolescents and adults, the disturbance is manifested by symptoms such as a stated desire to be the other sex, frequent passing as the other sex, desire to live or be treated as the other sex, or the conviction that he or she has the typical feelings and reactions of the other sex.
>   a. Persistent discomfort with his or her sex or sense of inappropriateness in the gender role of that sex. In children, the disturbance is manifested by any of the following:
>   ○ In boys, assertion that his penis or testes are disgusting or will disappear or assertion that it would be better not to have a penis, or aversion toward rough-and-tumble play and rejection of male stereotypical toys, games, and activities;
>   ○ In girls, rejection of urinating in a sitting position, assertion that she has or will grow a penis, or assertion that she does not want to grow breasts or menstruate, or marked aversion toward normative feminine clothing.

---

[341] American Psychiatric Association (2013)

○ In adolescents and adults, the disturbance is manifested by symptoms such as preoccupation with getting rid of primary and secondary sex characteristics (e.g., request for hormones, surgery, or other procedures to physically alter sexual characteristics to simulate the other sex) or belief that he or she was born the wrong sex.

b. The disturbance is not concurrent with a physical intersex condition.

c. The disturbance causes clinically significant distress or impairment in social, occupational, or other important areas of functioning.[342]

Symptoms must last at least six months. According to the DSM-5 (2013), the prevalence of Gender Dysphoria for natal males ranges between 0.005 and 0.014%. For natal females, the range is from 0.002 to 0.003%. GD is extremely rare, with 88-97.2% resolving before late adolescence.

> According to the DSM-5 (2013), the prevalence of Gender Dysphoria for natal males ranges between 0.005 and 0.014%. For natal females, the range is from 0.002 to 0.003%. GD is extremely rare, with 88-97.2% resolving before late adolescence.

GENDER IDENTITY DEVELOPMENT

Explaining to anyone that they have a debilitating physical illness, such as diabetes, cancer or Alzheimers, is usually met with resistance. While some people may receive such a diagnosis with a sense of relief—"I wasn't imagining it; I knew there was something wrong!"—many others experience a different reaction, and often withdraw into anger, denial and a process of grieving.

How much more is this process accelerated for those experiencing the symptoms described in the DSM? Many never seek professional help, and it is not unusual for individuals who do seek help to reject a diagnosis. For these individuals, it can often feel like a death of sorts.

Given the current atmosphere of affirming trans-gendering, Canadians specialists no longer treat GD with behavioural and psychoanalytic therapies to help the child resolve to their natal sex, even though such therapy has been highly successful and scientifically validated for many decades. I imagine it will

---

[342] American Psychological Association (2013)

be highly unlikely that we actually see a GD designation in the next edition of the DSM due to the backlash from the trans culture.

Until recently, it was assumed that children would identify as their biological sex, either male or female, but with the coming of the new millennium and the post-truth era, this assumption has been discarded in favour of an ongoing process of sexual identity development!

The idea goes like this: that a person's sexual self-identification and the preferred sex of partners can change over time. This is basically the concept of sexual fluidity.[343] As there is nothing new under the sun, I would suspect that the concept of sexual fluidity is actually a continuum of subjective feeling and experience. It is important to understand that even though a person may feel something, they are in no way bound to act on those feelings.

Pro-LGBT ideology states that it is in families that the beliefs of male, female, boy, and girl identification are being enforced and reproduced. What they mean by this is that you and I know that we are either male or female because our parents told us so (they called us boys or girls) and therefore we are male and female because our parents and cultural norms say so!

But is this true? Are we only male and female because this identification is enforced by our parents, or are we male and female by design? I don't think it is a stretch to believe what has been true for thousands of years—we are designed male and female. What happens to our minds to convince us otherwise is the social construct!

While how we express our masculinity or femininity is often a result of the family or environment we are raised in and the role models we have had, I maintain that our sexual design is binary: male and female.

Developmental course

Brain imaging research in the study of gender has been attempting to advance into new territory, as researchers endeavour to provide statistical evidence for a biological, genetic cause for Gender Dysphoria and/or transgenderism. As with the "gay gene," there is little evidence for a gene here. The problem is that most transgendered people have been acting, thinking and living for many years as the opposite sex; therefore, learned behaviour and the capacity of the brain to adapt may actually produce brain changes in transgendered individuals and make them different from others of their biological sex.

Such changes would not mean that they have been "born that way." The consensus of scientific evidence overwhelmingly supports the position that

[343] Better (2013)

a physically and developmentally normal boy or girl is indeed what he or she appears to be at birth.[344]

Developmental changes that occur in adolescence are complex, particularly with the onset of puberty. LGBT youth face the same challenges as their heterosexual peers, but in addition they face gender confusion and the stigma attached. Previously, efforts to survey young people about their sexual orientation have been fraught with difficulties at both the institutional review board and community levels. These barriers have impeded important developmental research.

Differences in mental and physical health have been observed in LGBT youth compared to heterosexual youth. These discrepancies are today considered by most researchers to be influenced largely by their experiences of stigma and discrimination during the development of their sexual orientation and gender identity and throughout the lifespan.

While I would agree that these children and adolescents often incur bullying of some form, they are far from unique in this aspect. We seem to have completely forgotten all the other children. For instance, those with mental or physical disabilities that have experienced bullying at school for decades. That's a whopping 13.7% of Canadians[345] whose childhood bullying is ignored so that the focus remains steadfastly on LGBT students. Another issue here is the fact that support staff at public schools have been drastically cut for those with such disabilities, while millions of tax dollars have been reallocated to develop new sex-education and provide specialized "desensitization" courses for teachers.

According to the DSM-V, rates of persistence of Gender Dysphoria into adulthood are very low. *Resolution of biological sex confusion occurs in 97.8% of boys and as many as 88% of girls.*[346] This means that these children no longer continue to exhibit signs of Gender Dysphoria.

Ontario psychologist and sexologist, Ken Zucker, found that children who cease their Gender Dysphoric behaviour often display homosexuality, while heterosexuality develops in a minority of these children. Because Gender Dysphoria seems to cease in most of these children, he concludes that Gender Dysphoria is influenced by psychological and social experiences, indicating that there is a degree of pliability in the disorder.[347]

---

[344] Mayer & McHugh (2016)

[345] Stroumboulopoulos (2013)

[346] American Psychiatric Association (2013 p. 455)

[347] Zucker (2004)

One longitudinal study[348] evaluated boys ranging in age 4 – 12 years old; two thirds of these boys were re-evaluated 10 years later. All the control group boys were other-sex attracted. In contrast, 75% of the feminine boys were classified as either bisexual or same-sex attracted. Of the boys who had interpersonal sexual experiences, 80% of the feminine boys had engaged in sexual activities with their same sex or both sexes, compared to 4% of the control group. The conclusion was that the highly feminine boys are more likely to become gay or bisexual adults than other boys.

Three outcomes regarding psychosexual variation have been identified[349]:

- Persistence of Gender Identity Disorder (GID) with co-occurring homosexual orientation
- Desistance (cessation) of GID with a co-occurring homosexual orientation
- Desistance of GID with a co-occurring heterosexual orientation[350]

Etiology (manner of causation)

When it comes to the topic of abnormal sexual behaviour, scientists like to stay away from using the word causation. One reason for this is that other than the definite observed biological sex of male and female, all other designations are purely theoretical. The overarching theory our society has been applying to these topics is that of social constructionism.

What is social constructionism? It is the *social construction of reality*. This denies any perspective of absolute reality within the universe. I indicated previously that our inner reality is made up of our perceptions of life and the world, and how we interpret and implement those perceptions in our lives. This is of course true on one level and it is where social constructionism stops. The current belief is that because we all devise our own "truth" or our own reality, we then need to acknowledge, affirm and defend everyone's reality. The problem with this is: how can each person's reality be right or true in the whole realm of nature? It can't. There must be an objective, absolute truth somewhere—whether one believes this or not.

There is no clear indication that Gender Dysphoria is caused by hormones or genes. This doesn't mean that we can absolutely rule out the probability of there being hormonal disruption in utero that could lead to gender confusion of which we are yet unaware. However, regardless of hormonal disruption, each person remains responsible for his or her own behaviour.

---

[348] Green (1987)
[349] Zucker & Bradley (1995)
[350] Ibid

Prenatal Sex Hormones

Attention has been given by scientists to the influential roles of the prenatal hormonal environment and its effect on psychosexual differences. There are various genetic disorders that affect the production of testosterone (for example, Klinefelter's Syndrome) and thus the development of the male child. The child is born male but doesn't pass normal male milestones (puberty, etc.), and needs testosterone to go through these necessary changes. There is a certain correlation between disorders like this and transgenderism/Gender Dysphoria. It is often disregarded because Gender Dysphoria is seen as a mental health disorder, and normative medical modelling isn't followed anymore due to social pressure to consider Gender Dysphoria normative to the person.

In the womb, prenatal hormones could account for future avoidance of rough-and-tumble play and low activity levels often seen in Gender Dysphoric boys. These traits, coupled with high anxiety and separation disorders, could set in motion a complex chain of events, thereby predisposing a young child to Gender Dysphoria.[351]

Left-handedness, sibling ratio (an excess of brothers to sisters), later birth order,[352] and lower birth weight have also been identified in many Gender Dysphoric boys. These are the same speculations that have often been considered in same-sex hormonal/genetic theories.

Endocrine Considerations

The endocrine system represents the glands that secrete hormones, which help to integrate the activity of the pituitary, thyroid, adrenals, ovaries and testes. These hormones regulate several actions in the body, such as growth, metabolism, and sexual development and function. The endocrine system is complex and consists of several "feedback loops" to help the body fine-tune various functions. Any one of these "loops" can be disrupted for a number of reasons, having an effect on the body.

At the onset of puberty, the hypothalmus gland releases natural chemicals into the child for the first time. Testosterone, the hormone responsible for sexual characteristics such as the a deepening voice for males, and estrogen, the reproductive hormone in females, are released. Puberty blockers affect the natural trajectory of the release of these hormones, shutting down the process of normal sexual development.

---

[351] Zucker (2004)
[352] Blanchard (1997)

Psychosocial Contributors

This category refers to the interrelation of social factors & individual thought/behaviour.

Again, due to limited number of female participants, psychosocial contributor studies have been primarily of boys. Suggestions of social reinforcement within the home have been explored. Can parents shape or influence sex-differences? Gender roles are usually seen within the parental home, but when parents of Gender Dysphoric children talk about their initial reactions to cross-gender behaviours, encouragement of these behaviours seems to be more common than negative or discouraging reactions. Therefore, initial parental intolerance or encouragement may in fact influence such behaviour.

Other theories of psychosocial contributors to Gender Dysphoria are similar to those I presented for same-sex attraction.[353] These include the mother's prenatal sex preference (I consider this as rejection in the womb or at birth). Rejection hurts. It can cause a neural alarm and disrupt the attachment system.[354] Among mothers of boys who had GD, and who had desired to give birth to daughters, a subgroup seemed to experience what has been called "pathologic gender mourning." These mothers often suffered from severe depression, which seemed to lift when their boys acted in a feminine manner.[355] Imagine a young boy seeking closeness to his mother and only being able to find it if he acts like a girl? This, indeed, affects brain mapping, and if continued it could lead to Gender Dysphoria. Mother-child and father-child relationships are also paramount in the development of secure attachment and psychological health. These relationships have been studied extensively in the development of homosexuality.

As is the case with homosexuality, boys with GD are referred to therapy more often than girls. I believe this developmental difference could be due to same-gender sexual abuse. It may also be that social factors play a role in more boys being referred, as adults are generally less tolerant of boys who exhibit cross-gender behaviour.[356]

A TRAJECTORY OF DEVELOPMENT

One will usually find that a researcher's bias affects the slant taken on the LGBT issue being studied. With this in mind the reader should still differentiate between interpretations based on solid research and unsubstantiated opinion.

---

[353] Gillies (2013)
[354] Eisenberger & Lieberman (2004)
[355] Zucker (2004)
[356] Cohen-Kettenis et al (2003); Zucker, Bradley, & Sanikhani (1997); Zucker et al (2002)

I have identified below what I believe to be multiple influencers in the sexual development of children diagnosed with Gender Dysphoria.

1. Childhood traumatic experiences

    a. Tragic death of a loved one
    b. Sexual or severe physical abuse
    c. Shock of viewing death or disfigurement
    d. Ritual abuse

2. Parental attachment systems

    a. Early childhood abuse
    b. Foster home experiences
    c. Adoption

3. Past or concurrent mental health problems

    a. Anorexia
    b. Autism Spectrum Syndrome
    c. Conduct Disorder
    d. Personality disorders
    e. Psychiatric disorders

Pathways of Disorders

"Pathways of disorders" is terminology I have used to describe the risk factors and outcomes for various diagnoses. There can be multiple pathways to the same or similar outcomes (see previous discussion of equifinality). This is the idea that one risk factor, such as extreme trauma—as in the case of chronic sexual abuse; rape; kidnapping; war experiences, etc.—can result in a variety of psychological and behavioural outcome.

Experiences such as chronic childhood sexual abuse often result in substantial psychological conditions[357] created by emotional dysregulation. These conditions include difficult to treat personality disorders like borderline personality disorder, paranoia, phobias, depression, anxiety, chemical addictions, sexual addictions, and many disorders. The trauma of physical abuse is often associated with

---

[357] Fergusson, Lynskey, & Horwood (1996); Putnam (2003)

later conduct problems, alcoholism, depression, criminality or other issues. Understanding the outcome that arises requires consideration of not only the initiating conditions, but also subsequent conditions.[358].

Gender Dysphoria, as well as sexual orientation, viewed from this perspective can be seen to be shaped and reshaped by a cascade of choices made in the context of changing environments and conditions.[359] This idea was once a well-accepted understanding of development, but it has now come under intense criticism and heightened intolerance, to the point where scientists who refuse to believe the politically correct stance of "born that way" (which empirical research has never proven) are largely silenced, and their warnings regarding gender-dysphoria largely ignored.

Let's turn our attention now to what I believe is the harbinger of the dilemma of Gender Dysphoria.

Childhood Abuse

Childhood abuse early in the lives of gender-confused individuals is often underreported. As found in a 2014 study, high psychiatric comorbidity (the simultaneous presence of two or more conditions present in a patient), particularly depression and suicidal ideation, is much more prevalent among these individuals than in the general population.[360] These conditions are also uniformly represented in an extremely high percentage of other trauma survivors. This study goes on to explain that clinical experience with these clients is filled with personal histories of abuse and neglect, often combined with common and sometimes extreme mental health conditions.

Although clinical experience substantiates high levels of abuse and neglect in early childhood among the Gender Dysphoric, the actual research on early childhood abuse is scarce for this population. Of course, one reason is that these individuals represent a very small percentage of the population. Another reason is that much available research focuses on the experience of bullying, birth order,[361] attachment wounds or genetic possibilities.

Traditional psychoanalytic theory understood Gender Dysphoria to be a psychological phenomenon occurring as a consequence of early trauma;[362] however, the popular approach of the moment is to embrace the concepts of gender fluidity and biological influence.[363] Early psychoanalytic theories of

---

[358] Sroufe et al (2005)
[359] Yarhouse (2004)
[360] Firth (2014)
[361] Blanchard & Bogaert (2004); Bogaert & Skorska (2011)
[362] Socarides, 1970, Meyer, 1982; Oppenheimer, 1991; Parfitt, 2007
[363] Kinnish, Strassberg, & Turner (2005)

Gender Dysphoria lacked an understanding of genetics and fetal and infant brain development, thereby suggesting that Gender Dysphoria, like sexual orientation, is determined both biologically and environmentally. Still, the evidence that Gender Dysphoria has a biological root is non-existent.[364]

In response to the more current evaluations, I would clearly defer to the traditional understanding, as the genetic and infant brain development theories have yet to be validated. Let's remember that while we may be genetically predisposed to a certain behaviour, this does not mean that we must act on that behaviour. In my opinion, the environment we live in bears a tremendous influence on outcomes of sexual development. The complexity of the transsexual phenomenon can be viewed, *as a product of our technology-based, individualistic culture*—a token of contradictions and a disease of our culture."[365]

Past or Concurrent Mental Health Problems

Gender dysphoric individuals have a history of mental health problems. The American College of Pediatricians states that their rate of maternal psychopathology, especially depression and bipolar disorder, is high by any standard. In addition, the majority of the fathers of these children feel easily threatened, exhibit difficulty with emotional regulation, and possess an inner sense of inadequacy, typically dealing with conflicts by overwork and distancing themselves from the family. Often the parents fail to support one another.[366] An intensified atmosphere of conflict and hostility pervades the home, leaving the child's sense of self-worth damaged. These situations set the child up for insecure attachment and a deep sense of aloneness, making them extremely vulnerable. As the child's anxiety and insecurity intensify, anger escalates, often restricting the child's identification with his/her biological sex.[367]

"The complexity of the transsexual phenomenon is a product of our individualistic culture - a token of contradictions. A disease of our culture."
Chiland, 2003
(paraphrased)

[364] Winograd (2014)
[365] Chiland (2003)
[366] Gregor, Hingley-Jones, & Davidson (2015)
[367] American College of Pediatricians (2016)

RAPID ONSET GENDER DYSPHORIA (ROGD)

There is only one accepted approach to Gender Dysphoria being advocated in our society—that of "affirming." Anything short of this is considered "transphobic" and hatemongering! How are parents, teachers, medical professionals and politicians to navigate and understand the overwhelming social agenda that is skewing research, even at the cost of our children?

Consider the newest dilemma in the Gender Dysphoria/transgender saga: Rapid Onset Gender Dysphoria (ROGD) in teenage girls and college aged women. This "diagnosis" is characterized by a sudden desire (without any previous signs of GD in childhood) to transition. In a 2018 study,[368] parents reported their children experiencing a rapid onset of Gender Dysphoria appearing for the first time during or after puberty. They described this development as occurring in the context of a peer group where one, multiple or even all of the child's friends developed Gender Dysphoria and came out as transgender during the same timeframe, often accompanied by an increase in social media/internet usage.[369]

> "Coming out" as transgender in the context of a peer group where one, multiple or even all friends have developed Gender Dysphoria and come out as transgender during the same timeframe.

These adolescents and young adults were predominantly female at birth (84.8%) and fifteen years of age when they suddenly announced they were transgender. Interestingly—and opposite to what has been become accepted as truth in the transgender community—for the majority, their mental well-being and relationships with parents worsened after their "coming out" announcement! These findings also contrast with existing research that suggests 61% of transgender adults describe improved relationships after coming out.[370]

The prevalence rate for transgender adults is now thought to have risen to 0.7% of the population. In the Littman study, in nearly 40% of the friend groups described, more than 50% of these groups had become transgender![371]

In the groups where activities were known, 63.7% of friend groups mocked people who were not transgender or LGBTQ, and 64.2% of these transitioning adolescents described an increase in popularity within their group after announcing they were transgender. Another disconcerting fact was that these

---

[368] Littman (2017)
[369] Littman (2017)
[370] Ibid
[371] Ibid

young people had received online advice that if they didn't transition immediately they'd never be happy![372]

Included in the Littman study were disturbing descriptions of LGBTQ-affirming groups in school, evidencing peer pressure of the worst sort. Analogous to descriptions of behaviour related to anorexia nervosa, the socialization surrounding these transgender-promoting groups was described as a "social contagion."[373] Further, those most at risk are youth who are already disadvantaged by mental health, complex trauma and/or attachment injuries, who, longing for a place to fit in, surrender their lives to further trauma—both physical and mental.

Especially sad is the fact that these children are being told that parents who disagree with their decision to take hormones are abusive and transphobic! In fact, many of these youth expressed distrust of anyone not transgender, stopped spending time with non-transgender friends, withdrew from family, and said they would only trust information about Gender Dysphoria that comes from transgender sources![374]

> They are being told that parents who disagree with their decision to take hormones are abusive and transphobic.

In 2016, a clinical social worker in Pennsylvania began offering consultations to parents of teens who suddenly announced they were transgender. She receives several calls a week, and the stories are strikingly familiar. Most have fourteen- or fifteen-year-old daughters who are smart, quirky and struggling socially—many on the autism spectrum. These girls are often asking for medical interventions that will likely render them sterile, with life-long physical complications.[375]

Parents talk of dealing with their fear for their child, while friends and family may blithely celebrate the child's "bravery." They describe thirty-minute consultations with physician's assistants at which the child is given an appointment to begin testosterone injections, with no explanation of physical or mental health complications and no caution regarding how hormone treatment might affect pre-existing physical and mental health diagnoses. All the child has to do in some of these clinics is sign a consent form stating that she identifies as a male and has "understood" the risks associated with testosterone! What fifteen-year-old is capable of understanding such risks when their mind is set on their objective?

---

[372] Ibid
[373] Littman (2017) p. 3; Marsden (1998)
[374] Littman (2017)
[375] Marchiano (2017)

These consultations often present the option to schedule "top surgery"—a double mastectomy![376] Then parents are told that their job is to support and affirm the decision, and often recommended to receive therapy to deal with their issues (transphobia) so they can better support their "son."

Michael Bailey, leading researcher on sexuality and gender, considers ROGD to be a distinct phenomenon from childhood-onset Gender Dysphoria, and declares it a socially contagious phenomenon.[377]

Protecting a child's health does not make one a bigot or transphobic. Taking the time to research unbiased scientifically validated studies on Gender Dysphoria and standing up for one's child shows a parental concern. How can parents say "no" to the mutilation of their child's body instead of caving to the pressure applied by our culture and now medical personnel?

A ***well-designed 2011 Swedish study***[378] indicated that postoperative transsexuals reported lower satisfaction with their quality of health and with the personal, physical and social limitations experienced following surgery. "Postoperative transsexual individuals had an approximately three times higher risk for psychiatric hospitalization than the control groups." In fact, this study indicated that ***beginning ten years after*** having sex reassignment surgery, the transgendered began to ***experience increased mental difficulties.*** Their ***death by suicide rate rose almost 20%*** above comparable non-transgender populations. This was after they thought they had "achieved their true self." The fact is that mortality from suicide is found to be very high among sex-reassigned persons. Post-surgical mental health is obviously quite poor, and actually worsens over time!

Nevertheless, although this is scientifically untrue, in 2017 the Elementary Teacher's Federation of Ontario declared that gender is not binary! This under the heading "How to become a Super Rad Gender Warrior Classroom Teacher!" This line of thinking serves to inundate teachers with this new but unsubstantiated doctrine. Taking a child's assumptions at face value, mental health evaluations are negated and medical treatment that would actually improve their lives may never be pursued.

What is the outcome of this GD affirming stance? Well, the GIDS Tavistock Clinic in London, England, reports a 42% increase in referrals received in 2016 after a 104% increase in referrals in 2015. There has been a twenty-fold increase in seven years.[379] While it may seem that the number of referrals is stabilizing in

---

[376] https://www.cpso.on.ca/DoctorDetails/James-Scott-Bradley-Martin/0024498-29320
[377] Bailey & Blanchard (2017)
[378] Dhejne et al. (2011)
[379] Tavistock and Portman Foundation (2017)

2017, consider that 2,016 children were referred in 2017 compared with 97 in 2009.

There seems to be little concern for the parent's pain or the number of family relationships being destroyed by a child's or adolescent's demands, blame and anger over the reception of their subjective assertions.

RAPID INCREASE IN LGBT POPULATION IN FIVE YEARS

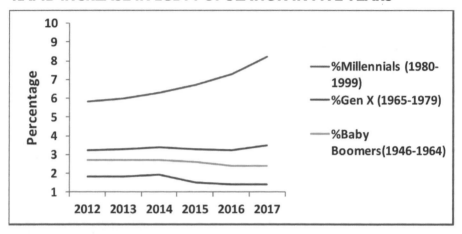

There is also an increasing trend among adolescents to self-diagnose as transgender after binges on social media sites such as Tumblr, Reddit, and YouTube. This suggests that social contagion may be at play. In many schools and communities, there are entire peer groups "coming out" as trans at the same time.[380]

Finally, strong consideration should be given to investigating a causal association between adverse childhood events, including sexual abuse, and transgenderism.

As previously mentioned, many professionals have left the *causation camp* and moved to a thought perspective believing Gender Dysphoria itself is the reason the individual encounters mental-health issues.

The causation section began with early childhood abuse, because, as you will find, most severe mental illnesses stem from being deeply traumatized—even if there may be some biological components. *My belief is that traumatic experiences, along with insecure attachment, can trigger genetic predispositions.*

While children and adolescents with Gender Dysphoria are markedly at risk for rejection by peers and discrimination, I maintain this is a result

[380] Youth Trans Critical Professionals (n.d.)

of their atypical gender behaviour—not the cause of it. In fact, most of the psychiatric diagnoses found with the Gender Dysphoric are also found in those experiencing early childhood abuse, especially chronic sexual and physical abuse.

A 2015 study found that the most frequent personality disorders diagnosed for those experiencing gender identity disorders (GID) are Depressive Personality Disorder, Obsessive-Compulsive Personality Disorders, and Borderline Personality Disorder, although no specific personality disorder seems to be specific to gender identity issues. Personality disorders can interfere with therapy and are related to more severe conditions. Along with Personality Disorders (which are inherently the most treatment resistant), other psychiatric disorders such as Post-Traumatic Stress Disorder (PTSD), Major Depression Disorder (MDD), Specific Phobia (SP), Body Dysmorphic Disorder (BDD), and Obsessive-Compulsive Disorder (OCD) were identified.[381] Narcissistic personality models have also been found in combination with GID.

Is there evidence...?

A 2008 textbook published on Gender Development[382] concluded there is *little solid, irrefutable evidence* of hormonal effects on gender identity development. The empirical evidence points to a complex, multifactorial (depending on several factors) pathway.[383]

There have been several studies[384] exploring a genetic component to the development of Gender Dysphoria, but as of this writing there remains no "hard" evidence of a biological root. Even so, schools are rushing to label pupils as transgender simply at a child's request, allowing them to change their names and identifying them quickly by their pronoun of choice.

In research utilizing case reports of Gender Dysphoric children, the focus seems to be narrowly placed on gender. The complex trauma along with insecure attachment found in these children is sometimes identified, yet is seldom now targeted as the underlying issue. This is very confusing to me, as complex traumatic stress symptoms seem to be found universally in this population.

In my opinion, focusing on the root of trauma would enable the therapist to identify the traumatic experiences the child has encountered. For example:

---

[381] Haver et al (2015)
[382] Blakemore, Berenbaum, & Liben (2008)
[383] Barkai (2017)
[384] Hare (2009); Rosenthal (2014); Van Beijsterveldt, Hudziak, & Boomsma (2006)

- rejection of sex at birth
- loss of parent(s) through removal by child services, death or divorce
- foster home experiences
- adoption/attachment losses
- insecure attachment with parent(s)
- parental triangulation (using the child as a mediator/go between)
- extreme, chronic sexual abuse
- extreme, chronic physical abuse
- extreme, chronic neglect
- rape
- kidnapping
- torture

Of course, not all individuals with complex traumatic stress display Gender Dysphoria, but almost all Gender Dysphoric individuals seem to manifest insecure attachment, sexual addictions, fear of sex, and fear of intimacy issues. How these issues interact is different for everyone, and I believe the manifestation of Gender Dysphoria is simply one of many possible outcomes of complex trauma.

The current cultural bias toward subjective (personal) gender identification, and the attempt to annihilate the biological mandate of male and female, make dealing with this issue extremely unpopular, as Dr. Zucker of Toronto recently experienced. Dr. Zucker is a renowned Ontario psychologist who for 30 years treated Gender Dysphoria in children and adolescents and was named Editor-in-Chief of *Archives of Sexual Behaviour* in 2001. He recently experienced this political agenda firsthand.

IMPERATIVE LABELLING

The perspective on the normalcy of Gender Dysphoria and transgender ideology has now led to the labelling of those who agree with a biological design of male and female as transphobic (or other negative designations). Of course, such labelling follows other LGBT groups and the derogatory labelling of those who might disagree with a minority group's understanding of self. The unquestioning acceptance of the transgender ideology, and the demonizing of those whose research rests on the observable phenomena of biological design, impact all of science, not just that of Gender Dysphoria.

For example, those who do not embrace the LGBT lifestyle due to either personal or religious beliefs have been repeatedly labelled as homophobic—

which means a fear or hatred of such individuals. These labels have been shouted so repeatedly in our media whenever anyone espouses a different opinion that they have effectively shut off any and all productive discussion. Labelling has definitely kept the Canadian public quiet and submissive to a new cultural mandate.

EMPIRICALLY VALIDATED RESEARCH

The book *Deconstructing the Administrative State: The Fight for Liberty*[385] details a now-common practice: designing and publicizing biased studies. The process goes like this: issue requests for research proposals that are slanted in favour of a particular outcome; then fund the studies, which reach the expected outcomes, and cite this research in studies continuing along this train of thought, claiming that a "growing body of evidence" supports the preferred policy. Such deceitful techniques, of which the general public is largely unaware, are now being executed in the treatment for gender dysphoria in order to attempt to produce "research" that will substantiate the new affirmation hormone therapies for Gender Dysphoric children.

> Doctors (and their clinics) primarily charged with conducting this longitudinal study are all strong advocates of affirming subjective feelings and using medical treatment to help kids transition.

When evaluating research, one must consider the fact that agenda-driven research has often been utilized to justify many things that end up being bad ideas.

The National Institutes of Health (NIH), which is the largest public funder of biomedical research in the world, is launching a new study in 2018 intended to produce evidence that supporting transgender affirmation therapy is safe and effective for Gender Dysphoric children.[386] The NIH is now funding a $5.7 million longitudinal study of children treated with affirmation therapy (hormones). That's a lot of money. This study is described as offering the "mental health, medical advocacy and legal expertise necessary to support a healthy transition."[387] The doctors (and their clinics) primarily charged with conducting this study are all strong advocates of affirming subjective feelings and using medical treatment (puberty blocks, hormones, and surgical treatment) to help kids transition.

[385] McGroarty, Robbins & Tuttle (2018)
[386] Robbins and Tuttle (2018)
[387] Ibid

These doctors are all deeply invested in this type of therapy and making sure the outcomes support their theories. In this study the "appropriateness of affirmation therapy is assumed, not evaluated."[388]

Another NIH study called the TransYouth Project (TYP)[389] is designed to follow several hundred transgender children whose parents "affirm" their Gender Dysphoria. There are early indications of bias. In an article for the *New York Times*, the lead researcher wrote about a child named John who used to have a girl's name because, as she puts it,

...when John was born his parents and his doctors said he was a girl.

The researcher's assumption is that doctors and parents did an injustice by recognizing the fact that this was a baby girl, effectively denying the biological reality of chromosomes and reproductive organs. "John's" parents and doctor said the baby was a girl because the baby *was* a girl.[390]

Endocrinologist Michael Laidlaw clarifies the thinking of the transgender teen Jazz Jennings, who claims, "I have a girl brain but a boy body. This is called transgender. I was born this way!"[391] This transgender narrative contradicts known medical facts. No genetic studies have ever identified a transgender gene or genes.

Jazz states that, "I have a girl brain." But Laidlaw, a board-certified physician specializing in Endocrinology, Diabetes, and Metabolism, has this to say:

There are billions of neurons that make up this magnificent structure [the brain]. Neurons are very specialized cells that transmit and store information. The control center, if you will, of every cell in the body is the nucleus, which contains DNA. The DNA is wound up into specialized units called chromosomes. There are 46 chromosomes in every human cell. Two of these are specialized chromosomes called sex chromosomes. Assuming normal development, females have two X chromosomes, and males have one X and one Y chromosome. These sex chromosomes are present in every cell in the body. They remain in the cells from conception until death and do not change.[392]

---

[388] Ibid
[389] See http://depts.washington.edu/scdlab/research/frequently-asked-questions/
[390] Ibid
[391] Laidlaw (2018)
[392] Ibid

Biologically, since every cell of his brain has an X and a Y chromosome (whereas a girl brain would have two X chromosomes), Jazz in fact has a "boy brain" right down to the very level of the DNA.[393] Although Jazz thinks he has a "girl brain," this is not the case.

One of the very disturbing facts about this case is that the book I am Jazz is now recommended reading for children in the primary grades in British Columbia. and is advocated as truth in the sex-ed curriculum.

Many previous empirically validated studies have shown the success of psychological therapy to help children experiencing Gender Dysphoria to affirm their biological sex,[394] but studies not concurring with the latest social agenda are ignored by policy makers.

Research has already established that administering cross-sex hormones after puberty suppression creates a multitude of harmful effects. These hormones will render the child infertile for life and also put them at risk for a host of other diseases and physical ailments.[395] Not only that—and this only stands to reason—adolescents who are placed on cross sex hormones will likely received such treatments for the rest of their lives, with great negative consequences.

One Atlanta pediatric endocrinologist[396] with extensive experience in the science of gender dysphoria states that there is *zero point zero evidence*[397] supporting the concepts of gender fluidity and gender identity. Van Meter, a thirty-seven-year member of the American Academy of Pediatrics (AAP), was outraged at the stance that there was no evidence linking health risks with LGBTQ lifestyles, and has withdrawn his membership with this academy.[398]

Van Meter now serves on the board of the American College of Pediatricians (ACP), where he states, "We are all about science; we are all about proofs." The ACP is not religiously funded nor politically affiliated, but instead *focused on genuinely seeking truth and what is best for the children rather than shaky science.*[399]

The prospective study designed by the NIH does not include a control group—something that is necessary in medical studies (unless of course it is

[393] Ibid
[394] American Psychiatric Association (2013); Zucker (2004); Zucker & Bradley (1995); Zucker et al. (1997); Zucker et al. (2002); Zukerman & Purcell (2011)
[395] The College of Physician and Surgeons has recognized such risks and even suspended the licence of a doctor found to be incompetent for failing to appropriately address the physical and psychological risks in transgender care. See https://www.cpso.on.ca/DoctorDetails/James-Scott-Bradley-Martin/0024498-29320
[396] https://health.usnews.com/doctors/quentin-vanmeter-445128
[397] Robbins & Tuttle (2018)
[398] Devine (2014)
[399] Ibid

deemed unethical to deny potentially life-saving treatment). The usually randomized "gold standard" of the scientific control study is being set aside. Further, the study is scheduled to be completed in five years, meaning that children who are eleven years old at the time of first interview will only be sixteen upon completion, hardly giving the child time to experience the world and their lives within a society that will not shape itself to accommodate their specific situations. Not only that, there would be no evaluation of infertility, life-threatening medical conditions from hormones or sex reassignment surgery destined to mutilate their bodies, nor post-op sex change regret.[400]

In the summer of 2018, a Brown University researcher (who received no funding for her study) released a study about the effect on teens participating in trans-affirming groups.[401] On Aug. 22, 2018, Brown University posted an article detailing the publishing of this study in the journal *PLOS ONE*.

However, on Aug. 27, Brown University removed the article from news distribution and issued the following statement regarding the decision:

> The School of Public Health heard from Brown community members expressing concerns that the conclusions of the study could be used to discredit efforts to support transgender youth and invalidate the perspectives of members of the transgender community and has withdrawn news about the study.[402]

There are two discussions happening here. The first, that Brown University pulled the article due to problems with methodology and analyses. OK, fair and square, if that is the truth—but remember that this is a noted university and the researcher is one of their own. Could they have made a mistake in posting a research study that was not checked and double-checked for soundness? Perhaps—anything is possible.

But the statement from the School of Public Health makes the pulling of the study suspicious. This statement seems to indicate that because the transgender community was disturbed by the conclusions and worried that the study could invalidate their perspectives, it was withdrawn.

The need to maintain a politically correct stance even when it is opposed by valid research is further nullifying the reality of biological determination, and exposing even more children to the invalidated assumptions of the transgendered.

[400] McGroaty, Robbins & Tuttle (2018)
[401] Littman (2018)
[402] Brown University (2018)

TREATING CHILDREN WHO HAVE BEEN DIAGNOSED WITH GENDER DYSPHORIA

Clinicians who treat gender-dysphoric kids utilizing proven therapeutic methods work now at their own peril in an increasingly hostile climate. Now, the prevailing trend is dedicated toward "gender-affirmative" approaches[403] regardless of data. One questions how those indoctrinating children in this new ideology will react as STDs mount, and as negative psychological, emotional and physical problems require increasing interventions.

The assessment process with Gender Dysphoric children was formerly rather comprehensive—usually three visits entailing in-depth psychological evaluations of patient and parents alike. Parents were sometimes encouraged to tweak family tendencies and habits that could be contributing to their child's distress,[404] which ruffled some feathers. Currently, the idea that a child with Gender Dysphoria even needs a full psychological examination is seen as inappropriate by those in the Kinsey camp.[405]

These children are not happy with the bodies they have, and are distressed that God got it wrong or their parents got it wrong. They are children with underdeveloped brain structures and, as all children, lack the ability to reason on an adult level. What happened to the idea that maybe, just maybe, these children are wrong?

HORMONE TREATMENT

The American College of Pediatricians states that:

> Puberty is not a disease and puberty blocking hormones can be dangerous. Such hormones induce a state of disease – the absence of puberty – and inhibit growth and fertility in a previously biologically healthy child.[406]

LGBT individuals and their allies are not only supportive of children seeking hormone therapy for Gender Dysphoria, but they have "gone to war" against the medical concept of "do no harm." Parents across Canada must stand up and resist such treatments that lead to life-long dependency.

Most doctors would be extremely cautious about using hormones on children in other circumstances, but they seem to have been pressured by LGBT

---

[403] Singal (2016)
[404] Zucker et al (2002)
[405] Ibid
[406] American College of Pediatricians (2016)

activists and unwitting parents into providing children as young as nine or ten with puberty suppressants such as Lupron.

According to the National Women's Health Network, Lupron® (leuprolide acetate) was a drug originally developed for advanced prostate cancer patients. It is now commonly used to treat women with endometriosis and fibroids, and to aid assisted reproduction procedures. Lupron® shuts down the pituitary gland, thereby reducing the amount of testosterone produced by men and estrogen produced by women. For women, this causes the rapid and artificial onset of menopause—potentially with incapacitating and long-lasting effects.[407]

The FDA reports that, as long ago as 1999, it had received adverse drug reports about Lupron®. Surveys conducted by the Endometriosis Research Center[408] (a patient advocacy group) with women who took Lupron® indicated that over half of the respondents (51.67%) experienced side effects lasting for longer than six months; for almost one-quarter (23%) of the women, side effects lasted longer than five years. Other clinical studies have found that almost three-quarters (72%) of women taking Lupron® experienced memory difficulties, and that these memory problems lasted as long as six months after the study was conducted.

Lupron® is a cancer chemotherapy drug and harmful to both cancerous and non-cancerous cells—particularly to pregnant women and developing fetuses. In addition to the harmful side-effects reported by women using Lupron® for its approved uses, there are concerns about its effects when used as part of assisted reproductive technologies, such as IVF.

Lupron seems to be the most widely used puberty-suppressing drug administered. The National Institutes of Health (NIH) and the Occupational Safety and Health Administration (OSHA) categorize Lupron® as a "hazardous drug" that health care workers should only handle while wearing protective gowns and gloves. They also recommend that "health care professionals who intend to conceive or father a child avoid handling Lupron® or other such hazardous drug for three months before conception."[409]

Some possible side effects of Lupron:

- bone pain, loss of movement in any part of your body
- swelling, rapid weight gain

---

[407] Finn & Millican (2008)
[408] Ibid
[409] Ibid

- pain, burning, stinging, bruising, or redness where the medication was injected
- feeling like you might pass out
- sudden chest pain or discomfort, wheezing, dry cough or hack
- painful or difficult urination
- urinating more often than usual
- high blood sugar (increased thirst, increased urination, hunger, dry mouth, fruity breath odour, drowsiness, dry skin, blurred vision, weight loss)
- sudden numbness or weakness (especially on one side of the body), problems with speech or balance
- sudden headache with vision problems, vomiting, confusion, slow heart rate, weak pulse, fainting, or slow breathing
- chest pain spreading to the arm or shoulder, nausea, sweating, general ill feeling

Rare but serious side effects may include:

- pain or unusual sensations in your back
- numbness, weakness, or tingly feeling in your legs or feet
- muscle weakness or loss of use
- loss of bowel or bladder control
- nausea, upper stomach pain, itching, loss of appetite, dark urine, clay-coloured stools, jaundice (yellowing of the skin or eyes)

Common side effects may include:

- acne, increased growth of facial hair
- breakthrough bleeding in a female child during the first 2 months of leuprolide treatment
- dizziness, weakness, tired feeling
- hot flashes, night sweats, chills, clammy skin
- nausea, diarrhea, constipation, stomach pain
- skin redness, itching, or scaling
- joint or muscle pain
- vaginal itching or discharge
- breast swelling or tenderness
- testicle pain

• impotence, loss of interest in sex
• depression, sleep problems (insomnia), memory problems; or redness, burning, stinging, or pain where the shot was given[410]

This is not a complete list of side effects, and others may occur. Cross-sex hormones are associated with dangerous health risks, according the American College of Pediatricians.[411]

CHEMICAL CASTRATION?

Chemical castration is identified as castration via drugs, to reduce libido and sexual activity, to treat cancer, or otherwise. Unlike surgical castration, where the gonads are removed through an incision in the body:

• chemical castration does not remove organs, nor is it considered a form of sterilization
• chemical castration is generally considered reversible when treatment is discontinued, although permanent effects in body chemistry can sometimes be seen, as in the case of bone density loss increasing with length of use of DMPA[412]

It is a human rights violation to sterilize minors who can neither consent nor understand what it means to give up that future right. It is not a stretch to see prepubescent hormonal intervention as a a type of sterilization of trans children—even if that is not the conscious intention. What's more, as many parents know, the decision to reproduce may come later in life, even if a person thought in their youth that they wouldn't want to have children. Naturally, most young people don't spend their time thinking about having children of their own; they have other priorities at that stage of life, as well they should.[413]

There were an estimated 1.4 million trans Americans (0.03% of the population) in 2017, and the demand is increasing for healthcare specific to them. Many doctors are now confronting the issue of fertility among trans communities, especially as children start voicing identity preferences at earlier ages. At this point, doctors may recommend that their trans patients preserve eggs or sperm for later use, according to Dr. Courtney Finlayson, a pediatric

[410] Finn & Millican (2008)
[411] American College of Pediatricians (2016)
[412] Chemical Castration (n.d.)
[413] Parents of 4thWaveNow (2017)

endocrinologist.[414] This is a bit tricky, especially since these youngsters haven't gone through puberty. Their bodies have not made mature eggs or sperm yet, therefore the treatment leaves their fertility prospects uncertain. "'You don't have that mature biological material for reproduction,' Finlayson said. She added that the effects of treatment on fertility was poorly understood and rarely addressed in the past for trans people."[415]

By blocking the onset of puberty in young people, endocrinologists create a situation where youth, who naturally yearn for puberty, watch their unblocked peers mature and move on. The solution: more high-tech, expensive medical intervention; earlier cross-sex hormones, and earlier sex reassignment surgery. This medical dilemma is created in the first place by suppressing the perfectly healthy bodies of young people.[416] Conditioning children into believing that a lifetime of chemical and surgical impersonation of the opposite sex is normal and healthful is child abuse![417]

Utilizing drugs and surgery in an attempt to remake a child who is unhappy with their body is nothing short of an unethical experiment—there is no evidence-based medical procedure for this. Most children, at some point in their development, are unhappy with their body image, yet they realistically understand the fact that we are all imperfect in some way. Being unhappy points to something far deeper than anything hormones or surgery can rectify.

DISMANTLING BIOLOGICAL DESIGN

As I mentioned previously, we as a society are being forced to deny the biological design of male and female. What is being promoted is that families are problematic to the concepts of sexuality fluidity, gender identity and gender expression!

Proponents of gender neutrality know that going too far too quickly would alienate acceptance of their views, so the destruction of family must be accomplished one brick at a time. Sexual identity, homosexual marriage, transgender identity and expression must all become "normal" in the Canadian mind in order for the LGBT agenda to continue.[418]

Cisnormativity is a word not yet found in Webster's-Merriam dictionary, but it is prevalent in LBGT language (which is like a language unto itself). It is a word used to describe a belief system that there are only two genders. To be

---

[414] Segal (2017)
[415] Ibid
[416] Parents of 4thWaveNow (2017)
[417] American College of Pediatricians (2016)
[418] Eichel & Muir (1990)

cisnormative means that you believe *your body defines your gender* and that your gender necessitates certain roles within family and society.[419] Being cisnormative, therefore, is counter-cultural in the millennial mindset.

Our culture is attempting to manipulate men, women, boys and girls into *a non-binary experiment* resulting in confusion and chaos, and driven by a demand for sex anytime, anywhere, anyhow. Science has indeed shown, and continues to confirm, that these individuals suffer from mental illness, and that it is probable that the mental illness precipitates Gender Dysphoria.

As evidenced by Dr. Zucker's expedited, unwanted expulsion from the Center for Addiction and Mental Health, transgender activists are now campaigning to stop Gender Dysphoric children from being considered as having a medical or psychiatric problem. Activist Hershel Russel, who helped get Zucker's Gender Dysphoria treatment clinic shut down, says, "It's not about mental health, so why does it belong in a mental-health institution. We don't want mental health assistance; we don't want to see a psychologist or a psychiatrist."[420] It is activists such as these who have been largely responsible for convincing many medical and psychological professionals of the viability of multiple genders.

To acknowledge transgender individuals as "normative" means to deny the mental health issues they face, and therefore no longer offer them the very services they need.

Such a perspective on the normalcy of Gender Dysphoria and transgender ideology has led to the labels such as transphobic being applied to those who agree with a biological design of male and female.

SPEAKING OUT

More people are speaking out than we hear about (due to media selectiveness). In 2016, gay British Actor Rupert Everett said:

> I really wanted to be a girl. Thank God the world of now wasn't then, because I'd be on hormones and I'd be a woman. After I turned 15, I never wanted to be a woman again.[421]

Everett is sounding a warning against transgender sex changes for children. Julie Bindel,[422] who grew up in the 70s, wanted to be a boy—boys had more

[419] Bauer (2009); Erickson-Schroth (2014)
[420] Singal (2017)
[421] Weatherbe (2016)
[422] Bindel (2016)

power, more freedom, more fun! Today, liberal teachers and social workers would probably tell her that she was trapped in the wrong body. Bindel is appalled at the new gender rules being imposed on parents if they don't affirm their child's preferences.

A young woman from the U.S. talks about her dad giving into his make-believe transgender impulses. When he left his family to chase after what he desired, he still wasn't satisfied, and he died a sad, confused, forgetful and regretful old man. Her father's desires left permanent scars in her life.

DONNA'S STORY

I was raised in a church-attending family. My parents got divorced when I was about 5 years old. I became known as a peculiar kid who was very expressive and talked like an adult. Around 7 years of age, I had my first crush on a girl in my dance class, but I didn't quite understand what those feelings were. A few years later, I began dressing up as a guy for Halloween.

Every year for about 6 years, I had a crush on new girls at school. I also began playing online games, to which I quickly became addicted. In these games, I had made a male character and dated girls from all around the world. Meanwhile, in reality, I was dating new guys constantly, trying to unsuccessfully to fall in love with any of them. I endured this double life during all my years of high school.

When I graduated and entered college, I decided that I would stop forcing myself to love men, because I obviously liked girls. I dated a few girls, but I felt very uncomfortable and even terrified until I had my first girlfriend at the age of 18. Our breakup happened nearly as soon as the relationship started, and it hurt me in a way that was far worse than expected. I fell into deep depression. Depression had already been part of my life for many years. But this time, I was planning suicide.

One day, as I was driving back home from Montreal, I was devastated from a very short and disappointing meeting with my ex-girlfriend, who, out of despair, I had decided to visit. Thinking about death in a much more serious way, I decided to pray to God and ask Him to show me His love for me.

I got back home and the next day, which was only about 9 hours later, I was driving to the gym with a friend and I got pulled over by a police officer because I accelerated to get through a yellow light. He asked for my papers, talked to me about my infraction, and asked me what the sticker in my back window meant, and I asked: "The 'Got Jesus?' one?" He said yes, and I answered: "Well it means, 'Do you have Jesus in your life?'"

Truth is, that's what I'd heard in church, way back when I used to go…so I considered myself a Christian and assumed that I knew what that all meant. He went to his car with my papers and came back about 5 minutes later, gave me my papers and said, "Well for today, it's only going to be a verbal warning. As the saying goes: 'Jesus saves.'" Then he said, "I'm a Christian too!" And at that moment, he removed his glove and pulled out his cross from under his vest. At that exact moment, I realized that God was real, powerful and cared deeply about *me*.

As I was still trying to survive depression, going through existential questions, I began searching for both God and my identity—but especially my identity, as I was offered so many options, some of which were very new and exciting. I was soon led back to what I had learned in my college class called "Psychology of Sexuality," where I was taught that transsexuality was making lots of people happy because it was the normal process for anyone dealing with a profound discomfort about being associated with their biological sex, also known as "Gender Dysphoria."

I researched it, and grew fascinated by how someone could be so drastically transformed in their physical appearance. I wanted that! I wanted some sort of… brand new start, and I also wanted to love myself more—especially physically.

I longed to date women with a clean conscience. I hated women's clothes, putting on makeup, dating guys, walking/talking/sitting like a girl—and I remembered how good it had felt to be seen as a guy in the online game and on Halloween. I remembered how badly I wanted to be the guy character in movies, and how I always chose Ken when it was time to play Barbie with my friends as a child.

It started making sense in my mind that I was like them, those Gender Dysphoric people! I joined an LGBT group where I could share my feelings and thoughts, and they suggested I try using male pronouns for myself and see what that would feel like. They suggested I ask others to do the same when I became more comfortable.

This quickly led me to give myself a new name, Don, along with changing my entire wardrobe, cutting my hair short, and eventually, starting to pump hormones intramuscularly. I was only on them for 9 months, but will suffer the effects for the rest of my life.

I was also dating a girl for a total of 1 year. She was a nurse and could therefore give me my injections. Everything seemed to be going fine, although I couldn't figure out what God thought about my transition. I was constantly praying with my girlfriend that we would receive a sign. Every time we got something that looked like a sign that we were on the right path, we rejoiced, assuming it was a confirmation. The problem was we always found ourselves praying again for a new sign because that one wasn't convincing enough.

Then on the 10th of May 2016, someone took the time to explain what it truly meant for Jesus to have died for us. Jesus was the only One who could sacrifice Himself and pay the price that *we owed* for our sin, so that we could put our feet in Heaven one day.

We realized that we thought that with enough "good deeds," we could earn it…but God didn't sacrifice His Son just as a symbol or a cute story for us to think about. God wanted us to experience total *freedom* from depression, anxiety, alcohol abuse, and addiction to porn. You name it, we were into it. But God never meant for us to live a life in any form of bondage.

Five days later, my girlfriend and I decided to give our entire life to the One who had laid down His for us. We didn't know at the time what it was going to mean for our relationship and my transition.

Two days later, on the 17th of May, I prayed. This time, I prayed that God would change my heart about transition if that wasn't His will for me. Nothing happened that day.

I simply went to work and forgot about what I had asked Him.

That night I had a dream about transition. It felt like I was struggling to remember it. When I woke up the next morning transitioning was the first thing on my mind and all the "good feelings" about transitioning left.

Suddenly I didn't want to wear men's clothes anymore. I didn't enjoy being called Don anymore. I didn't enjoy being seen as a guy anymore.

I thought the good feelings would come back throughout the day, but they didn't. They didn't come back the next day, or the next one, or the next one. On the 4th day after the dream, I began to watch some YouTube videos about other people who had experiences with God that were similar to mine.

All of a sudden it hit me! God *never created me a guy with a girl's body*, I had been trying to kill the girl inside me. He had answered my prayer. I began crying, and asked God to forgive me for what I had done to my body and how I had made Him grieve.

I went in my room and opened the only box that I had left of women's clothes and wore the first pieces on top. I called my girlfriend, who happened to be gone for the weekend, and told her that I wasn't going to take my injection on that day as I was going to stop transitioning. God had told me who I really was.

She told me that she knew it already and that everything was going to be fine. Just before my call, while she was driving, she received the same conviction in her heart and she declared it out loud: "Donna is a woman; we are living in a homosexual relationship. God, what do I do now?"

I stopped transitioning on May 21st, 2016. We peacefully and willfully broke up when she came back home, and we both got baptized at the same time! A few weeks later, we realized that we had both lost all desire for women.

It's now been over a year. We are now great friends but no longer lovers! I am continuing to sincerely heal in the deep areas I had been trying to bandage with a transgender persona.

Most people will never know what my story truly felt like, and for that I'm glad. My desire is to proclaim how God has truly set me (and many others) free from these sinful desires of the heart.

My prayer is that others would come to know Jesus through my testimony.

I also need to apologize to myself. Donna, *I am sorry.*

If I would've known your true value, I wouldn't have done that to you.

If I knew how much you were going to lose, I wouldn't have taken anything from you.

I've been imprudent. I've been impatient. I've been selfish.

I'm sorry for all the people that you made feel stupid about supporting you, once you came out as...your biological sex. I'm sorry for all the money you wasted on clothes and all the time you had to wait for your hair to grow back. I'm sorry for all the times you looked in the mirror and regretted the whole thing as your reflection was taking forever to look like *you* again. I'm sorry for your family and friends who followed you through it all without quite knowing what was going on and without having the time to adapt. I'm sorry for all the needles you poked your skin with, and all the times you got drunk to numb the pain.

And your voice...It was magnificent! I don't even know why it ever annoyed me.

Every tone you used, every note you sang, every poem you spoke...it was the most beautiful thing I had ever heard.

I'm sorry I gave it away, sorry that you trusted me with it and that I betrayed you. I told you about those feelings that I had, and although they were strong, they were only temporary. I was so convinced, myself, that I convinced you. I was ready to go all the way with this new life, because it all seemed to make sense once and for all, but I forgot about you. I forgot about what truly mattered. I think, perhaps, I even hated you. And...I'm sorry for that too.

But have faith that God will restore it! You have a good Father, and He wants the best for you! Believe that He will give you back what was stolen from you.

I hope it will happen before you get married, so your husband will call you all the time just to hear your voice because he misses it.

I hope it will happen before you have kids, so they will always be asking for mommy to read them stories because her voice is so sweet and comforting.

I hope there will be a big crowd that day, and they will all hear your voice crack and your pitch rise, and they will all stand up and applaud. I hope it will be worthy of God's glory and that it will change people's lives.

I know you have a hard time believing it most days.

I know I almost made you give up a few times, months ago.

I know that you fear phone calls, talking to guys your age, engaging with strangers, and singing in front of people now.

I know that you hate being misgendered by people and listening to yourself in videos because you know that you don't sound like a woman.

I feel your pain, but there is hope.

TRANSGENDER

Transgender is a broad category. The word is typically used to indicate any individual whose gender-related identification or external appearance either violates the conventional thinking (the design of biology of "male" or "female") or mixes biological descriptions of male and female. The description of male and female which through centuries has been considered binary (two distinct and opposite biological sexes) is now being disputed and dismantled within our culture. Young people like Donna are being encouraged to try out new ways of being—with devastating consequences.

While the term "sex" refers to biological differences—chromosomes, hormonal differences, internal and external sex organs—the word "gender" is used to *describe the characteristics* that a society or culture chooses to use to describe masculine or feminine traits. Gender defines more of a social role, either based on the sex of the person or their personal identification, i.e. transgender, of their own subjective awareness of their gender identity.

For the average individual, this can become incredibly confusing. As previously indicated, there are significant psychological, social and medical issues that face young people who identify as gay, lesbian, bisexual or transgender. Some researchers and academic societies say that almost all these issues arise from the stigmatization these youth face. Other theorists believe there are deeper, unexplored psychological issues. The psychological camp is once again divided on the "nature or nurture" aspects of transgender behaviour.

Gender nonconformity describes an individual who behaves in a manner contrary to the gender-specific norms of his or her biological sex.

The term *transsexual* is typically used to refer to individuals who *feel* that their true psychological gender is opposite of their biological sex, and who seek surgical or hormonal modifications to bring these two into alignment.[423] We need to be very aware that those who complete transsexual transitions are often disappointed in the results. Most people believe that changing gender will make "everything alright."[424] However, rates of suicide are 20 times higher among adults who use cross-sex hormones and undergo sex reassignment surgery.[425] It makes one wonder what compassionate person would subject a child to this fate, knowing these realities and that the vast majority grow out of their confusion. Cosmetic surgery cannot change chromosomes or make a man a woman; neither can it make a woman into a man, biologically.

There are better ways to help these individuals, but these require commitment, and time. Transgender people have been brainwashed. They no longer consider pursuing alternatives such as complex trauma therapy.

Redefining sex reassignment surgery as medical treatment rather than cosmetic surgery means that you and I as tax payers have to finance hormone treatment or surgery that supports an individual's delusionary concept of "being in the wrong body." The fact is these surgeries and hormone treatments do not magically make a man into a woman or vice versa. Nor do they automatically make the individual "happier."[426] In fact, research suggests that the suicide rate is at least as high or possibly higher after surgery. Why? Because the fact remains that surgery cannot change biology. Surgery, as Dr. Zucker has stated, does not cure unhappiness. What these people need is a hope and a purpose.

THE SOFT SELL...

using media to convey the message in such a way as to touch the heart. Ads depict beautiful, healthy infants with the caption, "We welcome Chestfeeding Parents."

THE REALITY...

"Photo of *trans dad chestfeeding his* son now celebrated as a brilliant image of a modern family!"[427]

---

[423] Henton (2006); Lawrence (2007); Sperber, Landers, & Lawrence (2005)
[424] Chiland (2003)
[425] American College of Pediatricians (2016)
[426] Meyer & Reter (1979)
[427] McCormick (2016)

The reality is a woman, head shaved, sporting a beard and with her chest covered in hair from hormone therapy, openly breastfeeding a newborn baby.

What this actually depicts is a woman on hormone therapy in the process of transitioning into a male persona—while still wanting to fulfill her biological desire to mother a child.

Taken altogether, it seems to me that this individual (biologically a woman) has a delusion of identifying as male; but is not willing to pay the price of losing the ability to give birth. This is how she has decided due to medical technology that she can have it both ways.

Overwhelming confusion abounds when it comes to Gender Dysphoria and transgender people. While Gender Dysphoria was once viewed as a subjective experience based on sexual confusion, it is now viewed as a normal developmental event that needs to be affirmed and encouraged. What once had commonly and naturally dissipated by puberty is now being not only accepted, but applauded and encouraged as normal development, so much so that parents are acquiescing to children's demands to be what they are not.

There are many psycho-social contributors to the development of Gender Dysphoria, which arises from an interrelation between social factors and individual thoughts and behaviours. Again, childhood trauma, sexual abuse, loss through death, and insecure attachment can all contribute to the child wishing they were someone else. Asperger's syndrome has been found to significantly contribute to Gender Dysphoria, and many of the Gender Dysphoric have been found to be on the autism spectrum.

As with the same-sex attracted, those with Gender Dysphoria struggle with[428] significant mental health problems that often go undiagnosed and untreated. This is becoming even more common, as there is now an attempt to suppress these struggles in order to normalize the behaviours for social acceptance.

Treatment for GD now focuses on hormone therapy, which is thought to expedite transitioning. Such therapy has high risks and is continued for life despite the risks involved. Exposing children to the risks of hormone therapy is child abuse, and yet as a society there is a greater outcry for these treatments—at ever-younger ages. Treatment guidelines need to consider Gender Dysphoria in minors in the context of severe psychopathology and developmental difficulties.

Transgender individuals experience heightened levels of mental illness and extremely high rates of suicide attempts. While most believe that changing their

---

[428] de Vries et al (2010); Pasterski et al (2014); Riittakerttu et al (2015); Strang et al (2014); VanderLaan et al (2015)

gender will make "everything alright," most are disappointed that their level of unhappiness continues. The reality—that no one can ultimately change their biological gender—remains steadfast.

CHAPTER 8

Lost at Sea: The Concept of Intergenerational Intimacy

In Darkness it's easy to believe a lie.
It's easy to embrace values that seem to be right, but aren't.
It's easy to believe that something that feels good, is good
In darkness it's easy to lose your way and stumble
You might even take a life-ending fall.[429]

I BELIEVE THAT WE ARE LIVING IN A TIME OF NEARLY IMPENETRABLE DARKNESS. Let me explain. This is a darkness that has been propagated by lies, the most serious of which is that there can be no absolute truth. This darkness is called relativism. Relativism means that knowledge, truth and morality exist in relation to culture, society or history. Such truth is not absolute. In fact, this truth depends entirely on us. You've maybe heard the phrase, my truth is my truth... your truth is your truth. This is relativism—the idea that we all create our own truth, therefore denying an absolute truth.

In the next few pages I want to expose the deep well that relativism has dumped us into. While we may have been able to keep our heads above the water for a time, we as a culture are now in jeopardy of drowning. We are drowning slowly as we stand by and watch the darkness surround us. We need someone to shine a light into this darkness and expose it for what it truly is. We need to

---

[429] Scott (2015, June 6)

be lifted out of this well of lies and get our feet on firm ground again, so that we can stand tall in the coming storm that is threatening not only us but future generations.

In chapter six, I shared that the human libido (sex drive) is not hardwired, but can be curiously fickle, easily altered by our thoughts, emotions, and the history of our sexual encounters. Sexual tastes, then, are altered by culture and personal experience. For the married couple maintaining sexual fidelity, their intimate bonding becomes mapped in the brain. For a man viewing porn and "masturbating his brains out," pornography becomes mapped in the brain. For the heterosexual pursuing casual, sexual experiences, they create a new brain map. For the man or woman engaged in homosexual or bisexual sex, this variation becomes mapped in the brain. For the individual excited by bestiality, sex with animals becomes mapped in the brain. For the person engaged in sex with children (the vast percentage are male), sex with children becomes mapped in the brain, becoming a compulsion that drives the individual to pursue more and more of the same experience.

Dr. Norman Doidge explains that the rewiring of our pleasure systems, and the extent to which our sexual tastes can be acquired, is most dramatically seen in such abnormalities as sexual masochism, which turns physical pain into pleasure.

To do this, he says,

> ...the brain must make pleasant that which is inherently unpleasant. This means that the impulses that normally trigger our pain system are plastically rewired into our pleasure system. People with perversions often organize their lives around activities that mix aggression and sexuality, and they often celebrate and idealize humiliation, hostility, defiance, the forbidden, the furtive, the lusciously sinful and the breaking of taboos; they feel special for not being merely "normal."[430]

If you remember, sexual masochism was touted as an acceptable variation of sexual activity in the Kinsey experiments. For most of us this type of behaviour would be unthinkable, but for those involved it becomes a compulsion, an addiction that requires greater and greater doses of the experience; it becomes novelty-driven. I would suggest that the same mapping in the brain happens for those who practice pederasty (sexual activity involving a man and a boy). The brain must make pleasant that which is inherently unpleasant. The activists

---

[430] Doidge (2007)

who support this practise would tell you, in an almost convincing style, that it is simply a good way to teach children how to experience their sexuality! These people believe in an ever-expanding relativism: my truth is my truth, and I will attempt to prove it to you, so that it can be your truth also!

Sexually abusing children is *inherently* wrong—there is no other way to say it. Here is a point where LGBT individuals and their allies and those supporting a spiritual and biological imperative behind sexuality can come together. None are more aggressive in defending the sexual sanctity of their children than the same educational theorists defining strict rules against teachers touching children, under any and all situations.

Just because someone has molded an individual's brain to seek after the forbidden (incest being the last taboo) doesn't mean that we as a society must join them in this atrocity! Calling it intergenerational love and intimacy is a devious way to insulate society from the *real truth*—of intergenerational rape. As a society, we can no longer believe that relativism provides the answer in protecting our children from societally approved rape.

According to neurobiologists, there are strategic times when we develop sexual and romantic tastes and inclinations get wired into our brains. This has a powerful impact on us for the rest of our lives. Freud was the first to argue that human sexuality and the ability to love have critical periods in early childhood. What happens during these critical periods has an inordinate effect on our ability to love and relate later in life! Child abuse, rape, trauma, and insecure attachment possibly have the greatest impact on the psyche of a child, and I believe we are seeing the effects in our young people with the eruption of anxiety and depression.

I believe that the horrific results of sexualization and the resulting insecure attachment of our children are going to create a condition similar to that experienced by the First Nations peoples, who still suffer the effects of being severed from their family systems after seven generations. While we commit to healing for our First Nations peoples, we simultaneously embark on sexual experimentation involving all society, and this without an iota of understanding as to the potential impact! Do we want to repeat our First Nations legacy? Have we learned nothing from history? We must turn the tide and listen to truth—absolute truth! Let me show you why.

MALE INTERGENERATIONAL SEXUALITY

Ken Plummer wrote the following in 1991:

Contemporary concern over pedophilia and child sexual abuse usually rests upon uncritical and under-theorized conceptions of childhood sexualities.[431]

So our concern over pedophilia and child abuse is basically because we don't know any better! Parents need to stop being concerned—it's perfectly normal, say the "professionals"!

In his article, Plummer examines these "uncritical and unsupported assumptions" in order to outline the "social constructionist"

> **Maintaining intergenerational [sic] incest is claimed to be in the best interests of the child!**

viewpoint. So, what's he saying? That society's concern over pedophilia and child sexual abuse is based on parents (you, me and your neighbour) not understanding childhood sexualities. And what sexualities is he talking about? The ones proposed by Kinsey—children are sexual from infancy. Can you see how far this relative darkness has projected?

Pedophilia, or "male intergenerational intimacy" (to soften the term as they are wont to do, though to be blunt, it is incest), uses the language of child love: consent, joy, willingness and choice—a language of desire. Plummer declares that such incest is in the best interests of the child. This view constructs a world of childhood where children are "naturally sexual" and adults may help them to joyfully explore their desires. Plummer wrote this in 1991. Just imagine how far we've trod this path of darkness; and how many have bought into this lie and how many children have been abused in the ensuing years.

Needless to say, there is a pedophilic movement afoot, fueled by many academics. Tom O'Carroll, who was charged with conspiring to distribute child pornography and authored *Paedophilia: The Radical Case,* claims that children's natural sexuality should not be denied. In fact, to do so would be to cripple these children.[432] O'Carroll, like others before and after him, advocates for pedophilic rights by muddying the waters to suggest that children will be less than fully developed—or worse, crippled—by not experiencing early childhood sex at the hand of adult males!

Plummer maintains and echoes Kinsey's words that sexuality is a biological potential in everyone at birth. He goes on to state that sexuality awaits a social environment to become significant; therefore it is constructed by society—an interesting comment. I can understand his line of thinking, but disagree

---

[431] Plummer (1991 p. 231)
[432] O'Carroll (1980)

vehemently. Sexuality is an innate part of our being, but it's not who we are or even what we become. It's simply part of our design. I believe, as I expect most of you do, that innate sexuality becomes significant at puberty and in early adolescence as hormones begin to intensify; that is, if the child is left to develop in a normative manner. However, the manner in which a child expresses sexual behaviour can be altered through their social environment. What we put into the brain will become mapped for future reference. Therefore, if a child is sexually violated by an adult, that event(s) can trigger earlier sexualization. This is exactly what people like Plummer and O'Connell are seeking.

Pedophilia and child sexual abuse have been highly publicized issues since the 1980s, and both are on the rise in Canada. Yet, according to Plummer, the pariah "child molester" has become the latest "folk devil" to produce anxiety in our culture. As a result of what he calls "moral panic," many feminists have left the camp of the sexual libertarians and aligned themselves with sexual conservatives and the child welfare lobby.[433]

Mothers have an innate desire to protect their young. There are more than a few times they've been identified as mother bears! May the desire to protect your children continues to intensify as you read this book.

Psychology and the media have bought in to the pedophilic agenda (which came out of the gay agenda), and often defend pedophilia by maintaining it is biologically-based. What irony. Part of the crowd advocating unbridled sexual freedom by denying the biological base for sex now claims their particular brand to be biologically-based!

In 2014, the New York Times ran an article called "Pedophilia: A Disorder."[434] In this report, the suggestion is made that we (society) think pedophilia is the same as child molestation. What pedophiles want us to believe is that this can be loving and kind if we mold the child as a sexual beings as early as possible. This article is suggesting that there are virtuous pedophiles—those who never act on the urge to molest children—then the author declares that pedophilia is not a choice, but rather a disorder that may have neurological origins. The idea, of course, behind this is that pedophiles are not responsible for their actions. Although there is *no scientific basis* for this suggestion, there is a growing momentum within the LGBT camp to propagate this idea, just as they did with the "born that way" idea—which, by the way, has been thoroughly debunked. It may surprise you, but there are groups who lobby and advocate for pedophilia, claiming it is a positive sexual experience, and they've been active since the 1950s.

---

[433] Plummer (1991)
[434] Kaplin (2014)

The American Psychological Association (APA) seems to be continuing down a slippery slope that began with the reclassification of homosexuality in 1973 creating a huge shift in public perception. The same thing is happening with Gender Dysphoria, and in 2014 there was an *attempt to reclassify pedophilia as a "sexual orientation"* in the *Diagnostic and Statistical Manual—DSM V!* This is unthinkable, yet it was happening! Fortunately, there was enough of a backlash from conservative family and Christian organizations that it prompted the APA to issue a statement insisting the designation was in error!

In error? The APA is an organization that goes over every document with a fine-toothed comb. There is a definite movement afoot to de-stigmatize pedophilia. If the APA had gotten away with this, it would have paved the way for social acceptance and the same specialized legal protection for pedophiles that is now allotted to the LBGT community. It seems that the ***acceptance of homosexuality as a sexual norm has widened the stream into a raging river of acceptance and affirmation of incest and pedophilia.***

Individuals who have accepted homosexuality as normal will now feel obligated to do the same for transgenderism, opening the door for pedophilia and creating incentive for it to be legalized. There is a pretty clear agenda to condition educators and the public toward the acceptance of all forms of sexual expression, including pedophilia. This is the agenda that, as parents, we need to stand up against! I'd like to give you examples to back up what I'm stating.

Duke University Official Caught in Alleged Sex Sting

A Duke University official, Frank Lombard, has been charged in federal court with offering his 5-year-old adopted son up for sex. He was associate director of the Center for Health Policy at Duke University.[435]

Lombard was charged with attempting to induce someone to cross state lines to engage in sex with a child, punishable by a maximum sentence of 20 years in prison. He allegedly used an adult Internet service to conduct his video chats. According to an affidavit in support of the arrest warrant, the Internet service indicated that Lombard's profile "stated he was interested in 'perv fam fun,' a reference to incestuous child molestation."[436]

A Washington, D.C., police detective who was investigating the case set up undercover chats with someone matching Lombard's description during which

[435] Date (2009)
[436] Ibid

the detective says he was *invited to have sex with the person's 5- year-old adopted child.*[437] According to the affidavit:

> "FL" told undercover investigators that *he had himself molested his child, whom he adopted as an infant,* and that he had *allowed others to molest his child.* "FL" stated that "the abuse of the child was easier when the child was too young to talk or know what was happening," but that he had drugged the child with Benadryl during the molestation. (emphasis added)[438]

Lombard was sentenced in 2010 to 27 years for these crimes against his adopted son. Thank God we still (at this point) have laws that uphold the protection of children. U.S. Attorney General R.C. Machen wrote: "The defendant betrayed the trust of his adopted child in the most deplorable way imaginable. His child became nothing more than a pawn..."[439]

San Francisco's Gay Icon Larry Brinkin Guilty of Felony Child Porn Possession

In 2014 Larry Brinkin, who worked at the Human Rights Commission (HRC) for the City of San Francisco for 22 years and was a prominent homosexual rights activist for more than 40 years, pleaded guilty to felony child pornography possession. Brinkin is expected to serve six months in jail, five years of probation, and register as a sex offender for the rest of his life when he is sentenced on Mar. 5. But he likely will get to keep his city pension because *possessing and viewing child porn apparently is not considered a crime of "moral turpitude"* (depravity) under San Francisco's retirement/pension rules.

According to police, Brinkin had photographic images of *children between the ages of 1 and 3 who were being sodomized and forced to perform oral sex on adult men.* (emphasis added)[440]

Meanwhile, in Canada...

---

[437] Ibid
[438] Ibid
[439] WRAL news (2010)
[440] Chapman (2014), emphasis added

Child sex offender Ben Levin said that he was in charge of crafting Ontario sex-ed curriculum

Benjamin Levin was a scholar and professor at the University of Toronto and the Ontario Institute for Studies in Education, as well as formerly serving as deputy minister of education for both Ontario and Manitoba. He was charged in 2013 with seven child pornography offences, and pled guilty to three. Levin was in direct charge of the Ontario school curriculum although his involvement was denied by the Liberal government.

> He stated: I was the deputy minister of education. In that role, I was the chief civil servant. I was responsible for the operation of the Ministry of Education and everything that they do; I was brought in to implement the new education policy.[441]

Levin was convicted in 2015 and sentenced to three years in prison on child porn charges. He was described by friends and family as a "kind, gentle and treasured" man.[442] Now that line is beginning to sound familiar! This 63-year-old father of three consistently claimed to have had sex with his own daughters, starting at age three—although, as he told one of the undercover officers, "I wish we'd started younger."[443] He essentially boasted about having achieved sexual *contact* (there's that word again!) with all three of his children, further incriminating himself by stating that his family knew nothing about his online activities. Levin sent one undercover office an image of a child in a short skirt and a top covering only her breasts. She was bound, hands behind her back, ankles in handcuffs, gag in her mouth and a leash dangling down in front. The image showed a woman standing over the girl. Levin wrote, "mmm, so hot to imagine a mother doing that to her girl to please her lover."[444]

Levin, according to The Sun news organization, has been paroled and found to be trolling academic studies on pornography, claiming he neither did anything wrong nor hurt anyone.[445]

---

[441] Blatchford (2015)
[442] Blatchford (2015)
[443] National Post (April 14, 2015)
[444] National Post (April 13, 2015)
[445] Mandel (Nov. 15, 2017)

OPP charge 80 people linked to Internet Child Pornography after days of raids; 274 offenses alleging sexual assault, making, distributing and accessing child pornography

OPP Chief Superintendent told reporters that the charges are a result of 27 police forces working together, including the RCMP, Canada Border Services Agency and U.S. Homeland Security. *"Child pornography is sexual abuse of our children and every image of child pornography is a revictimization of that child,"* he said.

The creation and distribution of images of child sexual abuse, the luring of young people by predators and the proliferation of internet sites where pictures of every imaginable sex act can be accessed by anyone, continues to be a major concern to police agencies worldwide.

One of the 80 people charged was a 37-year-old man who was released on bail on Monday after he was charged with possessing and accessing child pornography.

The man is an employee of the Milton Community Resource Centre, a daycare. (emphasis added)[446]

Nine People Across Central Ontario Charged

Nine people across central Ontario including a long time teacher face child pornography or sexual assault charges after police say they interrupted a network of online child predators that allegedly preyed upon two young sisters in Hamilton.

Hamilton Police says Children's Aid officials came to them after a seven-year-old girl told child welfare authorities she was being sexually abused by her mother's boyfriend.

Over the next four months, four other suspects (3 men and a woman) were arrested and charged with various child sex and pornography offences.

But after further investigation, one of the men is also now facing sexual assault and indecent act charges related to the unrelated historic sexual assault of another underage girl dating back to 2007 and 2008. This man previously *worked as a teacher* at Columbia International College—a boarding school in Hamilton—*as well as public schools in Hamilton, Guelph-Wellington, and Toronto.*

---

[446] CBC (2016)

Police executed a total of 14 search warrants and seized more than 100 computers and other devices as part of the investigation.

Between *2006 and 2016,* Ontario police services have embarked on *35,000 separate investigations into sexual exploitation of children,* leading to *12,700 charges laid against 3,665 suspects.* They've also located and assisted 1,160 child victims during that time. (emphasis added)[447]

And internationally…

Child Abuse Image Investigation Leads to 660 Arrests

More than 650 suspected paedophiles have been arrested as part of a six-month operation targeting people accessing child abuse images online.

The National Crime Agency (NCA) said among the 660 were *teachers, medical staff, former police officers, a social services worker and scout leader.*

More than 400 children have been protected as a result, the agency said.

Child protection experts warned they were *"the tip of the iceberg".* Arrests were made across the UK, with the majority of those held having had no previous contact with police. (emphasis added)[448]

Four men have come forward to accuse Ed Murray, Seattle's homosexual mayor, of rape

He was investigated in 1984 for sodomizing his foster son: "In the professional judgment of this caseworker who has interviewed numerous children of all ages and of all levels of emotional disturbance regarding sexual abuse, Jeff Simpson has been sexually abused by Edward Murray." The caseworker's conclusion led state officials to determine that "under no circumstances" should Murray be given another foster child.

The other men were also teens at the time of the alleged rapes.[449]

I want you to notice how many of those arrested for these crimes are parents and professionals, working in places where they have authority over children—teachers, social workers, doctors, and even scout leaders. Boy Scouts would be a

---

[447] Herhalt (2016)
[448] BBC (2014)
[449] Associated Press (2017); Lifesite News (2017, July 19)

great place for pedophiles to practice their sexual deviance, having access to many young boys. This is the tip of an iceberg so huge that it escapes imagination.

Pedophilia is polluting our society. It is polluting the minds of children.

The neurons that fire together, wire together! What this element of society is hoping to accomplish is to create future generations capable of perpetuating the same abuse on their own children, without moral restrictions. Our children are desperate for help. We must cry out.

Let me share some other statistics with you, ones that are largely ignored by the media and definitely denounced by the LGBT culture.

- In 1983-84, a random survey of 3,132 adults in Los Angeles found that 3.8% of men and 6.8% of women said that they had been sexually assaulted in childhood. 93% of the assailants were male, and only 1% of girls had been assaulted by females. Approximately *35% of the assaults were homosexual.*[450]

- Drs. Freund and colleagues at the *Clarke Institute of Psychiatry* in Toronto reviewed two sizeable studies and calculated that 34% and 32% of the offenders against children were homosexual. In cases they had personally handled, *homosexuals accounted for 36% of their 457 pedophiles.*[451]

- A 1986 survey asked 4,340 *adults to report on any sexual advances* and any physical sexual contact by elementary and secondary teachers (4% of those who were teachers in the survey claimed to be bisexual or homosexual)
  - *29% of the advances* by elementary teachers were *homosexual.*
  - In addition, 1 of 4 (25%) reports of actual sexual contact with an elementary school teacher were homosexual.
  - In high school, *22% of contacts between teacher and pupil were homosexual.* [452]

- A 1987 American 10-state survey found *199 sexual abuse cases involving teachers.*
  - In 59 of these cases, male teachers had abused male pupils, and in 4 cases, female teachers had abused female students (overall *32% were homosexual*).[453]

---

[450] Siegal et al (1987)
[451] Freund (1984)
[452] Cameron et al (1986)
[453] Serritella (2016)

○ One study found that "A disproportionate percentage—29 percent—of the adult children of homosexual parents had been specifically subjected to sexual molestation by that homosexual parent, compared to only 0.6 percent of adult children of heterosexual parents having reported sexual relations with their parent. ... Having a homosexual parent(s) appears to increase the risk of incest with a parent by a factor of about 50."[454]

• Of 52 child molesters convicted in Ottawa from 1983 to 1985, 31 (60%) were homosexual. [455]

• Even the Kinsey Institute found *that 25% of adult gays* studied admitted to having sex with boys aged 16 and younger. [456]

Study after study has produced estimates that those who identify as LGBT range between 2% and 3%. The proportion of lesbians in these studies is almost always lower, usually about half that of gays. So, overall, perhaps *2%-4% of adults regularly engage in homosexuality, yet they account for approximately 1/3 of all child molestation*. This potential makes the rate of homosexual molestation approximately 20 times higher than heterosexual molestation.[457]

Don't get me wrong—any incidence of child abuse is to be condemned, but there is a pattern here that suggests a prevalence of pedophilic behaviour among gay men. Even though the statistics regularly point to a 25 – 36% sex assault rate perpetrated by homosexuals, this fact seems shoved under the carpet. Given that, at most, those identifying as homosexual comprise less than 5% of the entire population, one wonders how these facts can be so ignored.

Perhaps the statistic that bothers me the most is that *29% of homosexual parents, compared to .6% of heterosexuals parents, abuse their children!* Remember the proportions here: heterosexual parents make up approximately 97% of the population and about .6% abuse children they raise, yet the 3% of gay parents abuse 29% of the children in their care.

Such statistics are called "myths" by LGBT activists, and the science is called "junk science." I believe these statistics show a heightened percentage of

---

[454] Cameron & Cameron (1986)
[455] Bradford et al (1988)
[456] Kinsey et al (1948)
[457] Family Research Institute (2009)

homosexual abusers. One fact to be aware of is that just because a man is married, this doesn't automatically exclude him from a propensity toward pederasty. Of course, this fact alone could lower the proportional rates as such individuals would not necessarily identify as LGBT even though they practice bisexuality.

Nevertheless, it should give us pause after we've discovered the long-standing agenda of some influential bisexual and homosexual figures toward pederasty. Yet facts such as these don't seem to move secular "progressives" in acknowledging the undeniable interplay between homosexuality and childhood sexual abuse.

If homosexuality can be presented as a healthy, good and normal "lifestyle," in the face of overwhelming evidence to the contrary, so can pedophilia. It wasn't fact that brought us to this place in history—it was activism!

The rewiring of our pleasure systems through sexual experimentation can change our sexual "tastes," resulting in what is now called sexual fluidity. In the case of sexual masochism, the brain must make pleasant that which is inherently painful and unpleasant, as Dr. Doidge explained.

Rewiring a child's latent sexuality through the experience of sexual abuse is abhorrent. Sexually abusing children is still viewed as a crime in Canada, yet the undercurrent of sexual indoctrination that began with Kinsey is pushing us further into the grips of pedophilia. Incest is the last taboo, but one that is now being dubbed as intergenerational love and intimacy.

The fact that Kinsey adherents downplay societal concern regarding child abuse should be a sounding gong to parents and educators of the increased need to protect the most vulnerable of our society. The attempt of the APA to remove pedophilia as a disorder shows the slippery slope we are racing down.

Recounting the surge in sex crimes, especially among high-profile individuals, speaks to the pervasiveness of incest and pedophilia that is surging through society. Truly we are in a flood zone when it comes to increasing levels of sexual perversion and child abuse. This is a direct result of the sexual revolution in which we find ourselves enveloped. The high percentage of child sexual abuse perpetrated by homosexual parents is staggering. How do we protect these children against the concept of intergenerational intimacy accepted by many gay people?

CHAPTER 9
Societal Storm Waters: What Comes Next?

Yesterday's sinners have become the new secular saints
Yesterday's sins have become virtues – positive expressions of freedom[458]

THE TITLE READ: LGBT COMMUNITY CELEBRATES 8-YEAR-OLD DRAG QUEEN. The world of female impersonators is celebrating an eight-year-old Montreal boy who performs as a "drag queen" under the stage name "Lactatia." He became a social media star after appearing on stage in late May, 2017, with drag queen "Bianca Del Rio," at the Montreal stop of the *Werq the World Tour*.[459] Del Rio tells the boy (wearing red eye-liner, lipstick, painted nails, a curly, blond wig and dressed in a black woman's gown with sequins)—that he is "[f—k—g] adorable."[460]

Historically an important part of gay culture, drag shows are now a fixture of urban entertainment, attracting both homosexuals and straights. In a "Best Kept Montreal" video (now approaching 700,000 views), Del Rio jokes about giving the boy "a shot" (of liquor) and calls him a "bitch," applying the typical drag vernacular term to the child. After "Lactatia" picks another drag queen as his favorite, Del Rio says, "Even though I'm not your favorite, you're my [f—k-n'] favorite."[461]

---

[458] Eberstadt (2016 p. 23)
[459] James (2017)
[460] LaBarbera (2017)
[461] Ibid

In a follow-up video put out by "LGBT in the City," the eight-year-old's mother is shown happily applying exaggerated makeup to the boy's face as they prepare for the Montreal drag show. His parents are fully supportive of Nevis' dream to be a drag star. In an interview with the parents, Best Kept Montreal writer Riley James gushes, "To see a family so in tune with their child's inner superstar is something very special, we must take note. I was lucky enough to have a chance to speak with the up-and-coming drag star's parents, and the love I felt in their words about Nemis (the boy's real name) and Lactatia (drag name) is overwhelming!"[462]

What do you think:

Progressive parenting or child indoctrination?

Societal change has opened the way for a further redefining of relationships beyond the classifications of heterosexual and homosexual behaviour. Such changes are affecting all levels of social interactions: changes in the self, redefined meanings of relationships, and new ways of experiencing pleasure and understanding our bodies through socialization. These social changes present new potentials for identity and intimacy.

Looking ahead to the ever-expanding sexual revolution, we can predict a snowball effect of gender expression within our society. What does this look like, you ask? You may have heard of some of these forms of non-monogamy before. But let me give you a run down from Psychology Today, 2014. It states that:

non-monogamies are more diverse forms of sexual relationships, and vary by degrees of honesty, sexual openness, importance of rules/ structure, and emotional connection[463]

According to this magazine, there is significant overlap of non-monogamous practices with other unconventional subcultures such as pagans, geeks, gamers, science fiction enthusiasts, and practitioners of Bondage and Discipline, Submission and Masochism (BDSM—previously known as sadomasochism, which entails sexual gratification from the infliction of physical pain or humiliation either on another person or on oneself).

Just in case you think I've been a bit extreme in my projecting, I recently came upon an article called "Man in threesome marriage: This could be the future of relationships."[464]

---

[462] Ibid
[463] Sheff (2014)
[464] Hodges (May 22, 2017)

According to the man being interviewed, three parents are better than two, since "normal" two-parent couples are often too exhausted and struggle to keep up with work and children—so three people is logistically easier and makes so much sense!

Can you hear what's being said? "It's too difficult to parent children in a two-parent family"—so the excuse for a threesome marriage is to make it easier for the parent. Is parenthood at times exhausting? Absolutely. That's why grandparents, relatives and friends lend helping hands when moms bring home a new baby, many providing babysitting services throughout the life of the child.

Would any one of you mothers out there like to bring your baby home from the hospital (knowing your "husband" has in all likelihood been having sex with the other woman while you were delivering his child) and handing your newborn over to this woman to parent? I don't believe these "progressive thinkers," as they like to call themselves, have much awareness of human emotions, nor do they consider the confusion for children. In their minds, because a polygamous arrangement has been going for five years, it proves that they're a real family with healthy, happy kids! (By the way, the family in question has a two-year-old, and at the time of the interview they were expecting a second child)

These three also admit that they will sometimes bring in a fourth sex partner. "We're still open to fun when it comes along."[465] They also enjoy time going to strip clubs together. This is what, they conclude, being a happy family consists of.

I believe that such families will eventually implode. Here is a young man in a polygamous relationship for 5 years—admittedly having sex outside of the relationship, telling the rest of us what marriage should look like. Jealousy is a human emotion. I believe we were designed for monogamous male and female marriage, one where you are completely safe and securely attached to one another. Deep bonding in the new types of relationships is unlikely to occur.

MONOGAMISH

The term "monogamish" was popularized by Dan Savage in a few years ago.[466] It is an umbrella term for primarily monogamous relationships that allow varying degrees of sexual experiences with others. Each couple has their own set of rules, which allows them the freedom to shape their relationship exactly how they want. For example, only allowing one night stands, only kissing (maybe second or third base) but no home run, or only when the partners are traveling and may be away from each other for a period of time. Hey, it's your relationship; you

[465] Ibid
[466] Savage (2015)

should get to set the rules that work for you. My query is…what if your partner doesn't feel the same way?

POLYGAMY

Like polyamory, this is a type of relationship where one person has multiple spouses or partners. Either polygyny, where the man has several wives, or polyandry, when the woman has multiple husbands, or group marriage, which combines the two.

Alongside monogamy, cultures throughout the world have long practiced polygamy—a form of marriage consisting of more than two persons. The most common form of multiple partner marriage is polygyny, a marriage of one husband and multiple wives who are each sexually exclusive with the husband. Worldwide, Muslims are most likely to be polygynous, with the highest concentrations of contemporary polygyny in the Middle East and parts of Africa.

OPEN

Open relationships are varied enough to be an umbrella term for consensually non-monogamous relationships based on a primary couple that is "open" to sexual contact with others. The most common form of open relationship is that of a married or long-term committed couple that takes on a third (or sometimes fourth or fifth) partner whose involvement and role in the relationship is always secondary.

A couple practicing this relationship type might engage in sexual activity with the secondary partner together or separate, or they may each have independent outside relationships with different secondary partners—regardless of the specific parameters, the primary couple always remains a priority. Generally rooted in specific rules, expectations, and communication between those involved, open relationships may take a variety of forms and may evolve over time as needed to meet the needs of those persons involved. Swinging, monogamish, polyamorous/polyfidelitous, and anarchistic relationships can all be considered "open."

SWINGING

This is the best-known, and seems to be the most popular, form of non-monogamy. Generally, swinging involves "*entirely committed*" couples exchanging partners (consensually, of course) specifically for sexual purposes. It can range from strangers at sex parties or clubs to groups of friends who have known each other for years and just happen to live a similar lifestyle.

Swinging began as the practice of "wife swapping" among US Air Force pilots after World War II, and has spread across the globe and become quite popular on the Internet. Generally a heterosexually-focused subculture, swingers have a reputation for being much more open to "girl on girl" same-sex interaction but often explicitly reject sexual contact between men at swing clubs or parties .

POLYAMORY AND POLYFIDELITY

In 2010, Newsweek featured an article on Polyamory, calling it the "Next Sexual Revolution"! It reads like this...

Terisa Greenan and her boyfriend, Matt, are enjoying a rare day of Seattle sun, sharing a beet carpaccio on the patio of a local restaurant. Matt holds Terisa's hand, as his 6-year-old son squeezes in between the couple to give Terisa a kiss. His mother, Vera, looks over and smiles; she's there with her boyfriend, Larry. Suddenly it starts to rain, and the group must move inside. In the process, they rearrange themselves: Matt's hand touches Vera's leg. Terisa gives Larry a kiss. The child, seemingly unconcerned, puts his arms around his mother and digs into his meal.

Terisa and Matt and Vera and Larry—along with Scott, who's also at this dinner—are not swingers, per se; they aren't pursuing casual sex. Nor are they polygamists of the sort portrayed on HBO's Big Love; they aren't religious, and they don't have multiple wives. But they do believe in "ethical non-monogamy," or engaging in loving, intimate relationships with more than one person—based upon the knowledge and consent of everyone involved.

Terisa, 41, is at the center of this particular polyamorous cluster. Twelve years ago, she started dating Scott, a writer and classical-album merchant. A couple years later, Scott introduced her to Larry, a software developer at Microsoft, and the two quickly fell in love, with Scott's assent. The three have been living together for a decade now, but continue to date others casually on the side. Recently, Terisa decided to add Matt, a London transplant to Seattle, to the mix. Matt's wife, Vera, was OK with that; soon, she was dating Terisa's husband, Larry. If Scott starts feeling neglected, he can call the woman he's been dating casually on the side. Everyone in this group is heterosexual, and they insist they never sleep with more than one person at a time.[467]

---

[467] Bennett (2009)

Bennett goes on to say that it's enough to make a monogamist's head spin… but traditionalists better get used to it! Books like *Open, Opening Up,* and *The Ethical Slut* are the modern "poly" bible. And then there's the online polyamory magazine called "Loving More."

Carla Bruni, supermodel and former first lady of France, has become somewhat of an official spokesperson for polamory as creator of a comic series on the internet, called "Family." Polyamorists have now come to the foreground since legislation on gay marriage passed, but they seem reticent to jump into the political foray to crusade for their civil rights (at least so far).

As with other sexual anomalies, polyamory came into vogue during the sexual revolution of the 1960s and 70s. Although the term polyamory was coined in the 1990s, it didn't enter dictionaries until 2006.

But humans are hard-wired to be jealous, and though it may be possible to overcome this, polyamorous couples are "fighting Mother Nature" when they try, says biological anthropologist Helen Fisher, a professor at Rutgers University who has long studied the chemistry of love.

It's complicated, to say the least: tending to the needs of multiple partners, figuring out what to tell the kids, making sure that nobody's feelings are hurt. "I like to call it polyagony," jokes Haslam, the Kinsey researcher, who is himself polyamorous. "It works for some perfectly, and for others it's a f—king disaster."[468]

And of course, as with the transsexual population, polyamory comes with its unique pronouns, such as:

- Triad; vee (i.e. Treisa is the center of the V and Scott and Larry are the tips of the arms of the V)
- Spice (the plural of spouse)
- Polygeometry (how a polyamorous group describes their connections)
- Polyfidelitous (folks who don't date outside their "group")
- Quad – a four member grouping

The Seattle-based Center for Sex Positive Culture claims that polyamory shakes up people's world view, and suggests the practice is more natural than we think: a response to the challenges of monogamous relationships, whose shortcomings are clear, they say. Everyone in a relationship wrestles at some point with an eternal question: can one person really satisfy every need? Polyamorists think the answer is obvious—and that it's only a matter of time before the monogamous world sees there's more than one way to live and love.

---

[468] Ibid

So there we have it—legalized polyamorous marriages on the horizon. Why?—because "everyone" knows that this will resolve the challenges of monogamous relationships!

RELATIONSHIP ANARCHY

Relationship Anarchy is basically the opposite of any kind of relationship. It is pretty much exactly what it sounds like. It takes all standard and culturally-accepted rules and distinctions of a romantic relationship and throws them out the window. RA claims to focus just as much importance on the love in a relationship as on the sexual aspect and believes that no relationship, whether platonic or not, is more important than another. It rejects the rules of a "standard" relationship and will never require either partner to compromise or sacrifice anything in order to sustain it.

Given the anarchist nature of this relationship philosophy, it is difficult to pin down an exact definition of relationship anarchy (RA), but two themes appear regularly in the writings of people who discuss it. First, relational anarchists are often highly critical of conventional cultural standards that prioritize romantic and sex-based relationships over non-sexual or non-romantic relationships. Instead, RA seeks to eliminate specific distinctions between or hierarchical valuations of friendships versus love-based relationships, so that love-based relationships are no more valuable than are platonic friendships. Each relationship is unique and can evolve as participants require; if conflict arises, people deal with the issues or the relationship comes to an end. Because love is abundant (they say), people can have many concurrent meaningful and loving relationships that are not limited to the couple format.

> No one should have to give anything up or compromise in order to sustain a relationship, according to RA.

Another important theme within RA is the resistance to placing demands or expectations on the people involved in a relationship. Whereas swingers and polyamorists often create specific rules and guidelines to structure their relationships, RA rejects such rules as inevitably leading to a hierarchical valuation of some partners over others. In RA, no one should have to give anything up or compromise in order to sustain a relationship; rather, it is better to amicably separate than to sustain an unhappy and unfulfilling relationship.

ANYTHING YOU CAN IMAGINE

Gender has become a catchword in our post-truth; post millennial generation and has come to mean whatever the individual considers it to mean for them. An extreme example of this comes from an article I read recently.[469] Vinny Ohh is in the final stages of becoming a genderless alien. He plans on having his testicles removed. At 22 years of age, he has had 110 surgeries to transform him into a genderless extra- terrestrial who is now looking for a surgeon who will remove his genitals, nipples and belly button.

"I want to be a sexless alien being, I want my outside to reflect how I feel on the inside," he said. "The overall image I want to do is an alien. I want to be a hybrid, not male or female. I've wanted to be sexless and genderless since I was 17."[470] His statement sounds very much like the declarations made by transgendered individuals, who want to reflect on the outside (in appearance) what they feel on the inside. But did you really hear his words? He feels like a sexless alien! What does it take for an individual to arrive at such a place in his life?

We will either capitulate to the sexual ethics of the world's system or we will stand firm in our understanding about the binary categories of male and female and the normalcy of heterosexuality, if for no other reason than the survival of our society and eventually the human race itself.

You may have noticed in all this discussion that there is little to no mention of family or childrearing. The new sexual elite appear not interested in raising a family, with all its resulting demands.

Understanding the direction of the sexual revolution gives one pause. What does it mean for this generation, and for future generations? Putting children on display as drag queens would have been unthinkable a few short years ago. The parents would have been challenged. Children's Aid would have moved in. In 2017, it's had the opposite effect. The child is sensationalized, the parents applauded, and naysayers chastised as hatemongers.

The snowball effect of continued exploration and experimentation with sex at younger and younger ages and in diverse relationships is simply an extension of our sex-consumed society. Relationship anarchy—anything goes—is already here! Are people happier? Absolutely not. Just turn on the six o'clock news and you find the reality. People are angrier, more hate-filled, more easily offended, and more unpredictable than ever before.

---

[469] Postmedia Network (2017)
[470] Postmedia Network (2017)

The problem with the sexual revolution is that it has attempted to destroy the very foundation of what made society strong—marriage and family. If we continue on this trajectory we will become increasingly self-destructive.

CHAPTER 10

Artesian Wells Springing Up: Findings from
The New Atlantis Report

In a time of universal deceit,
telling the truth is a revolutionary act.
Attributed to George Orwell

SUCH IS THE CURRENT STATE OF OUR ENTIRE CULTURE ON MATTERS OF
sexuality.

I am beginning this chapter in much the same way I began chapter two, by
describing the scientific researchers responsible for the New Atlantis Report on
Sexuality and Gender. I quickly acknowledge that some of my readers may want
to skip this chapter, as it tends to be more scientific and academic, but I would
encourage you to at least scan it. The Atlantis Report is not a fly-by-night, shot-
in-the-dark, haphazard reflection of some kind, but a genuinely credible scientific
report. I believe understanding the academic background of the researchers gives
credence to their report and clarifies much of the backlash that came from the
LGBT culture when it was released.

LAWERENCE MAYER, M.B., M.S, PH.D

Let me begin with Dr. Mayer, who is a scholar in residence in the Department of
Psychiatry at the Johns Hopkins University School of Medicine and a professor
of statistics and biostatistics at Arizona State University. He is a *biostatistician*

(biostatistics is a specialized branch of the statistics field that collects and examines data related to living things) and *epidemiologist* (an expert in the branch of medicine which deals with incidence, distribution and possible control of diseases) who focuses on the design, analysis, and interpretation of experimental and observational data in public health and medicine, particularly when the data are complex in terms of underlying scientific issues. He earned an M.S. in mathematics from Ohio State in 1969 and a Ph.D. in statistics and biostatistics from Ohio State in 1971.

Mayer has been published in many peer-reviewed journals (including *The Annals of Statistics, Biometrics, International Journal of Geriatric Psychiatry,* and *American Journal of Political Science*) and has reviewed hundreds of manuscripts submitted for publication to many of the major medical, statistical, and epidemiological journals. He has also testified in dozens of federal and state legal proceedings and regulatory hearings, in most cases reviewing scientific literature to clarify the issues under examination.[471]

Mayer is a full time academic involved in all aspects of teaching, research and professional service. He is a research physician and has been a full-time tenured professor for over four decades having held professional appointments at eight universities, including Princeton. The University of Pennsylvania, Stanford, Arizona State, John Hopkins University Bloomberg School of Public Health and School of Medicine, Ohio State, Virginia Tech and the University of Michigan. He has also held research faculty appointments at several other institutions, including the Mayo Clinic. His full time and part-time appointments have been in **twenty-three disciplines**, including statistics, biostatistics, epidemiology, public health, social methodology, psychiatry, mathematics, sociology, political science, economics, and biomedical informatics, with research interests varying far less than his academic appointments, the focus of which has been to learn how statistics and models are employed across disciplines, with the goal of improving the use of models and data analytics in assessing issues of interest in the policy, regulatory, or legal realms.[472]

He has dedicated his work on this report to the LGBT community, which bears a disproportionate rate of mental health problems compared to the population as a whole.[473]

---

[471] Mayer & McHugh (2016)
[472] Ibid
[473] Mayer & McHugh (2016)

PAUL MCHUGH, M.D.

Dr. McHugh's professional biography reads like a Who's Who of American psychiatry and medicine. A Harvard College and Harvard Medical School graduate, Dr. McHugh was Henry Phipps Professor and Director of the Department of Psychiatry and Behavioural Sciences at the Johns Hopkins University School of Medicine, and Psychiatrist-in-Chief at Johns Hopkins Hospital from 1975 to 2001. McHugh is credited with major research discoveries, including being "the first to describe increased cortisol secretion associated with depression, an accomplishment that led to the development of a test to identify serious depression by physical means," according to the National Academy of Science (NAS).[474]

He is the author of many books, including *The Perspectives of Psychiatry*, described by the NAS as "a treatise on practice methods and principles, [which] has been lauded as one of the most influential psychiatry texts in the last century."

In 1998, the Johns Hopkins School of Medicine, rated by U.S. News & World Report as one of the top medical schools in the world, named Dr. McHugh the University Distinguished Service Professor. In 2015, it named a new program after him, as he became the inaugural Director of the Paul R. McHugh Program for Human Flourishing, located within the Department of Psychiatry and Behavioural Sciences, according to the school's website. Dr. McHugh was elected to the National Academy of Sciences' Institute of Medicine in 1992, and in 2008 received its Sarnat International Prize in Mental Health for "outstanding achievement in improving mental health."

In 2001, he was appointed by President Bush to the President's Council on Bioethics and in 2002 by the United States Conference of Catholic Bishops to the National Review Board for the Protection of Children and Young People, investigating the homosexual sex-abuse scandal.

McHugh also served as Professor of Psychiatry at Cornell University School of Medicine, Clinical Director and Director of Residency Education at the New York Hospital Westchester Division, and Professor and Chairman of the Department of Psychiatry at the Oregon Health Sciences Center, according to his Johns Hopkins bio.[475]

This world-renowned psychiatrist is the leading mental health expert speaking out against radical "gender ideology." Last year, the editors of *The New Atlantis*, in publishing a special edition on sexuality and gender in their journal co-written

---

[474] Swaab (2008)
[475] Mayer & McHugh (2016)

by Dr. McHugh, called him "arguably the most important psychiatrist of the last half-century."[476]

Despite McHugh's impeccable credentials, or perhaps because of them, LGBT activists became incensed, as one would expect when a report's findings are unwelcome. Whatever the case, this group refuse to dialogue in a respectful manner about scientific findings that might disagree with their preconceived ideas. Instead they used their normal tactics of name calling. It's a joke, really, when you consider who they're talking about. They know they can't dispute the findings, so they go on the attack.

In a recent interview with LifeSiteNews,[477] McHugh, 85, said he was "amused" by the Human Rights Campaign (HRC)'s online attack-site demonizing him, and said he will not be intimidated from speaking out against the current "craze" of transgender surgeries and hormone therapies pursued by gender-confused people seeking to "become" the opposite sex. We need more people like him who won't be intimidated by the gay agenda.

"I'm proud of what I've achieved," he said, noting in particular his election to the prestigious National Academy of Science's (NAS) Institute of Medicine, and the recognition and honours he has received from colleagues in the psychiatric and medical fields. "I've been a part of American psychiatry for more than 50 years."

So what do the LGBT activists have to say about Dr. McHugh? Here's a sample...

"McHugh's effort to give a veneer of academic integrity to *transphobic junk science* is part of a broader disturbing trend: the use of misleading, badly designed or completely unscientific "research" to attack LGBTQ people and their families," says Human Rights Campaign press secretary Sarah McBride, on its anti-McHugh site.[478]

Badly-designed or completely unscientific "research"?! This kind of rhetoric has become a common line of attack by the LGBT culture whenever they are confronted with research that opposes their point of view. The Human Rights Campaign is the world's largest and best-funded homosexual-transgender lobby organization, and it has a long history of demonizing opponents of LGBTQ activism, such as researchers like McHugh who do not line up with LGBT goals.[479]

Dr. Tonia Poteat, also a professor at John Hopkins, is a certified AIDS specialist. In an interview she claims that there is no certifiable research suggesting

---

[476] Keiper (2016)
[477] LaBarbara (2017, May 15)
[478] Human Rights Campaign (n.d.)
[479] LaBarbera (2017, May 15)

that homosexuality is a choice.[480] What she is suggesting is that homosexual orientation and behaviour are innate and immutable. As you read in chapter six, this is not the case, but such controversy surrounding scientific research is common, which of course leads to subsequent confusion for the public and makes it easy for the media to jump on the LGBT bandwagon.

This being said, one needs to look at qualifications of the researcher as well as the statistical significance of the research itself, hence my "journal" about the qualifications of Mayer and McHugh.

McHugh's comment regarding the controversy—"These [the statistical significance of research] are things the Human Rights Campaign wouldn't even understand," he said. "They want to portray me as some kind of crank!" Dr. Cretella, president of the American College of Pediatricians (AcPEDs) said the HRC's attacks are most often directed against a person in an attempt to discredit them and their research. The attacks contain misrepresentations of science and of what has actually been written or said.[481] These attacks are factually baseless and are deployed as character assassination.

As many are aware, this kind of attack against any opposing opinion has increased exponentially in the last 10 years, and seems to be part of an ongoing strategy to intimidate anyone, especially those in the academic field, who might be brave enough to challenge error. LGBT activists rely on factually inaccurate and distorted information (such as the Kinsey report) to smear anyone opposing them. Using phrases like "exporters of hate," and labelling highly credible individuals with the invented terms of transphobic or homophobic or a multitude of other names, is meant to silence all opposition, and it has to this point been very effective.

Ryan Anderson, senior research fellow at the Heritage Foundation, tweeted, "attacks on Dr. McHugh are amazing: It's not the man who thinks he's a woman who has mental issues, it's the doctor who dares speak truth."[482]

This kind of malicious and hateful behaviour from LBGT spokespersons is one more reason of why truth needs to be brought to light. With this in mind let me continue now to explain what was compiled in the New Atlantis Report.

THE NEW ATLANTIS REPORT

In the fall of 2016, *The New Atlantis*—a journal of technology and society—issued a special 116-page report entitled "Sexuality and Gender: Findings from the

---

[480] Human Rights Campaign (n.d.)

[481] Haverluck (2017)

[482] LaBarbera (2017, May 15)

Biological, Psychological and Social Sciences," authored by Mayer and McHugh. This report is divided into three sections: Sexual Orientation; Sexuality, Mental Health Outcomes and Social Stress; and Gender Identity.

The focus is on scientific evidence—what it shows and what it does not show. It examines concepts such as heterosexuality, homosexuality, bisexuality, Gender Dysphoria and transgender issues. I want to remind you again that Mayer, whose impressive credentials were explored above, was the chief statistician.

For this chapter I will focus on the findings for the Gender Dysphoric population.

According to the American Psychological Association (APA):

> Sex is assigned at birth and refers to one's biological status as either male or female. Gender on the other hand refers to the socially constructed roles, behaviours, activities and attributes a given society considers appropriate for girls/women and boys/men[483].

This definition seeks to advocate that gender is wholly "socially constructed" and detached from biology. I keep asking myself—how did we find ourselves in this dilemma? Detaching gender from biology is causing tremendous confusion, especially for our children.

Mayer & McHugh share the example of Thomas Beatie, who made headlines as a man who gave birth to three children between 2008 and 2010.[484]

Beatie was born a woman, and underwent a surgical and legal transition to living as a man before deciding to have children. Because the medical procedures he underwent did not involve removal of his/her ovaries or uterus, Beatie was capable of bearing children, much like the trans man in chapter nine. The state of Arizona recognizes Thomas Beatie as the father of his three children, even though biologically he is their mother.

> Beatie's ability to have children does not represent an exception to the normal ability of males to bear children. The labelling of Beatie as a man, despite his being biologically female, is a personal, social, and legal decision that was made without any basis in biology; nothing whatsoever suggests Thomas Beatie is a male.[485]

---

[483] Mayer & McHugh (2016)
[484] Ibid (2016 p. 90)
[485] Ibid

Physicians considering therapeutic interventions for children with Gender Dysphoria should consider the probability that children may outgrow cross-gender identification.[486] Family relationships and the social environment play a significant role in the development and persistence of gender nonconforming behaviour.

So what does this mean? Parents, particularly mothers, can play a large role in this area of gender nonconformity; as witnessed in recent media, we are seeing more and more parents affirming their child's ideas of being in the wrong body, to the point where the parents of such children are now pressuring medical staff for early childhood interventions (see discussion in chapter 8). These children are being sentenced for life to unnecessary drugs, surgeries, and emotional issues, due to a false belief about their identity. The larger cost to the child (and society) will be the subsequent medical interventions, which do not alleviate the emotional pain incurred. A systematic review of 28 studies, which examined 1,833 patients who underwent sex reassignment

> The prevalence of suicide attempts among transgendered individuals was 41%, vastly exceeding the overall population who report a lifetime suicide attempt rate of 4.6%.

procedures including hormone therapies, found that there was a very low quality of evidence that sex reassignment via hormone interventions improves Gender Dysphoria or psychological functioning. In fact, four of the studies reviewed reported worsening quality of life. [487]

The American Foundation for Suicide Prevention and the Williams Institute summarized findings on suicide attempts among transgender and gender-nonconforming adults in a national sample of over 6,000 individuals. One of the major findings was that the prevalence of suicide attempts among transgendered individuals was 41%, vastly exceeding the overall population who report a lifetime suicide attempt rate of 4.6%. This is also higher than the 10-20% of lesbian, gay and bisexual adults who report attempting suicide.[488]

Sex change surgery has become a big industry in the USA, and the clientele is growing in Canada as well. McHugh states that

---

[486] Zucker (2004)
[487] Mayer & McHugh (2016)
[488] Haas, Rodgers, & Herman (2014)

People who undergo sex-reassignment surgery do not change from men to women or vice versa. Rather, they become feminized men or masculinized women. Claiming that this is a civil-rights matter and encouraging surgical intervention is in reality to [sic] collaborating with and promoting a mental disorder.[489]

A well-designed 2011 Swedish study[490] indicated that postoperative transsexuals reported lower satisfaction with their quality of health and with the personal, physical and social limitations experienced following surgery. "Postoperative transsexual individuals had an approximately three times higher risk for psychiatric hospitalization than the control groups. Most alarmingly, sex-reassigned individuals were 4.9 times more likely to attempt suicide and 19.1 times more likely to die by suicide. Mortality from suicide is found to be very high among sex-reassigned persons."[491] Post-surgical mental health is obviously quite poor, as shown by the high number of suicide attempts.[492]

It would seem that sex-reassignment surgery does not rectify the poor health associated with transgender individuals. A 2009 study examining post-surgery quality of life of transsexuals 15 years after surgery also found that post-operative transsexuals have lower general life satisfaction in their quality of health.[493] Even with this scientific data on the outcomes of sex reassignment surgery, transgender advocates are pushing to proceed with sex reassignment at younger ages.

> "In all the times I cried out for help, I never once received honesty or sound mental or medical help."
> Serritella, 2016

SEX CHANGE REGRET

In one study, three out of the 17 people interviewed regretted sex reassignment procedures, with two of the three seeking a reversal of procedures. This translates to a 17.65% regret rate in this study.[494]

There is definitely the potential that adults undergoing sex reassignment surgery may at some point want to return to their biological gender, which indicates that reassignment surgery comes with increased psychological and

---

[489] Lifesite News (2016 p. 3)
[490] Mayer & McHugh (2016 p. 111)
[491] Ibid
[492] Mayer & McHugh (2016 p. 108)
[493] Mayer & McHugh (2016)
[494] Ibid (p. 112)

physical risk. According to Mayer and McHugh, "patients' pre-treatment beliefs about an ideal post-treatment life may sometimes go unrealized."[495]

The 2011 Swedish study indicated that, beginning about 10 years after having sex reassignment surgery, the transgendered began to experience increasing mental difficulties. Their suicide mortality rose almost 20 % above comparable nontransgender populations.[496] Many of those with sex change regrets have been intimidated by LGBT activists in order to silence them. But, some are speaking out. In fact there is now a website named www.sexchangeregret.com where you can read the testimonials of those who will not be silenced. As you can imagine, it would not be good for the LGBT cause to have those within their ranks desiring to return to their original biological design. I believe we will see a new wave of these disheartened and dissatisfied individuals coming to the same conclusion as Donna did—that they, in essence, have rejected themselves. I will share a little bit here of one man's comments after his own regret over sex reassignment surgery.

> When contemplating a transition from one gender to another it is important to seek and obtain wise and unbiased counsel. Variant opinions are needed. Balance the media-hyped stories of the high-profile transgendered elite with the reality of the struggling, regretful and dead transgendered people. Anxiety and depression should be treated or excluded. Addiction, personality disorders, dissociative traits and mental derangements need to be identified and dealt with. In all the times I cried out for help, I never once received honesty or sound mental or medical help. There are frankly too many "yes practitioners."
>
> As a physician I know the horror of disease, and this whole notion of Gender Dysphoria and its treatment has spun out of control. Lives are being ruined and devastated.
>
> *It has become a cancer.* (emphasis added)[497]

The work of Drs. Mayer and McHugh is a landmark piece of credible scholarship. Instead of being spread all over the media for its wisdom, it has been denigrated by LGBT activists who are threatened by what it exposed. The study was immediately decried as junk science by the LGBT lobby, despite the vigorous research methods and validity of the study. Character assassination was then employed in an attempt to disqualify the researchers. The consistent

---

[495] Ibid (p. 111)
[496] Ibid (p. 111)
[497] Serritella (2016 p. 180)

efforts of this group to deny legitimate science and denigrate anyone who speaks in opposition to their opinion, while at the same time expounding invalidated research, are unbelievable. These kinds of attacks against credible science have increased as part of an agenda to intimidate those who would espouse a different perspective. Phrases like "exporters of hate" are common and quickly shut down opposition, which, of course, is the purpose of such attacks.

Mayer and McHugh's credentials should speak volumes to those questioning the validity of the transgender agenda. Here is a study once again confirming what most of us realize on a common sense level—birth sex is biological; gender refers to roles, behaviours, and expressions of biological sex; and Gender Dysphoria is gender confusion. The truth is that most children will outgrow Gender Dysphoria—at least 88% of them.

The study also confirms that gender reassignment does not change biological sex, nor does surgical intervention lead to greater life satisfaction or happiness. In fact, it seems to increase the risk of psychiatric hospitalization. The lack of media representation of the facts allows our society to continue embracing erroneous representation of the transgender population as normal and content.

CHAPTER 11

Finding the Source: What Does Attachment Have to Do with It?

Love is the tension of grace and truth.[498]
C. Kaltenbach

ATTACHMENT BEHAVIOUR IS BELIEVED TO CHARACTERIZE HUMAN BEINGS from "cradle to grave'."[499] John Bowlby described attachment behaviour as any form of behaviour that results in a person attempting or retaining proximity to another individual, usually one conceived as stronger and/or wiser (primarily mother and father). Although it is most frequently and intensely displayed by infants and young children, it continues to be manifested throughout life, especially when distressed, ill or afraid.[500]

No form of behaviour is accompanied by stronger feelings than that of attachment. If a child is in the unchallenged presence or within easy reach of a principal attachment-figure, he/she feels secure. A threat of loss creates anxiety, and actual loss creates sorrow; both, moreover, are likely to arouse anger.[501] Attachment is a theory of emotional regulation which begins in infancy through the interaction between baby and primary caretaker—most frequently the parents, and initially the child's mother. It is here, in the first years of life,

---

[498] Kaltenbach (2015 p.30)
[499] Bowlby (1973, 1979 p. 129); Beniot & Parker (1994)
[500] Ainsworth, & Bell (1970); Ainsworth (1989)
[501] Bowlby (1969 p. 209).

that a child builds connection through interaction. If the child finds security, protection and safety, they will feel the freedom to explore their world and will learn the process of regulating their emotions.

As new attachments are built, these representations help the child build a pattern for perceiving, interpreting and reacting to attachment signals and situations. The chief goal of attachment theory is one of protection and safety.

Early parent-infant interactions create a foundation for future interactions and other behaviours.[502] The tables following illustrate the attachment arousal-relaxation cycle.

Attachment and sexuality "impinge on each other and influence each other." There is also an "overlap between attachment, parenting and sexual behaviour".[503] The early years merit special attention because the initial adaptations they promote become the starting point for subsequent transactions.[504]

Risk in early childhood remains a significant predictor of behaviour problems, even when risk in middle childhood is controlled. This is an important example of the power of early experience.[505] "Problems in developing initial attachment have been assumed as a predisposing factor for problematic sexual behaviour. A template of the opposite-sex parent is likely to play a critical role in influencing the choice of mate."[506]

Attachment theory suggests that disruptions in primary relationships, due to absence, injury, trauma, or death, can create insecure infant and child attachment, and that subsequent trauma in later years also has a definite impact on the person. From this perspective, one can gain insight into how the lived experience of LGBT individuals has progressed. Attachment theory, along with its category of disorganized attachment, which is often seen in this group, provides a starting point for understanding, as well as showing the need for the healing of life-long emotional injury.

The power of traumatic experience is well documented in attachment theory, and the subsequent impact on the child, especially before age five, is extreme. I have spent considerable time in this book linking childhood abuse (especially sexual abuse), pedophilia, and the propensity of the gay population toward incest, to empirically validate outcomes that devastate children, predisposing them to a

---

[502] Ainsworth (1963, 1967); Ainsworth, Bell, & Strayton (1974); Ainsworth et al (1978); Beniot & Parker (1994); Bowlby (1969, 1973); Bretherton (1992); Bretherton & Munholland (2008); Clinton & Sibcy (2006)

[503] Bowlby (1969)

[504] Sroufe, Coffino & Carlson (2010)

[505] Ibid

[506] Morehead (1999 p 368).

lifetime of insecure attachment.[507] I believe it is a longing for secure attachment that often drives LGBT individuals to a life of sexually addictive behaviour

Below are two charts depicting secure and insecure attachment. My theory remains that it is insecure attachment, most often accompanied by sexual abuse and /or dissociated trauma, that creates an atmosphere for gay, lesbian and Gender Dysphoria to develop as individuals search in vain for a valued sense of identity. Finding identity will be discussed in a subsequent chapter.

Secure attachment to caregivers in childhood leads to well-adjusted adolescents who are able to navigate the turmoil of youth within the safety net of healthy family relationships. Secure individuals are self-confident, self-assured, and self-reliant, while at the same time other-aware. What I mean by this is that they are sensitive to emotional cues and able to respond with appropriate care for others while maintaining personal boundaries. Such individuals are good at developing and maintaining friendships. They are wise with whom they place their trust.

Those who are insecurely attached in childhood tend to become more easily angered. These individuals either trust too much or are overly suspicious. They are more easily coerced as children, more vulnerable, and more easily victimized. The lack of self-esteem arising from insecure attachment often predisposes an adolescent to be vulnerable to peer pressure, especially in the area of sexuality.

What creates secure attachment? It takes parents who are totally committed to one another and who respond in an appropriate manner to a child's pain or needs with love and compassion. Even trauma in the child's life can be minimized by parental care and the security of family.

Family is still the bedrock of safety and the building block of society.

---

[507] Gillies (2013)

The Arousal-Relaxation Cycle

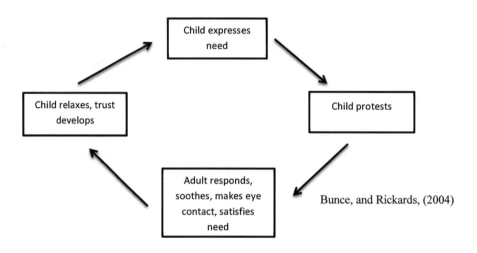

Bunce, and Rickards, (2004)

The Disturbed Attachment Cycle

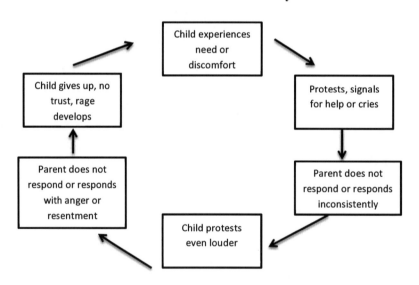

Bunce, and Rickards, (2004)

CHAPTER 12

The Flood Plains: A Political Arena

*In a free country we punish men for
crimes they commit,
but never for opinions they have.*[508]
Former US President Henry S. Truman

*There is no moral high ground in putting
Butchers and Bakers and Candlestick Makers
in the legal dock for refusing
to renounce their religion;
or in stalking and threatening Christian pastors
for being Christian pastors;
or in denigrating social science that doesn't fit
preconceived ideology about the family...*[509]
Mary Eberstadt

THE YEAR WAS 1807. THE PLACE: THE BRITISH HOUSE OF COMMONS. THE man: William Wilberforce. The campaign: the injustice of slavery. The battle for justice: 18 years. The result of his resilient approach: the Abolition of Slave Trade Act 1807.

---

[508] Eberstadt (2016)
[509] Ibid

Wilberforce was a British politician and philanthropist. In 1785, Wilberforce underwent a spiritual conversion. He turned to evangelicalism and promised to dedicate his life to the service of God, thereafter devoting his life to the abolition of slavery after coming into contact with anti-slave trade activists Thomas Clarkson, Granville Sharp, Hannah More and Charles Middleton in 1787.

These activists convinced him to take on their cause, and he subsequently headed the anti-slavery parliamentary campaign for some 20 years, until the passage of the act a mere three days before his death! For twenty years he battled against the powers of the legislature. Sometimes the battle for justice is long and difficult.

The LGBT culture has been campaigning for their manifesto for a long time—the battle has been intense. Many of them might compare their battle to that of Wilberforce's—injustice to justice. In fact, they have modeled the campaign on that used to abolish the slave trade. There are elements that may at first glance seem similar—but in fact, they are vastly different. Whereas Wilberforce was fighting to free slaves and save lives, the LGBT are not only fighting for the freedom to practice any form of sexual expression, but also that these practices would be taught to our children.

LBGT activists would say, but our lives are at stake! It's true that a number of them have been targeted by angry individuals, but let's take a closer look—are they (as a culture) currently in constant danger for their lives due to Canadian law? No. They fought for recognition and they won the battle. So what is the battle that they are engaged in now?

Gender mainstreaming has become a high priority at every level of politics. At the same time, what does this term really mean? Under the pretext of equality and justice, equivalency is manufactured between men and women until genders are no longer distinguishable.[510] The term on the streets: gender bender.

As a child, did you read the Hans Christian Anderson tale *The Emperor's New Clothes?* Canadians are very much like the officials of this story, having come to believe in something that isn't real—that is an illusion, a delusion. We can no longer simply consider ideas according to the rules of logic and evidence, but are now forced to consider the political and hostile forces that surround them.

The desire of the LGBT culture to crush any and all opposition is virtually unprecedented. The LGBT culture takes intolerance to unprecedented levels. Accusations of hatred and bigotry, media shaming, bullying, and harassment from activist leaders in this group have been repeatedly minimized and discounted.

---

[510] Ruby (2015 p. 97)

LGBT activists endeavour to place responsibility for their atrocious behaviour on the backs of all Canadians, and especially religious groups, claiming "we" have caused their problems just by virtue of who they are.

It was Voltaire who said, "I disapprove of what you say, but will defend to the death your right to say it!"[511] Yet in Canada we have squelched that very right. Freedom of Speech and Freedom of Religion are now in great jeopardy in the West.

Christian believers today are being charged with afflicting society. History shows that society has been at the point of eradicating Christianity before. Many times there have been attempts to silence biblical truth when it conflicts with social lifestyles. If our culture continues to attempt to eradicate those who would question ethic, morals and values, then they can impose their own standards on all. What are the standards proliferating today?

THE KINSEY STANDARD

Kinsey's data has been reviewed and dissected elsewhere in this book, and we have seen that it is based on the sexual abuse of innocent children. I suggest that you watch the video "The Children of Table 34." Some takeaways from the video:

- Systematic molestation of over 300 children
- Ideas about "normal" childhood sexual development come from illegal research
- Sex educators are trained based on the Kinsey model
- Co-author Pomeroy's book sexualizes children
- Kinsey describes infants and young children having "orgasms"
- Reisman's study shows a huge number of images associating sex with children and violence in pornographic magazines[512]

Kinsey's study set in motion a new standard for sex education in the West— one that sexualizes children and prepares our minds for the possibility of sex from infancy onward.

A HOMOSEXUAL STANDARD

Listen to what Michael Swift, a self-described gay revolutionary, wrote in the Boston Gay Community News in 1987:

---

[511] Voltaire 1765
[512] YouTube (2015)

We shall sodomize your sons, emblems of your feeble masculinity, of your shallow dreams and vulgar lies. We shall seduce them in your schools, on your dormitories, in your gymnasium, in your locker rooms, in your sports arena, in your seminaries, in your truck stops, in your all-male clubs, in your houses of Congress, wherever men are with men together. Your sons shall become our minions and do our bidding. They will be recast in our image. They will come to crave and adore us... All laws banning homosexual activity will be revoked...If you dare cry faggot, fairy, queer at us, we will stab you in your cowardly hearts... all churches who condemn homosexuals will be closed. Our gods are handsome young men...We shall be victorious because we are fueled with the ferocious bitterness of the oppressed...[513]

Lester Kirdendall states that "Programs of the future will probe sexual expression with same-sex partners and even across generational lines. With a diminished sense of guilt, these patterns will become legitimate. And the emphasis on normality and abnormality will be much diminished with these future trends."[514] This has already transpired.

But there is so much more. I am going to share excerpts from *The Homosexual Manifesto*—written by Michael Swift and drawing on earlier works:

- The 1972 "Gay Rights" platform[515]
- The 1993 "Gay Rights" platform[516]
- *The Overhauling of Straight America*[517]

These complete documents can now be accessed via internet search. To begin with, it has been suggested that the homosexual manifesto by Swift was penned as satire, but as you read it in 2017, you will see much has come to fruition (as with the gay rights platform and *The Overhauling of Straight America*). I will save my comments till the end of the excerpts from these four manuscripts.

I begin with quotes from *The Homosexual Manifesto*:

All laws banning homosexual activity will be revoked; legislation will be passed that engenders love between men. We shall write poems of love

---

[513] Swift, (1987)
[514] Blackburn (2012)
[515] National Coalition of Gay Organizations (1972)
[516] Lively (2009)
[517] Kirk & Pill (1987)

between men; we shall stage plays in which man openly caresses man; we shall make films about the love between heroic men. Our writers and artists will make love between men fashionable and de rigueur, and we will succeed because we are adept at setting styles. *We* will unmask the powerful homosexuals who masquerade as heterosexuals. You will be shocked and frightened when you find that your presidents and their sons, you industrialists, your senators …your priests are not the safe, familiar, bourgeois, heterosexual figures you assumed them to be. We are everywhere, we have infiltrated your ranks.

And further…**those who oppose us will be exiled.** The **family unit,** which only dampens imagination and curbs free will, **must be eliminated.** All churches who condemn us will be closed. Our only gods are handsome young men. We are free to live our lives according to the dictates of the pure imagination. *For us too much is not enough.* One of the major requirements for a position of power in the new society of homoeroticism will be indulgence in the Greek passion.

We shall rewrite history…we shall portray the homosexuality of the great leaders and thinkers who shaped the world. We will demonstrate that homosexuality and intelligence and imagination are inextricably linked and that homosexuality is a requirement for true nobility, true beauty in a man. *We shall be vicious* because we are fueled with ferocious bitterness… (emphasis added)[518]

EXCERPTS FROM THE 1972 GAY RIGHTS PLATFORM:

Amending all Civil Rights Acts, other legislation and government controls to prohibit discrimination in employment, house, public accommodation and public services; prohibiting the military from excluding for reasons of their sexual orientation. Federal funding of aid programs of gay men's and women's organizations designed to alleviate the problems encountered by gay women and men…

Immediate release of all gay women and men now incarcerated in detention centers, prisons and mental institutions because of sexual offence charges relating to victimless crimes or sexual orientation. Enactment of legislation so that child custody, adoption, visitation rights, Foster parenting and the like shall not be denied because of sexual orientation or parental status.

[518] Lively, (2009); Swift, (1987)

Repeal of all laws governing the age of sexual consent. [It is noteworthy here to mention that the fight was on the platform of pedophilia!] *Repeal all legislative provisions that restrict the sex or number of persons entering a marriage unit*; and the extension of legal benefits to all persons who cohabit regardless of sex or numbers. (emphasis added)[519]

Platform of the 1993 March on Washington (The 1993 "Gay Rights" Platform)
The LBGT movement demands:[520]

1. *We demand* the passage of LGBT civil rights bills...to repeal all sodomy laws and other laws that criminalize private sexual expression between consenting adults.

2. *We demand* legislation to prevent discrimination against LBGT people in the areas of family diversity, custody, adoption and foster care and *that the definition of family includes the full diversity of all family structures.*

3. *We demand* a full equal inclusion of LGBT people in the educational system and the *inclusion of LBGT studies in multicultural curricula.*

4. *We demand* the right to reproductive freedom and choice, to control our own bodies, an end to sexist discrimination; unrestricted, *safe, and affordable alternative insemination.*

5. *We demand* an end to discrimination and violent expression based on actual or perceived sexual orientation identification, race, religion, identity, sex and gender expression, disability, age, class, AIDS/HIV infection: a*n end to consideration of Gender Dysphoria as a psychiatric disorder; an end to censorship*

THE OVERHAULING OF STRAIGHT AMERICA

The first order of business is the *desensitization of the American public* concerning gays and gay rights; to help the public view homosexuality with indifference, instead of emotion. You can forget about trying to

---

[519] National Coalition of Gay Organizations (1972)
[520] Smith (2013)

persuade the masses that homosexuality is a good thing, but only if you can get them to think that it is just another thing, a shrug of their shoulders, then your battle for legal and social rights is virtually won. A large-scale media campaign will be required.[521]

So here is the strategy LGBT activists employed:

1. Talk about gays and gayness as loudly and often as possible; *almost any behaviour begins to look normal if you are exposed to enough of it at close quarters and among your acquaintances.* The way to *benumb raw sensitivities about homosexuality* is to have a lot of people talk a great deal about the subject in a neutral or supportive way. Open and frank talk makes the subject seem less furtive, alien, and sinful, more above board. Even rancorous debates between opponents and defenders serve the purpose of desensitization. The main thing is to talk about gayness until the issue becomes thoroughly tiresome. In the early stages of any campaign to reach straight America, the masses *should not be shocked and repelled by premature exposure to homosexual behaviour itself. Instead the imagery of sex should be downplayed and gay rights should be reduced to an abstract social question as much as possible.*

2. *So far gay Hollywood has provided our best covert weapon to desensitize the mainstream...*while public opinion is one primary source of mainstream values, religious authority is another. First, we can muddy the moral waters... publicizing support for gays by more moderate churches, raising theological objections of our own about conservative interpretations of biblical teachings and exposing hatred and inconsistency. Second, we can *undermine the moral authority of homophobic churches by portraying them as antiquated backwaters, badly out of step with the times and with the latest findings of psychology.*

> "Groups on the farthest fringe of acceptability such as NAMBLA (North American Man-Boy Love Association) must play no part at all in such a campaign."
> Kirk & Pill, 1987

---

[521] Kirk & Pill (1987); Kirk & Madsen (1990)

3. *Gays must be cast as victims in need of protection* so that straights will be inclined by reflex to assume the role of protector. We must forego the temptation to strut our "gay pride" publicly when it conflicts with the Gay victim image. A media campaign to *promote the Gay victim image* should make use of symbols which reduce the mainstream's sense of threat. It goes without saying that *groups on the farthest margin of acceptability such as NAMBLA* (North American Man-Boy Love Association) must play no part at all in such a campaign—suspected child molesters will never look like victims. Mr. and Mrs. Public must be given no extra excuses to say, "They're not like us." *Our campaign should not demand direct support for homosexual practices,* should instead take anti-discrimination as its theme...

4. To make Gays look good, you have to portray him as Everyman. The campaign *should paint gays as the pillar of society.* Yes, yes, we know—*this trick is so old it creaks...*

5. Long after the other gay ads have become common-place, it will be time to get in touch with *opponents. To be blunt they must be vilified.* First, we need to *replace the mainstream's self-righteous pride about its homophobia with shame and guilt.* Second, we intend to make antigay look so nasty that the average American will want to dissociate themselves from such types. The public should be shown images of ranting homophobes...images like the Klu Klux Klan, demanding that gays be burned alive or castrated; bigoted southern ministers drooling with hysterical hatred; menacing punks, thugs, and convicts speaking coolly about the "fags" they have killed.

6. Solicit funds

7. Without access to TV, radio and the mainstream press, there will be no campaign. Because straightforward appeals are impossible, the National Gay Task Force has had to *cultivate quiet backroom liaisons.* We must continue to encourage the appearance of favourable gay characters in film and TV. Through political campaign, the mainstream would get over the initial shock of seeing gay ads. If we behaved ourselves courageously and respectably, our drive would gain legitimacy...and the major networks themselves would be readied for the next step of our program.

8. It is time to ask the networks to accept gay sponsorship of certain ads and shows. Networks will be forced to say no unless we make their resistance look patently unreasonable, and possibly illegal. We'd propose "gay ads" patterned exactly after those currently sponsored by the Mormons and others. Viewers would be treated to squeak-clean skits on the importance of family harmony and understanding and the narrator would end by saying, "This message was brought to you by—The National Gay Task Force". All very quiet and subdued. *The core of our program is a media campaign to change the way the average citizens view homosexuality.* (emphasis added)[522]

Mission accomplished! The average citizen now believes that homosexuality is a normal expression of sexuality. I'm sure as you've read through the excerpts of these documents you've experienced at least two things: shock at the propositions of the agenda and possibly surprise at how far three percent of the population have managed to impose their values on the 97%. Let me expand on some of my thoughts about this material.

Mr. Swift (like other homosexual activists) has a definite agenda. Mr. Swift seems quite capable of the seduction of our children (as he states): making our sons into minions to do their bidding. Not only that, but much of what he has written—i.e. legislation being passed that engenders love between men—has taken place in the last 40 years. Although the LGBT-identifying population is small, they have found a loud voice in our media and politics. We have definitely seen the ferocious bitterness, anger and hatred of LGBT activists poured out upon any who might stand up to them.

Swift's threats are not to be taken lightly. His wish to eliminate the family unit is well on its way to fruition. The explosion of teen pregnancy,[523] divorce, co-habitation, and single parenting, have all led to a dismantling of marriage and an instability of family life—creating generations of fatherless children (or weekend dad/moms) and disrupting the secure attachment needs of our children, all of which can lead to a future inability to emotionally connect with spouse and/or children.

Basic human rights prohibit discrimination against anyone, but this group goes way over that line when it demands that laws be changed in regard to gay marriage; solicitation (prostitution); repeal of laws governing age of sexual consent (see NAMBLA's internet sites for what this could mean); repeal of laws restricting the sex or number of persons in a marriage unit—which is where

---

[522] Kirk & Pill (1987); Kirk & Madsen (1990)
[523] Singh & Darroch (2000)

our country is now headed; and the extension of benefits to all who cohabit regardless of sex or numbers (polygamy, polyamory).

This, of course, takes me to another political demand: that Gender Dysphoria be removed from the psychological bible (DSM) as a psychological condition! Just because a fraction of the population becomes transgender (0.03%) does not mean that we should remove the condition or the possibility of treatment. Yet, this is already happening in Canada, as trans individuals push hard to be identified as "normal." There is no way to normalize self-destructive behaviour. Many people struggle with a multitude of mental health issues— most are willing to undergo, and even expect, psychological intervention, therapy and medication.

Remember Swift's Homosexual Manifesto? Let me remind you of his words from 1987 "…we shall demonstrate that homosexuality and intelligence are inextricably linked; homosexuality is a requirement for true nobility"!

In case you are becoming discouraged by the idea that in order to have a higher intellectual standing you must be gay, listen to what else another activist has to say: "the trouble is that Jesus wasn't a very intellectual person, rather one with profound insight."[524]

He's talking about Jesus here. The man who, for 2000 years, has impacted society with the moral code of love, respect and forgiveness. Well, I guess if God's son (because he wasn't gay?) wasn't an intellectual person, then we needn't take offence.

This is exactly the understanding that is being propagated: if you dare to believe that human beings are born male and female and that marriage should be between a biological male and a biological female, you are an imbecile, uneducated, and have a lower order of intelligence.

University of Toronto Professor Jordan Peterson[525] has issued a stark warning for anyone "out of step" with society's politically correct agenda—*Tremble!*

We are bombarded with accusations (part of the agenda, remember) that cause us to pause and wonder if we really are "against" homosexuality. What does being against homosexuality mean anyway? I'm not an advocate of same-sex marriage. Does that mean I hate gays? Absolutely, according to the propaganda and the repulsive hate-mongering against anyone who disagrees with the LGBTQ agenda. But it's not true! Am I concerned for them, yes; do I like or agree with their sexual behaviour—no.

One is not allowed to have a different opinion, let alone advocate for a different agenda— such as a moral stance to sexuality. If you dare to believe

[524] Zerrilli (2010)
[525] Gyapong (2016)

human beings are born male and female by biological design you are not only out of touch, but you are wrong! If you believe that marriage should be between a biological male and a biological female, you are declared a homophobe, uneducated, and definitely not someone to be listened too.

Where is the outcry against *the gay manifesto,* and such a malicious, intolerant and arrogant opinion? Where are the ones who have stood for the created order of male and female copulation and procreation? Where are the researchers of the past who explored causation and considered homosexuality and transgenderism to be abnormal lifestyles? Where are those who attempted to bring to light the scores of diseases, caused by male to male sex? Where is the Christian church?

The intimidation of a movement intent on remaking us in their image has prevailed; rational thought has been reviled and the Christian church declared the enemy. As a result, we have chosen silence.

SILENCED!

Silenced through opposition,
Silenced through intimidation,
Silenced through ridicule,
Silenced through lack of knowledge,

Silenced through a public outcry based on the erroneous message
of the perceived normalcy of homosexuality, transgenderism and other
such sexual behaviours.

Silenced by a minority that is intent on having what it wants,
when it wants.
Silenced by individuals determined to express themselves in
whatever manner they wish and with the expectation that those who
don't agree with them need to get themselves in line—because this
minority is right!

I'm not suggesting this is new to humankind, for there truly is nothing new under the sun; rather, the newly espoused theories of "pure relationship and plastic sexuality" coming from feminist and queer theory proponents expand the limits of sexuality to embrace all levels (or contingencies) of sexual expression.

The postmodern western world has become a product of the gender and sexual liberation movements. Individuals, especially children, are learning new ways of experiencing their bodies, sexual identities and relationships, coming with an astronomical price tag in the lives of those affected.

RESTRICTING FREEDOM OF SPEECH AND FREEDOM OF RELIGION

One Ontario Father
The following case transpired in an Ontario court in 2016. It should shake you to the core! A Christian father, who simply asked for notice of questionable same-sex teachings on sexuality in his children's classrooms, was refused by the school board.[526] This man was brave enough to take this ruling to the Ontario Superior Court. He asked the Court to rule that the board's decision violated his Charter Rights of Freedom of Religion, and to declare he had final authority over the education of his children. The result?

> The court concluded the school board's refusal to grant religious accommodation, including giving him notice, was "reasonable," given the board's statutory obligations—particularly those outlined in the Equity and Inclusive Education Strategy launched by [provincial Premier] Kathleen Wynne in 2009. The judge also tossed out this father's request that the Court declare that, as a parent, he has the final authority over the education of his children. Apparently, the judge stated that "parental rights" are "a matter of some nuance."

This same judge also suggested that this parent has the option of taking his kids out of public school if he is worried about "false teaching." This ruling essentially says that parental rights are subordinate to the State's rights. How did we get to this place? I believe that the church has "dropped the ball." We've become weary of the homosexual debate. The Christian church, after all, is not a militant group by nature of their theology, and is certainly not to be compared to LGBTQ extremists.

An update on this Steve Tourloukis's seven-year battle came on June 29th, 2017 as his case landed in Ontario's appeal court this week.

---

[526] Hamilton Spectator (2016)

"This appeal is about protecting the rights of parents to direct their children's education, and to protect the religious freedom of parents and their children," states Tourloukis' appeal factum.[527]

Mr. Tourloukis made it clear in his 2012 legal challenge that he did not object to his children being taught facts, or to discussions and opinions by classmates on these subjects. But he did *object to teachers, who are authority figures, making "value judgments" in class, such as presenting homosexuality as natural, or abortion as morally acceptable.* This father believes same-sex sexual relations are not God's intention for sex and that there are but two genders, male and female; that marriage is a sacred institution; and he must raise his children according to the Christian faith and God's holy law.

The board's lawyer argued that a public school is not allowed to "indoctrinate" students, but that Ontario's public schools have statutory obligation to create safe schools, including Bill 13. The lawyer stated that accommodating Tourloukis would directly impact the ability of Ontario public schools to provide students with a positive, inclusive, and supportive educational environment.

The Elementary Teachers' Federation of Ontario's lawyer argued

teachers are mandated by law to embed positive examples of homosexuality, lesbianism, transgenderism, and queerness throughout the curriculum, and to teach children not just to "tolerate" LGBTQ lifestyle, which has a negative connotation, but to "honour and respect" and "celebrate" it.[528]

This was the sex education law implemented by the then-minister of education, for whom Ben Levin served as deputy minister—a man who, as I previously mentioned, consistently claimed to have had sex with his own daughters, starting at age 3. He was convicted of three child pornography-related charges, including counseling another person to rape a minor.

At least one teacher has openly admitted to embedding LGBTQ material throughout the curriculum. A Mississauga elementary school teacher told a pro-gay conference she uses math class to push the homosexual agenda.[529] Is this really something that we want pushed on our children in every class?

[527] Laurence (June 29, 2017)
[528] Ibid
[529] Laurence (June 29, 2017)

Parents are confused and basically have no idea where they stand. We've been sold a "bill of goods" by our media's false representation of scientific "fact" and have come to believe that homosexuals, bisexuals, pansexuals, and transsexuals are all "born that way"! Our children are being indoctrinated into what can only be called "false belief."

Because of this, our society has been bullied into accepting every form of sexual expression as "normal," and we are now afraid to stand up to these ideas. We've been told that we must not only agree with and accept every perceived gender identity, but we also must affirm these thoughts, emotions and behaviours!

Individuals can practice any form of hedonism they wish, but should they expect people of deep moral convictions and faith to subscribe or support their beliefs, or worse yet, have these practices taught to our children?! While I believe in decency and respect for all, I don't believe that I or anyone else should have to subscribe to the LGBT agenda.

The ruling against this Christian father is an example of this type of "integrated" totalitarianism in the guise of sexual freedom, inclusiveness, and a progressive society. Parents, faith groups, and religious institutions are fighting with their hands tied behind their backs. We've been bombarded with so much confusing LGBT marketing that we just wearily succumb due to lack of time and energy.

A Bakery Owner in the United States

Also on June 29th, 2017, I read an updated story about the owner of Masterpiece Cakeshop, Jack Phillips, who ignited a national debate after he refused to create a wedding cake for a gay couple in 2012. Phillips, who had served this gay couple for many years and considered them friends, simply stated his belief in the biblical mandate of marriage being between one man and one woman. Phillips didn't refuse the couple service, and offered to sell them anything in the store. But when it came to actively participating in the couple's wedding, that's where Phillips drew the line.

Instead of graciously accepting this man's genuine belief and going to another bake shop, these men took him to court. Since then, Phillips has lost a chunk of his business revenue, received death threats, and been subjected to vile online reviews.[530]

> "In all of this, the worst part is that I have to answer the phone so they're not threatening my wife or my daughter when they pick it up," Phillips said. "They don't wait to see who's on the phone. You pick up the phone,

---

[530] Schallhorn (2017)

they're already talking." Phillips added that he also tries to shield the other employees at the bakery from negative comments directed at him.[531]

Phillips has also been told that he doesn't "deserve to live" and that "Christians should be thrown into the Roman Colosseum with lions." One of those threats, Phillips said, came just a few weeks after he refused to bake the cake—long before the story garnered national attention. A man called to say that he knew Phillips' daughter, Lisa, was working at the bakery. The man proceeded to give point-by-point driving directions to the bakeshop, where he would murder them. Phillips has also been accused by a member of the Colorado Civil Rights commission, who compared him to a perpetrator of the Holocaust![532]

These statements are deeply offensive and unjustified. Consider a different scenario. Recently my husband was asked by an acquaintance to sign an assisted death (euthanasia) form for him so that he could then have the permission needed to end his life. My husband told him that he would not sign due to his belief that it is God who gives us life and it is God who decides when we die. The man's response? He thanked my husband for being honest and said he totally respected my husband's beliefs! This man did not become hostile or manipulative. There was no name calling; there were no threats; no calls to the civil rights commission. Instead there was acknowledgment of belief. A few days later the man died after finding someone else to sign for him.

Could not the gay men have chosen a similar route? Why did they find it necessary to persecute this man for his belief? Instead, they and their friends have entered into character assassination along with death threats. Are they being charged with threatening death? Not to my knowledge. What would happen if the tables were turned?

BACK TO CANADIAN POLITICS

Dr. Berger, a renowned Ontario psychiatrist and expert in the field of mental illness, was asked to make a statement regarding a Canadian legislative bill (Bill C-279—initially defeated, and in 2016 reworded as Bill C-16, which was largely supported). His point, which may seem harsh to those who are trying to embrace the LGBT lifestyle, is spoken from a place of education and experience. From a scientific perspective, let me clarify again what "transgender" means. Transgender people claim that they truly are, or wish to be, people of the opposite sex to which

[531] Ibid
[532] Ibid

they were born, or to which their chromosomal configuration attests. Sometimes, some of these people have claimed that they are "a woman trapped in a man's body" or alternatively "a man trapped in a woman's body." Scientifically, there is no such thing. Therefore, Berger points out, anyone who truly believes this notion is deluded and psychotic. The medical treatment of delusions or psychosis is not by surgery.[533] He is talking about observable scientific fact.

There are many complicated questions that we are no longer answering in a scientific or rational context. Our culture has become gender-affirming, and we have seen sweeping parliamentary changes due to activists lobbying for such affirmation while disregarding established research. Attempts to understand the transgender phenomenon from a scientific or scriptural basis have collided with a resounding impact, one that has marginalized a redemptive and scientific understanding. The cause of feeling something that has no biological or scientific support, is, as Berger suggests, unhappiness! The treatment for unhappiness, again, is not surgery.

In January 2016, BBC produced a documentary featuring Dr. Zucker, despite over 11,000 signatures by LGBT activists claiming that this show would trigger more prejudice and bullying against Gender Dysphoric children. Kudos to the BBC for standing up against these activists!

The film presents evidence that most kids with Gender Dysphoria overcome it without gender reassignment. This truth is not what the LGBT activists want you to hear. I highly recommend this documentary to you. It's called *Transgender Kids: Who Knows Best?*[534]

Gay Star News[535] declared, "there are fears a BBC documentary on trans children will be 'blatant transphobic propaganda,'" which, of course, was not the case. Others were concerned the documentary could potentially mislead people by suggesting GD is an illness in need of treatment! Such sentiment displays the *scales over the eyes mentality* that permeates the LGBT culture.

Diversity of family structures is not in the best interests of children. Of course, children can adapt to all kind of situations, but that doesn't mean exposure to those situations is healthy for them, as research and common sense have repeatedly shown. Being raised in a home where the parent changes their sex partner regularly or adds others to the marriage bed does not make for family stability.

Any reasonable, rationally-thinking parent who doesn't want their children exposed to the lifestyle of the homosexual culture is vilified. The agenda is

---

[533] Berger (2013)
[534] Conroy (2017)
[535] Morgan (2017)

to denigrate anyone who opposes them. Their prime target is the Christian Church—the last vestige of morality, that has at its foundation a belief in absolute truth, including the creation of male and female, the covenant of marriage and the blessedness of family.

I believe it is time for parents in Canada to shake off their complacency and stand up and be counted. Remember Jordon Peterson's warning for anyone "out of step" with society's politically correct agenda: *Tremble!* It's time to protect Canada's children.

POLITICAL DIVERSITY, ONE PURPOSE

From the most unlikely sources come common allies! In early 2017, five women formed an unlikely alliance against transgender ideology and formed a panel called "Biology isn't Bigotry"![536] These women were able overlook immense differences. Miriam Ben Shalom is a lesbian educator and activist best known for being the first woman reinstated into the U.S. Military after she was discharged for being an open lesbian. Triller Haver is a rape survivor and advocate for women's privacy rights. Kami Mueller is the Communications Director for the Republican Party in North Carolina. Mary Lou Singleton describes herself as a long-time leftist and women's liberation activist. Emily Zino is a stay-at-home Catholic mom of seven who fights to protect women and children's privacy. Together, they are fighting for truth and reason. [537]

As a teacher, Shalom believes pushing transgender activism on children is child abuse. "In this culture you cannot vote until you're 18 or drink until you're 21," she points out.[538] Yet children in kindergarten are given all kinds of chemicals.

Singleton knows several adults who are now upset that their parents let them undergo sexual transitions as children. As a midwife who has delivered babies at home for years, Singleton rejects the notion that gender is merely a social construct. That's a talking point of many liberal and transgender activists, but "The cognitive dissonance is mind blowing to me," she says. She tells conservatives, "Don't just fight on the basis of religious freedom," noting that the transgender ideology poses a threat to the non-religious as well as to people of faith.[539]

The real issue here is male violence. If "transwomen"—biological males identifying as females—were really women, they would sit down and talk civilly

---

[536] McArtor (2017)
[537] Ibid
[538] Ibid
[539] Ibid

with women concerned about their demands. Instead, they force women to give up their private, safe spaces, all while men-only spaces are still left uncontested.[540]

With Mueller, the fight chose her when the city decided to allow biological men in women's restrooms. "The idea that my niece would be approached perhaps in a shower or to see male genitalia for the first time as a young girl grieved me."[541]

These women are working together to shed light on an issue affecting not only the United States, but Canada, too—the legal erasure of women and girls. But there's a cost to standing up. Singleton says she has been called a bigot, received death and rape threats, and been the victim of a campaign calling for the removal of her medical license. She was even accused of a hate crime for refusing to honor the preferred pronouns of a serial child rapist.[542]

While these women are standing up for women, I believe we also need to see women stand up for men! Many decent men in our society have been beaten down, demoralized, dishonoured, disrespected, maligned, and even marginalized in the job market—just for being men! Is this what we really meant by equality?

Women are feminizing men; gays are feminizing men; trans are feminizing men. While I applaud the progress of men taking more responsibility in the home and especially with fatherhood, I think they are getting a bad rap overall. Let men be men. Let women be women.

Having traversed the rugged ground of the Kinsey study and the resulting destruction of sexual morality, it is now time to focus on the quest of the Gay Rights movement. You may have discounted Michael Swift's tirade about sodomizing your sons as just blowing off steam, but for the Homosexual Manifesto he later developed.

When we read this material, we recognize that the proclamations of 1972 and 1993 have been largely realized. Truly as a society we have been the frog in the boiling pot, sitting there as the temperature rises, to the point of no longer being able to escape the immensity of the revolution. What has transpired on our watch?

- Laws banning homosexual activity: revoked
- The family unit: in shambles but not totally decimated at this point
- Churches condemning homosexual practice: not yet closed, but definitely reviled
- Rewriting of history by portraying the homosexuality of great leaders: attempted

---

[540] Ibid
[541] Ibid
[542] Ibid

- Demonstrating that homosexuality is intellectually superior: attempted
- We shall be vicious: absolutely
- Amending the Charter of Rights and government legislation: done
- Federal funding of gay organizations: done
- Releasing LGBT people from incarceration for sexual offence charges: not universal at this point
- Enactment of child custody, adoption, and foster parenting: done
- Repeal of all laws governing age of sexual consent: attempted
- Demanding full equal inclusion of LGBT in the educational system and LGBT studies in curriculum: done
- Reproductive freedom, surrogacy etc.: done
- An end to the designation of Gender Dysphoria as a psychiatric disorder: attempted
- An end to censorship: attempted
- Desensitizing the public to help them view homosexuality with indifference: done
- Incorporating large-scale media campaigns: done
- Eliminating the shock factor of homosexual behaviour by downplaying the imagery of sex: done
- Raising theological objections and their own interpretations of biblical teaching: done
- Undermining moral authority of "oppositional churches" by portraying them as out of step with the times and modern psychology: done
- Casting LGBT people as victims in need of protection; anti-discrimination theme: done
- Portraying LGBT people as everyman, the pillars of society: done
- Opponents must be vilified: done
- Making the "anti-gay" look so nasty others will want to distance themselves: done
- Cultivating backroom liaisons with media: done
- Gay ads patterned after those of the Mormons, showing squeaky clean skits of family harmony; sitcoms: done
- Changing the way average people view homosexuality: done

Truly the Gay Rights agenda has met with success. Any opposition has been threatened, and most has been silenced. Truth has been replaced with relativistic personal feeling. Freedom of speech and freedom of religion are now compromised and largely denied in our institutions of power—universities and government.

Those who have spoken out have been ridiculed and ostracized. Parents have been forced from the educational forum, and no longer have the right to educate their child in the public system according to their beliefs.

The last vestige of morality—the Christian church—has been sidelined as archaic and out of touch with reality.

WISE POLITICAL INVOLVEMENT - WHAT DOES IT LOOK LIKE?

First, it's value driven. We speak for those who cannot speak for themselves: the children. Next, we need to be loving and kind. We don't participate in slander, gossip, name-calling, or violence of any form, seasoning our comments with grace and kindness. For those of faith: be prayerful. Pray for those in authority over us—regardless as to whether we agree with their view of not, pray for wisdom. And lastly, be peaceful and respectful.

I provide more information on this in the next chapter.

CHAPTER 13
Stemming the Flood: Enough is Enough – Parents Unite

I am a Canadian, free to speak without fear,
Free to worship in my own way,
Free to stand for what I think is right
Free to oppose what I believe wrong
Or free to choose those who shall govern my country.
This heritage is the freedom I pledge to uphold
For myself and all mankind.[543]
John Diefenbaker

Nearly everything you do
You do because of beliefs in your heart[544]
S.K. Scott

I HAVE WRITTEN THIS BOOK AS A RESPONSE TO WHAT I SEE HAPPENING IN our culture. Beliefs of the heart have shaped our land. The basic principle that shaped Canada's beliefs is this: do unto others as you would have them do onto you. This belief comes from the book of Matthew in the Holy Bible:

---

[543] Hutchinson (2017)
[544] Scott (2015, June 14)

So in everything, do to others what you would have them do to you, for this sums up the law and the prophets. (Matthew 7:12, NIV)

Another belief that shaped Canada for 450 years was that of divine design or creation. This belief was acknowledged long before white men came to this country. The indigenous peoples of our land intimately understood the divine Creator, along with the belief that mother, father and children created the best family atmosphere. They believed that male and female are designed to complement one another in the unity of marriage, and that children are a blessing, an inheritance of God. While a few individuals may have held to different beliefs, there was a distinct unity in the concept of marriage and family.

Christianity is our best defence. Until recently there has been a broadly shared understanding that Judeo-Christianity was a cultural template of inescapable value—historically, morally, aesthetically and otherwise—even among those who weren't card-carrying churchgoers.[545]

IMPACT OF A CHRISTIAN LIFESTYLE ON SOCIETY

Religion, and Christianity in particular, has come under vigorous attack in the media and in our nation. Many claim that Christianity itself is the cause of so much "homophobia." Christianity, once considered an important component in the life of families across this nation, is now considered to be a detriment. In fact, fueled by the LGBT agenda, politicians, businesses, and individuals are increasingly hostile to the Bible and Christian tradition.

But is it true that Christianity is of no value to society? Although the following data comes from the 1800s, it is historical confirmation of the impact of Christian lifestyle—not simply church attendance, but individuals "practicing what they preach"!

Let me share this case[546] as we talk about history and morality. The story is based in the United States and was originally written by R.A. Dugdale in 1874. If you've heard this one before, please bear with me. It is a history of two men both born in the early 1700s. One was Jonathan Edwards, the other Max Jukes.

Let's start with Jonathan Edwards, who was born in 1703 to parents Timothy and Esther Edwards. Jonathan's father was a pastor, his mother a pastor's daughter. In his early childhood Jonathan was instructed at home and began the study of Latin at the age of six. Jonathan entered Yale College at 13 and graduated with honors, becoming the pastor who started the Great Awakening revival.

---

[545] Eberstadt (2016, p. xxvii)
[546] Winship (2005)

His is a history of the work of redemption. He resolved early in life to …

never do anything which I should be afraid to do if it were the last hour of my life.[547]

Jonathan and Sarah similarly placed high value on training their children in the Bible and education system of that day. Their descendants followed in their footsteps, leaving an outstanding legacy of church and public service that is recorded in the annals of history.

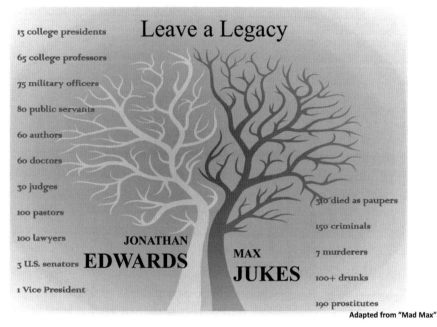

Adapted from "Mad Max"

The childhood of Max Jukes, aka Mad Max, is a little sketchy. Max would not go to school and became a loner, leaving home early to take to the woods, and in 1750 (or thereabouts) he built a shanty on a beautiful lake in New York State. Apparently, he simply wanted to get away from people, to be where he would not have to work and where he could not be preached to. Mad Max had thirteen children, none raised in church nor with a strong moral home environment. They were trained to put themselves first in life. This beautiful location in the woods became a "notorious cradle of crime."[548]

An in-depth study revealed the details of some 1,200 of Max's descendants, covering 5 generations. The traits of this family were idleness, ignorance and

---

[547] Federer (2011)
[548] Winship (2005)

vulgarity, the characteristics of which led to disease and disgrace, to pauperism (poverty) and crime. Many were insane. The sick and weak were almost all paupers; the strong and healthy of the family became criminals.

Further facts from the Jukes lineage: 310 of the 1,200 were professional paupers (living in what was then called poor houses); 300 more died in infancy from lack of care (neglect); 50 of the women lived lives of notorious debauchery; 400 men and women were physically wrecked early in life by their own wickedness; 7 were murderers; 60 were habitual thieves, who on average spent 12 years each in lawless depredation! This family cost the state more than $1,250,000.

Denison[549] studied 1,026 of Max's descendants, finding that 300 wound up in prison, 190 became prostitutes, and 509 alcoholics.

Two families—two very different trajectories! The first family committed to faithfully serving God and country; the second committed to excluding God and robbing community.

Christianity has transformed lives for over 2000 years, and for more than 450 years, faith has shaped the human landscape of Canada. It has shaped how we live our lives, how we see our neighbours, how we fulfill our social responsibilities, and how we imagine our life together. A Christian lifestyle is one that honours God and puts precedence in the moral absolutes of the Bible, teaching these to one's children. It also values good education—"training up a child in the way he/she should go." In the words of John Webster Grant,

> Canada grew up under the tutelage of its churches. The pulpit, the school and the press were the leading forces in moulding the Canadian character…by preaching, editorializing and founding universities, the church sought on one hand to lay the moral and spiritual foundations of nationhood, and on the other, to act as a conscience to the state.[550]

After reading to this point, it may be a good time to consider what your moral gauge is built on. What beliefs do you hold dear for yourself, for your children? Why? It is important to first examine our own beliefs, thoughts and actions before we impart them to our children.

Take again the issue of sex education in our schools. Do you believe it is the parent's responsibly to protect children from exposure to sex and sexual ideas perpetrated by others? Do you believe that your children have the right to experience sexual pleasure at any age, in any manner? Let me put it bluntly—

---

[549] Denison (2015)
[550] Grant (1967 p. 63)

should your six-year-old have the right to pursue sex with adults? Or, more likely, should adults have the right to pursue sex with your six-year-old? Do you believe you have a responsibility to raise your children as moral agents? How important to their education, future employment, family, and quality of life is the teaching of anal sex experience (among other forms of sexual expression) to a thirteen-year-old? Do you believe that it is up to you, the parent, to teach young children about sexual matters in the safety and confidentiality of the home?

In 1989, LGBT activists *set out a plan for the eradication of truth.* The book *After the Ball: How America will Conquer its Fear and Hatred of Gays in the 90s,*[551] offered a twofold plan:

1. Discussion to undercut rationalizations, and raising serious theological objections to conservative biblical teachings

2. Undermining the moral authority of the *homo-hating* church by portraying these institutions as antiquated backwaters, out of step with the times

Undercut rationalizations, create theological confusion, undermine moral authority by labelling the Christian church as homo-haters. Use slander, misrepresentation, and, if necessary, outright lies to incapacitate moral authority of any kind.

Desensitizing and sexualizing our society was the very thing that Kinsey, Pomeroy and their associates were pushing toward in the 50s and 60s. Kinsey and his associates were also normalizing pedophilia and incest.[552] Now we see these very things proliferating in our society.

As a parent, I can't imagine that you want your children to either experience or be a perpetrator of such acts.

Should your young children be taught unhealthy and self-destructive sexual activities by describing, exploring and removing all boundaries and/or moral guidelines? Is it any wonder that sexual promiscuity, pornography, sexual exploitation, teen pregnancy, and sexual diseases continue to rise?

Have you been shocked and challenged by some of the things that you've learned in this book? Do you think I'm "out to lunch" or perhaps even fear-mongering? You don't have to believe me, of course, but perhaps understanding what is transpiring throughout our world will help:

[551] Kirk & Madsen (1989 p. 179)
[552] See Pomeroy (1976)

Parents in Hawaii found it difficult to get access to the Planned Parenthood (PP)-promoted sex education curriculum, which teaches children in middle school (ages 9-12) about oral and anal sex and same-sex relationships. These parents then complained to their state representative. When he attempted to secure copies of the entire curriculum from the Department of Education, his request was denied. He then approached the University of Hawaii, which had developed and implemented the sex education program (in partnership with PP, receiving almost $1,000,000 in a teen pregnancy prevention governmental grant). The state representative was turned down again, by a spokesperson who apparently told reporters that

"the curriculum is sensitive in nature and can be misinterpreted!"[553]

This elementary school curriculum is so sensitive that a *state representative is not allowed to read it,* yet our children are being taught it! Parents, faith groups, and religious institutions have been fighting with their hands tied behind their back—mostly because they've been bombarded with so much confusion that they simply capitulate to the LGBT agenda due to lack of time and energy. Elementary and high school teachers have been bombarded with this curriculum, and like it or not they teach it or lose their jobs.

PARENTS – UNITE.
PARENTS – STAND UP.

Our children are being assaulted with sexual material that is way beyond their need to know at such sensitive ages, being taught in co-ed class rooms, and being shamed into complete compliance.

Do you remember when you were nine years old? Talking about sex with the opposite sex was embarrassing. In fact, we didn't do it. Sharing intimate details about sexual activity would have made us blush.

> Remember, Kinsey believed: children are sexual beings from infancy onward, and they can and should have pleasurable sexual interaction with adult "partners."

Children should enjoy this age of innocence before puberty. They should be able to enjoy being children; not intimidated into becoming sexual objects. I

---

[553] Diller (2014)

realize this may come as a shock to some—but our identity is not in how, why, when or where we have sex. We are much more than sexual beings.

It's time!

PARENTS – STAND OUT.

It's OK to disagree with what is happening in our schools, communities, cities, nations, and across the industrialized world. In fact, it's OK not to let political correctness damage our children. It's OK to speak up on behalf of our children. In fact, that's our responsibility—to protect our children. Our children are being sexually maltreated by what would have been perceived as pornographic material just ten years ago. Children are being exposed to public nudity, depictions of sexual intercourse, and the wild behaviour of Pride Parades that a decade ago would have been considered lewd and inappropriate. It's not just children, of course. Adults have become sexually desensitized to the point of acceptance, without thinking of the future lifelong consequences.

Our brains—and especially those of our children—are being changed through indoctrination. The warning signs are obvious. This sexualized dam is about to break and the flood will be absolutely devastating. Are you comfortable standing by and waiting for the flood, or are you stirred to do something?

PARENTS – STAND FIRM.

This is not a time to back down just because you are called a name, ranted at, or ridiculed for your beliefs. If your child were being beaten in front of you, would you stand by and watch? Of course not—yet we have hidden our heads in the sand and tried not to look at what is being done to them in the name of education and inclusivity.

The floodwaters are already beginning to overflow the dam, and it's your children and grandchildren who are being carried away to drown in a sea of self-centeredness and sexual addiction. They are being groomed in exactly the way Kinsey instructed—to be encouraged by adults to engage in any and every form of sex possible. Remember his words: "children are sexual beings from infancy onward,"[554] and they can and should have pleasurable sexual interactions with adult partners! The basis for this claim? Kinsey eliciting stories of sexual abuse from offenders, and observing infants and children being masturbated for hours

---

[554] Starr (2011)

at a time, then calling their responses pleasurable (see chapter two). Are you really ready for these lies to be the legacy of our children?

From 1950 to the present decade, parents have refused to subject their children to such reprehensible abuse. Now Kinsey's legacy has permeated our universities and governments in such a way that basic humanity is being redefined, yet few are crying foul! Our governments and universities have succumbed to "the frog in the pot of boiling water" syndrome, and it's nearly too hot to escape.

Anyone questioning these new definitions of human nature is immediately labelled—homophobic, transphobic…you pick a name. Solid citizens with good minds and common sense have been silenced by intimidation. The price: your children are being sacrificed on the altar of sexual slavery. They will be swallowed by a lifetime of physical and psychological and emotional pain. The cost to our medical systems will be astronomical: diseases yet unheard of will emerge; sex change surgery will become rampant.

There will never be enough psychiatrists, psychologists, psychotherapists, counsellors and mental health care workers to facilitate care for our indoctrinated and abused children as they paddle in leaky canoes over the flood waters of adult life, crippled by the teachings of their childhood.

John Kennedy quoted Edmund Burke, Irish philosopher of the 1700s, when he said…

The only thing necessary for the triumph of evil
Is for good men to do nothing…

But wait a minute! I have some encouraging news fresh out of Australia.

New South Wales public school teachers have been banned from teaching gender theory in the classroom after an independent review into the state's sex and health education resources.

Students will no longer be taught that gender is a "social construct," or that sexuality is "non-binary," occurring on a continuum and "constantly changing." An edict encouraging teachers to "de-gender" their language will also likely be scrapped, along with sexually explicit case studies and teaching aids such as the "Genderbread Person," which promotes the idea that there are "infinite possibilities" of gender identity.[555]

Announced in September, 2016, the review by professor Bill Louden followed reports in *The Australian* that the Teacher Toolbox, a sex education resource for

---

[555] Urban (2017)

delivering content related to diversity of sex, sexuality and gender, was promoting Safe Schools materials, possibly in contravention of federal guidelines. Further revelations about Crossroads, the state's compulsory sex education program for Years 11 and 12 that was also pushing gender theory, prompted then-education minister Adrian Piccoli to order a review into the research base and scientific underpinning of the material.[556]

One of the items in the Teacher Toolbox, called Opposite Ends of the Pole, encouraged students to consider various case studies, including "Joseph," a man married with three children who "masturbates [and] fantasises only about men" as well as "Alex," who had sex with girls as a teenager but has developed a relationship with a man since moving to a country town.[557]

What did it take to get this junk removed from the education system? One board member getting involved, discovering verifiable truth, and taking a stand! Just see what can happen when people read the science and grasp reality!

PARENTS – STAND TALL.

To moms, dads, grandparents, aunts, uncles and cherished friends – time is running out… let nothing dissuade you. Now is the time to turn the tide. We do it by being united. So…

PARENTS– UNITE.

PARENTS – STAND UP.

PARENTS – STAND OUT.

PARENTS – STAND FIRM.

PARENTS – STAND TALL.

Canadian culture has maintained a belief in divine design for over 400 years. Before that, our First Nation folk believed the same way. There was a common belief that mother, father, and children provided the best family model for society. There was definitely a distinct unity in the understanding of marriage and family. The impact of a Judeo-Christian lifestyle on Canadian society produced not only

---

[556] Ibid
[557] Ibid

family cohesiveness, but also generated the workforce, and has proven successful throughout all of history.

The LGBT agenda promotes a minority group to the level of majority, and has attempted to depict all sexual behaviour as equal and healthy. The truth of this claim is dubious at best and completely destructive at worst. Are you willing to stake the lives of your children on this new social experiment?

CHAPTER 14

Hope on the Horizon

For I am not ashamed of the Gospel,
for it is the power of God for
salvation to everyone who believes
Romans 1:16 (ESV)

And they overcame him [Satan]
by the blood of the Lamb,
And by the word of their testimony;
And loved not their lives unto the death.
Revelation 12:11 (KJV)

GOD KEEP OUR LAND – Glorious and Free!

IN 1965 PIERRE BERTON WROTE A BOOK CALLED *THE COMFORTABLE PEW: A Critical look at the Church in the New Age.*[558] A few of you might remember it. His thought on the mainline churches of his day was that

> Large numbers of nominal Christians are no longer either very hot or very cold, for the virus that has weakened the church is apathy.

---

[558] Berton (1965)

While I might dispute the fact that nominal Christians could be very hot in the first place, his point is well-taken. What weakened the whole of the Christian Church, from Catholic to Evangelical, was apathy[559]—something for which Canadians are well-known.

As I suggested earlier, the Judeo-Christian framework created a cultural pattern of inescapable value throughout history. It has shaped history, yes; but it has also shaped morality. It is this ethic that is being bombarded by radical activism, to the point where proclaiming a Christian ethos in Canada is likely to get one fired from their job or even jailed. Individuals and churches upholding these values have been persecuted in the past, and it is likely to happen again. In fact, it is only increasing in this century.

The Christian church in Canada (and in many places around the world) has become ashamed of the Gospel! The very Word of God that gives life to believers and truth to the world is once again being suppressed. Until fairly recently, Christians of all traditions have assumed the complete trustworthiness and truthfulness of God's Word, as the Apostle Paul stated:

> *All scripture is God-breathed and is useful for teaching, rebuking, correcting and training in righteousness, so that the man of God may be thoroughly equipped for every good work.* (2 Timothy 3:16-17, NIV)

Rosaria Butterfield commented that, "The internal mission of the Bible is to transform the nature of humanity."[560] God's will for human sexuality is clearly written, and, contrary to public opinion, Jesus' point of view is not outdated. The truth of scripture concerning various sexual behaviours provides a safety net for our children called purity. Young people who realize and practice purity will not only escape many of the physical health issues of this generation, they will likely also avoid the pervasive mental health problems identified throughout this book.

We need to get this straight: we are all sexual sinners at some point in our lives, be it in thought or action. Not only that, but our feelings often overwhelm and deceive us. There are many Christians who have or still struggle with same-sex attraction, and there are many same-sex strugglers have given up the fight and decided to embrace a gay identity just because the alternative is difficult. On the other hand, there are many men and women who have

---

[559] Hutchinson (2017)
[560] Butterfield (2015)

managed their brokenness and had great victory. We all have experienced brokenness, sexual or otherwise, in our lives. Perhaps you've heard it said that in life all good things are difficult to achieve. The struggle against sin affects every person on the planet. In itself the struggle is not sinful, but woe to those who call evil good.

The church must return to its biblical foundation, unafraid to proclaim truth and the good news of the gospel. We must take a stand and proclaim with the apostle Paul, *"I am not ashamed of the Gospel, because it is the power of God for the salvation of everyone who believes"* (Romans 1:16, NIV)! So many have wandered from this path of truth, simply because it offends some in our society! Even the very suggestion of the word "sin" now meets with public outcry! So what do so many believers now do in 2017? We back down and cower in our closets in fear.

The LGBT agenda is attempting to subjugate the Judeo-Christian ethic of morality.

> Freedom of religion and freedom of speech are under threat of extinction in Canada at the intersection of culture and law regarding family rights (e.g. the Hamilton father). There is a direct challenge to the Judeo-Christian worldview of parental rights, particularly the right to impart these values and sexual ethics to one's own children.[561]

SPEAKING OUT

Common cause has brought leaders from all sides of the religious factions together in the past, and I want to suggest it can again. The common cause will likely come when the correct understanding of what the indoctrination of our children is doing to our society hits home. Hopefully the pot will not be at a full boil before this happens!

> If you listen to the media, God is dead and the Christian Church is supposedly destined to self-destruct.

Christianity is still the largest religion in Canada; with Catholics included, it tips the scales at 67.3%[562] of the population—who knew! Evangelical Christians alone number about 12%.[563] Yet, if you listen to the media, God is dead and the Christian Church is supposedly destined to self-destruct. The church hasn't

---

[561] The Public Discourse (2016)
[562] Religion in Canada (n.d.)
[563] Hutchinson (2017 p. 70)

helped its image either. It seems we at times have minored on majors and majored on minors—issues that is.

In 1993, sociologist and pollster Reginald Bibby painted a rather dreary picture of where Canada's churches would be by about 2015. His thoughts were that congregations would be older, birth rates wouldn't keep up with death rates, and many, if not most, children weren't being socialized into a faith. It was a linear decline, plain and simple. "The writing was on the wall for religion, it looked pretty much over."[564]

When 2015 finally came around, Bibby decided to revisit his book and check on his predictions. He discovered that for many religious groups, he was quite off-target. Catholics, for example, are building new churches in some parts of the country. Evangelicals increased their total numbers as Canada's population grew. He had accurately forecasted a long, drawn-out decline for the United Church of Canada and the Anglican Church. "What I screwed up on—it sounds so naive looking back—[is] I didn't allow for the immigration variable," Bibby says. "The thing that pumps new life into religion in Canada has been this mammoth entrance not only of Muslims, but also Catholics." [565]

THE POWER OF ENGAGEMENT

The God of the Bible understands the power of engagement. You may recognize the following words from the Bible…

For God so loved the world that he gave his one and only son, that whoever believes in him shall not perish but have eternal life. For God did not send his Son into the world to condemn the world, but to save the world through him. (John 3:16-17, NIV)

Talk about engagement! God was so in love with His created ones that He actually sent His own son, Jesus, to die a horrible death on the cross—crucified by the very ones He loved—in order to bring them redemption and give them the hope of eternity! Of course, the story is about more than the cross—it is about His resurrection. If Jesus was still in the grave, the story would have ended there, but Jesus rose again. It is when we put our trust and faith in Jesus, that he gives us eternal life. He longs for the entire world to acknowledge, receive Him and live in obedience to His Word. May John 3:16-17 be the cry of our hearts to

[564] Bibby (1993)
[565] Bibby (2015)

a lost, lonely and hurting world. May we become the hands and feet of Jesus to the very ones who revile us!

> *…God demonstrates his own love for us in this: While we were still sinners, Christ died for us.* (Romans 5:8, NIV)

For the church to engage society in twenty-first century Canada, it must approach society like an outsider reaching out to the lost. That's how Jesus approached those He encountered. Christian believers must never forget the principle of *imago Dei*—all humanity is created in the image and likeness of God. Even with our differences, and especially in our discourse, we must treat others with dignity.

It's important to see the lost as lost, not as wrong. That's not easily done, when we who have walked in truth are opposed by those demanding that their their own truth, often based on subjective feelings, overrides scripture. When feelings are not translated through biblical wisdom, we become unmoored.[566] God's Word is not considered authoritative by those who do not embrace it. The principles of Scripture must be translated into the language of listeners who reject or are unaware of its Author.[567]

Immediately, two parables stand out for me: the parables of the lost sheep and the lost coin.

> *Now the tax collectors and sinners were all gathering around to hear Jesus. But the Pharisees and the teachers of the law muttered, "This man welcomes sinners and eats with them."*
>
> *Then Jesus told them this parable: "Suppose one of you has a hundred sheep and loses one of them. Doesn't he leave the ninety-nine in the open country and go after the lost sheep until he finds it? And when he finds it, he joyfully puts it on his shoulders and goes home. Then he calls his friends and neighbors together and says, 'Rejoice with me; I have found my lost sheep.' I tell you that in the same way there will be more rejoicing in heaven over one sinner who repents than over ninety-nine righteous persons who do not need to repent.* (Luke 15:1-7, NIV)

Jesus loves the lost. He loved you and me when we were astray from His flock. When we consider those who, according to scripture, are living sin-filled

---

[566] Butterfield (2015 p. 45)
[567] Hutchinson (2017 p. 21)

lives, we also need to consider what Jesus said about them; they are lost, like sheep without a shepherd...

The Bible says that all we like sheep have gone astray; there is no one who is perfect.

> "It's important to see the lost as lost, not as wrong."
> Hutchinson, 2017

"Desires for things God has forbidden are a reflection of how sin has distorted me, not how God has made me."[568]

Every one of us is in need of a Saviour to rescue us from our own selfishness and bring us into relationship with Almighty God.

One phrase I regularly use is that it's either the "*Word or the world.*" God or culture—the church can't love both! Yes, we love people *in* the culture, but our first love needs to be directed toward God and scripture. It seems to me that the Christian church has abandoned God's Word to become politically correct!

Because the Christian church stopped exercising its voice, our society has been bullied into accepting every form of sexual expression as "normal." Society as a whole, and the church in particular, is now afraid to stand up for biblically-expressed moral behaviour. We've been told that we must not only agree and accept every perceived sexual expression or gender identity, but we also must affirm these thoughts, emotions and behaviours!

Parents across this nation, many of whom are people of deep moral convictions and faith, are being forced to expose their children to hedonism. I believe in decency and respect for all, but I don't believe that I, or anyone else, should have to subscribe to the LGBT agenda of indoctrination—yet here we are!

I believe it is time for the church in Canada to shake off its complacency and stand up and be counted. To do so, we need to stand on the inerrancy of scripture as well as on empirical scientific research into sexuality.

ULTIMATE DECEPTION - THE GAY CHRISTIAN MOVEMENT

> *Cheap grace is the grace we bestow on ourselves.*
> *Cheap grace is the preaching of forgiveness, without repentance*
> *Baptism without church discipline...*
> *Cheap grace is grace without discipleship,*

---

[568] Allberry (2013 p. 32)

Grace without the cross,
Grace without Jesus Christ, living and incarnate[569]
Dietrich Bonhoeffer

The Gay Christian movement, active within Catholic, mainline, and now evangelical churches, is a form of deception we have not, in modern history, experienced before. The Bible is very clear about sin, and especially sexual sin.

Romans chapter one identifies those who have been deceived and *have chosen to reject* God and His truth:

For since the creation of the world God's invisible qualities—his eternal power and divine nature—have been clearly seen, being understood from what has been made, so that men [and women] are without excuse. (Romans 1:20, NIV)

Because humankind turned their backs on God, they no longer wanted to be in the sheepfold. The apostle Paul goes on to say that

...their thinking became futile and their foolish hearts were darkened...they became fools and exchanged the glory of the immortal God for images made to look like mortal man, birds, animals and reptiles.

Therefore God gave them over in the sinful desires of their hearts to sexual impurity for the degrading of their bodies with one another. They exchanged the truth of God for a lie, and worshiped and served created beings rather than the Creator...

Because of this, God gave them over to shameful lusts. Even their women exchanged natural relations for unnatural ones. In the same way the men who also abandoned natural relations with women and were inflamed with lust for one another. Men committed indecent acts with other men, and received in themselves the due penalty for their perversion.

Furthermore, since they did not think it worthwhile to retain the knowledge of God, he gave them over to a depraved mind, to do what ought not to be done. They have become filled with every kind of wickedness, evil, greed and depravity. They are full of envy, murder, strife, deceit and malice. They are gossips, slanderers, God-haters, insolent, arrogant and boastful; they invent ways of doing evil; they disobey their parents; they are senseless, faithless, heartless, ruthless. Although they know God's righteous decree that those who

---

[569] Bonhoeffer (1959 p. 99)

do such things deserve death, they not only continue to do these very things but also approve of those who practice them. (Romans 1:21-32, NIV)

There are no biblical examples of a person identifying with their sinful brokenness and then adding Christian to it. Just imagine saying, "I am an angry, unbelieving, porn-addicted Christian!" Yet this is exactly what the "gay" Christian is doing. You can't have it both ways. The fact is that we are all driven by selfishness, we all desperately want a Jesus who will take our side, defend our opinions, and make us comfortable with ourselves! We will only love Jesus as long as He conforms to our image.

> "Those who leave homosexuality and maintain a repentant heart have a different goal than those who embrace a Gay Christian identity. They embrace a state of overcoming which fosters a mature understanding of sanctification. It requires a lifelong conformity to live like Jesus."[570]

In the midst of sexual darkness you either give in and choose to walk away from Jesus, or you resist temptation and draw close to Jesus. We are all faced daily with the same choices.[571] When diagnosing sexual sin, Jesus always pointed people back to God's original design—Adam and Eve.

Yet many LBGT activists are so impassioned by the forces of sin in their lives that they will stop at nothing to silence those who challenge their behaviour. They desire to stop God's followers from teaching the truth of the Word of God to their families and society.

It will only be by the power of Jesus that the tide is turned in this generation. Yet, I believe with all that is within me that He *will* turn the tide as we speak the message of the cross: Christ crucified and risen for the redemption of sin—yours, mine, and the world's. There is a better identity than a gay identity—it's a Christ identity!

A CHRISTIAN IDENTITY

Jesus' command to "love your neighbour as yourself"
does not have an exception clause for
a gay neighbour![572]
C. Kaltenbach

---

[570] Black (2017 p. 86)
[571] Barr & Citlau (2014)
[572] Kaltenbach (2015 p. 5)

CLOSING THE FLOODGATES

Christian men and women encountering same-sex attraction are led either toward or away from loving communion with God.[573] Although conflict regarding homosexual behaviour continues for Jesus followers, the church is now being assailed with the newly recognized fluidity of sexuality.

According to Dallas & Heche,

> Theories claiming homosexuality springs from family dynamics are suggesting something the Bible neither confirms nor denies, so at least they can be considered, whereas, theories insisting that homosexuality is normal and to be accepted because it's observable in nature, are to be rejected on the basis of equating the morality of mankind with that of the animal kingdom, as scripture is clear in its distinction between human beings and animals.[574]

When we talk about LGBT culture, the conversation often comes around to identity! How one "identifies" sexually becomes the basis of their personal identity. Christians also have an identity: a new identity is formed when we choose to believe in Jesus.

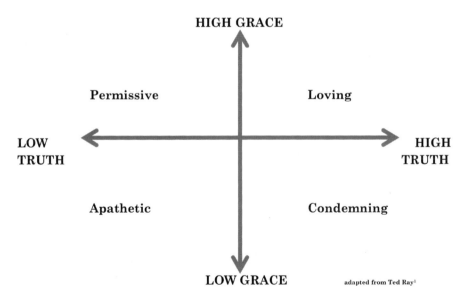

adapted from Ted Ray[1]

---

[573] Jones & Yarhouse (2000)
[574] Dallas & Heche (2010 p. 178)

Mark Yarhouse recognizes an "identity in Christ script"[575] for believers, no matter what their sexual background. An identity in Christ occurs when intrinsic God attachment transpires. God, throughout scripture, is identified as Father—Abba. We enter into the deepest father/child relationship imaginable upon salvation. God is the perfect father; the perfect attachment figure. He is the epitome of Love, Grace, Mercy, Truth and Justice. While I go into the subject of God Attachment much deeper in my book, Deep Impact,[576] suffice to say this relationship begins a process of love, forgiveness and healing throughout our life. Our Christ identity is counter-cultural to the sexual identity script.[577]

Same-sex attractions may be part of our experience, but they are not the defining element of our identity. We can choose to integrate our experiences of attraction to the same sex into a gay identity, or we can choose to center our identity on other aspects of our experience, including our biological sex, family, love and God. The most compelling aspect of the personhood of the Christian is one's identity in Christ, a central and defining aspect of what it means to be a follower of Jesus.[578]

A Jesus follower's essential belief system and faith-shaping events can be described in God attachment terms, with personal relationship and God experiences being seen as transformational. It is within these experiences that same-sex attracted individuals can find true acceptance, love, and security, as well as spiritual and emotional healing. This is the heart of the gospel—to turn from our sin (repentance), and receive God's forgiveness and true acceptance, living out a life securely fastened in the love of God.

The Holy Bible, Judeo-Christian thought and tradition, and even other religions teach that homosexuality is diametrically opposed to created design. The gay Christian movement, part of the LGBT agenda, has not only challenged biblical interpretation, but also attempted to reinterpret Christian history on this issue. It's time to sound the alarm, as segments of the Christian church who have adopted this reverse theology are approaching apostasy.[579]

We are indeed living in an age where what Christ followers through the ages have regarded as the truth about sexuality, marriage, fidelity, and biblical authority is under violent attack. The only group that has consistently stood "in the way" of accomplishing the LGBT mandate is people of faith standing on the

---

[575] Yarhouse (2010)
[576] Gillies (2016)
[577] Yarhouse (2010)
[578] Ibid
[579] Fortson & Grams (2016)

truth of God's word. Unfortunately, malicious and insidious picking away at the essence of biblical truth has eroded their impact.

GLAD ALLIANCE

The GLAD alliance arose in 1970 from the abundant fields of the gay rights movement. It is a gay advocacy group within the Christian church directed at transforming Christians to be openly affirming of homosexuality and working for inclusion of all gender and sexual identities. This group has recently changed their name to Disciples LGBTQ Alliance.

Let me share their mission statement: [580]

We, the GLAD Alliance, are members of the Christian Church (Disciples of Christ), called to join in God's work of transforming the Christian Church (Disciples of Christ) into a just and inclusive church that welcomes persons of all gender expressions and sexual identities into the full life and leadership of the church.

We openly welcome persons of all sexual orientation, gender expression, socioeconomic status, family configuration, age, national origin, race, religious or non-religious background, and physical or mental condition. We embrace all people at any point in their faith journey and recognize each person's spiritual gifts. We proclaim God's inclusive welcome to the Communion Table, and affirm that full and equal participation in the life and leadership of our church is open to all. We seek to continue to learn and grow in our efforts to be a movement for wholeness in a fragmented world.

The 2014-2017 Strategic Vision of the GLAD Alliance:[581]

Supporting the mission of the GLAD Alliance and responding to the call of the Christian Church (Disciples of Christ) to become a people of grace and welcome to all, the GLAD Alliance commits itself to:

• *increasing the number of Open & Affirming Ministries*, creating communities of grace and welcome, including congregations, regions, higher education institutions, seminaries, ministry partners, and general units;

[580] Disciples LGBTQ+ Alliance (n.d., a)
[581] Ibid

- *educating and supporting the Open & Affirming Ministries* with resources to expand their pastoral care of LGBT persons with renewed commitment to bisexual and transgender persons;
- *empowering the Open & Affirming Ministries* and the members of the Alliance to respond to justice issues such as marriage equality, employment non-discrimination, and opposing bullying;
- and, to enable this plan, *expanding the resources of the Alliance* by increasing individual membership, contributions, and volunteer involvement. (emphasis added)

Although I don't see anything about God, Jesus the Holy Spirit or the Bible expressed in their statements, there are numerous mandates to increase the LGBT agenda—one that is directly opposed to the God of the Bible. I see the Gay Manifesto snaking its way into full acceptance.

How do the GLAD mission and vision statement line up with the Christian church and Scripture? Firstly, the absolute lack of scripture on their website astounded me! There doesn't seem to be a statement of faith either. On the other hand, let me highlight the creeds from the Catechism of the Catholic Church.[582]

The Apostles' Creed	The Nicene Creed
I believe in God, the Father almighty, creator of heaven and earth.	We believe in one God, the Father, the Almighty, maker of heaven and earth, and of all that is, seen and unseen.
I believe in Jesus Christ, his only Son, our Lord.	We believe in one Lord, Jesus Christ, the only Son of God, eternally begotten of the Father, God from God, Light from Light, true God from true God, begotten, not made, one in Being with the Father. Through him all things were made. For us men and for our salvation, he came down from heaven:
He was conceived by the power of the Holy Spirit and born of the Virgin Mary.	by the power of the Holy Spirit he was born of the Virgin Mary, and became man.
He suffered under Pontius Pilate, was crucified, died, and was buried. He descended into hell.	For our sake he was crucified under Pontius Pilate; he suffered died and was buried.

[582] Seper (1975)

On the third day he rose again.	On the third day he rose again in fulfillment of the Scriptures;
He ascended into heaven and is seated at the right hand of the Father. He will come again to judge the living and the dead	he ascended into heaven and is seated at the right hand of the Father. He will come again in glory to judge the living and the dead, and his kingdom will have no end.
I believe in the Holy Spirit, the holy catholic Church, the communion of saints, the forgiveness of sins, the resurrection of the body, and the life everlasting. Amen.	We believe in the Holy Spirit, the Lord, the giver of life, who proceeds from the Father and the Son. With the Father and the Son he is worshipped and glorified. He has spoken through the Prophets. We believe in one holy catholic and apostolic Church. We acknowledge one baptism for the forgiveness of sins. We look for the resurrection of the dead, and the life of the world to come. Amen.[1]

And now, the statement of faith of the Christian and Missionary Alliance in Canada.[583]

1. There is one God, who is infinitely perfect, existing eternally in three persons: Father, Son and Holy Spirit.

2. Jesus Christ is true God and true man. He was conceived by the Holy Spirit and born of the Virgin Mary. He died upon the cross, the Just for the unjust, as a substitutionary sacrifice, and all who believe in him are justified on the ground of his shed blood. He arose from the dead according to the Scriptures. He is now at the right hand of the Majesty on high as our great High Priest. He will come again to establish his Kingdom of righteousness and peace.

3. The Holy Spirit is a divine Person, sent to indwell, guide, teach and empower the believer, and to convince the world of sin, of righteousness and of judgment.

4. The Old and New Testaments, inerrant as originally given, were verbally inspired by God and are a complete revelation of his will for the salvation of people. They constitute the divine and only rule of Christian faith and practice.

---

[583] The Christian and Missionary Alliance in Canada (n.d.)

5. Humankind, originally created in the image and likeness of God, fell through disobedience, incurring thereby both physical and spiritual death. All people are born with a sinful nature, are separated from the life of God, and can be saved only through the atoning work of the Lord Jesus Christ. The destiny of the impenitent and unbelieving is existence forever in conscious torment, but that of the believer is everlasting joy and bliss.

6. Salvation has been provided only through Jesus Christ. Those who repent and believe in him are united with Christ through the Holy Spirit and are thereby regenerated (born again), justified, sanctified and granted the gift of eternal life as adopted children of God.

7. It is the will of God that in union with Christ each believer should be sanctified thoroughly thereby being separated from sin and the world and fully dedicated to God, receiving power for holy living and sacrificial and effective service toward the completion of Christ's commission. This is accomplished through being filled with the Holy Spirit which is both a distinct event and progressive experience in the life of the believer.

8. Provision is made in the redemptive work of the Lord Jesus Christ for the healing of the mortal body. Prayer for the sick and anointing with oil as taught in the Scriptures are privileges for the Church in this present age.

9. The universal Church, of which Christ is the Head, consists of all those who believe on the Lord Jesus Christ, are redeemed through His blood, regenerated by the Holy Spirit, and commissioned by Christ to go into all the world as a witness, preaching the Gospel to all nations.
The local church, the visible expression of the universal Church, is a body of believers in Christ who are joined together to worship God, to observe the ordinances of Baptism and the Lord's Supper, to pray, to be edified through the Word of God, to fellowship, and to testify in word and deed to the good news of salvation both locally and globally. The local church enters into relationships with other like-minded churches for accountability, encouragement and mission.

10. There shall be a bodily resurrection of the just and of the unjust; for the former, a resurrection unto life; for the latter, a resurrection unto judgment.

11. The second coming of the Lord Jesus Christ is imminent and will be personal and visible. As the believer's blessed hope, this vital truth is an incentive for holy living and sacrificial service toward the completion of Christ's commission.

Let's compare the creeds and statements of the Christian Church with those of the GLAD movement.

GLAD (Christian Church—Disciples of Christ) doctrine (no creed identified) vs historical Christian creedal belief:

We are members of the Christian Church (Disciples of Christ) [GLAD has no explanation of what this means. No reference to God, Jesus or Holy Spirit on their site.]	There is one God, Father, Son and Holy Spirit. Jesus Christ is true God and true man. He died upon the cross, and all who believe in Him are justified on the ground of His shed blood. He arose from the dead according to the Scriptures. He is now at the right hand of God. He will come again to establish His kingdom of righteousness and peace. The Holy Spirit is a divine Person, sent to indwell, guide, teach and empower the believer, and to convince the world of sin, of righteousness and of judgment. The Bible—Old and New Testaments—was verbally inspired by God and is a complete revelation of His will for the salvation of people, constituting the divine and only rule of Christian faith and practice
We are called to join in God's work of transforming the Christian Church (Disciples of Christ) *[into the acceptance of all things LGBT+]* [No description of sin and reference to it and therefore no need for salvation?]	All people are born with a sinful nature, are separated from the life of God, and can be *saved only through the atoning work* of the Lord Jesus Christ. Salvation *has been provided only through Jesus Christ.* Those who repent and believe in Him are united with Christ through the Holy Spirit and are thereby regenerated (born again), *justified, sanctified* and granted the gift of eternal life as *adopted children* of God.

GLAD Alliance commits itself to: increasing the number of Open & Affirming Ministries, creating communities of grace and welcome, including congregations, regions, higher education institutions, seminaries, ministry partners, and general units [not sure what this means]	It is the will of God that in union with Christ each believer should be sanctified thoroughly, thereby being separated from sin and the world and fully dedicated to God, receiving power for holy living and sacrificial and effective service toward the completion of Christ's commission.
educating and supporting the Open & Affirming Ministries with resources to expand their pastoral care of LGBT persons with renewed commitment to bisexual and transgender persons	The local church, the visible expression of the universal Church, is a body of believers in Christ who are joined together to worship God, to observe the ordinances of Baptism and the Lord's Supper, to pray, to be edified through the Word of God, to fellowship, and to testify in word and deed to the good news of salvation both locally and globally. The local church enters into relationships with other like-minded churches for accountability, encouragement and mission.

GLAD makes no recognition of sin or the need for salvation on their site. What I did find were books by Patrick Cheng. *Radical Love: An Introduction to Queer Theology*[584] describes a "love so extreme that it *dissolves our existing boundaries*—gay/straight, male/female, life/death, divine/human." *Radical Love* is described as "an excellent introduction into how queer theology works."[585] Another book by Cheng is listed—*From Sin to Amazing Grace: Discovering the Queer Christ.*[586] "Struggling with the doctrines of sin and grace, Cheng argues that people need to be liberated from the traditional [as he calls it] crime-based model of sin and grace and proposes a Christ-centered model that is based upon the ancient doctrine of theosis, or deification, in which sin and grace are defined in terms of what God has done for us through Jesus Christ."[587]

The Eastern Orthodox Church uses the term theosis in the understanding of a transformative process, the aim of which is to depict the likeness of union with God. The last line fits into the Christian belief, but I think the issue here is what

---

[584] Cheng (2011)
[585] Disciples LGBTQ+ Alliance (n.d., c)
[586] Cheng (2012)
[587] Disciples LGBTQ+ Alliance (n.d., b)

is believed about sin. At the heart of discipleship is a self-denying submission to Jesus as Lord.

BUT HOW DO I RESPOND TO MY NEPHEW WHO IS PRACTICING A GAY LIFESTYLE?

What is perhaps the most confusing to the average Christian is when a Christian relative or friend comes out. Firstly, it is important to differentiate between someone identifying as a sexually active gay man and someone who is experiencing same-sex attraction but may not be acting on their feelings. Attraction and behaviour are two different things.

Oftentimes, believers in Jesus are accused of being unloving and/or homophobic if they suggest that they disagree with the individual's behaviour! But think of this. Do you ever disagree with *your* children's behaviour? Does your disagreement mean that you are unloving, unkind, oppositional, or phobic? Well, in their young eyes, perhaps. But is that true?—no! It's because of your love for them that you set guidelines for their behaviour. That's what God has done for us as well. The Bible actually says that He disciplines those He loves…just as a loving parent does with their children.

Oh, how far we have fallen. The argument now goes like this—Jesus's teaching on Love trumps explicit biblical prohibitions of homosexual, bi-sexual, transsexual, pansexual, and other illicit forms of sexual expression. The reality? Jesus's teaching on love comes with behavioural limits. He calls sin "sin," even in the midst of expressing love:

> *The teachers of the law and the Pharisees brought in a woman caught in adultery. They made her stand before the group and said to Jesus, "Teacher, this woman was caught in the act of adultery. In the Law Moses commanded us to stone such women. Now what do you say?" They were using this question as a trap, in order to have a basis for accusing Him.*
>
> *But Jesus bent down and started to write on the ground with his finger. When they kept on questioning him, he straightened up and said to them, "Let anyone of you who is without sin be the first to throw a stone at her." Again he stooped down and wrote on the ground.*
>
> *At this, those who heard began to go away, one at a time, the older ones first, until only Jesus was left, with the woman still standing there. Jesus straightened up and asked her, "Woman, where are they? Has no one condemned you?"*

"No one, sir,' she said.

"Then neither do I condemn you," *Jesus declared.*

"Go now and leave your life of sin." (John 8:3-11, NIV, emphasis added)

This scripture is a beautiful portrayal of the love, grace, mercy, and truth of Jesus. There is no longer condemnation of past sin, but there is an admonition to leave the life of sin one is involved in. This is the unchanging message of the gospel. You can't have it both ways and walk with Jesus.

Gay "Christians" want to talk about the injustices they face and their commitment to monogamy (which, as you have discovered through reading, is rarely the case). They consistently minimize discussions of sexual promiscuity, practice, violence and abuse. Their sexual identity becomes more important than their relationship and obedience to God or their submission to His revealed will.[588]

I believe that we are to engage with those caught in the hedonistic practices of our culture, in the same manner that Jesus did in his time. He offered the way of redemption—without minimizing the sin or the person. He, of course, offered perfect love, grace and mercy along with unchanging truth. If you have practiced your faith in the past, your friends and relatives already understand what you believe. They may attempt to change your mind or challenge your beliefs, but those beliefs are based on the irrefutable Word of God. Stand firm. The world all around is building on shifting sand—when their house falls, they are going to need the security of your consistent faith and the security of Jesus in their lives.

Keep in mind that *sexual experimentation of all forms is highly valued* in our present culture and *highly reprimanded in God's Word*, so it is not only homosexual practice or bisexual, but also heterosexual fornication and adultery which can be painted with the same brush stroke of immorality.

Christian believers have always been called to a distinct set of beliefs and particularly sexual practices, based on God's Word. Here we find lifestyle expectations and specific directives regarding sexual behaviour. The call to live a distinctly Christian life is the call to sacrifice. Dietrich Bonhoeffer[589] said,

When Christ calls a man, he bids him come and die.

---

[588] Fortson and Grams (2016)

[589] Bonhoeffer (1959)

Many believers have literally given their lives for Christ; many more have lived their lives for Christ, dying to their own selfish desires. Sexual purity comes at a cost—death to self-gratification.

Sexual purity became a symbol of the Christian community, and consistently, throughout the ages, the church has denounced immoral acts as incompatible with Christian faith. The Christian church historically has distinguished itself from non-believers in this foundational ethical element, while *maintaining that believers could receive forgiveness* for these and other sins and overcome them by the Power of the Holy Spirit.

The early church's powerful sexual ethic and teaching turned the Roman world upside down in a radical reversal of the cultural norms of the day, by maintaining that sexual relations were only acceptable within heterosexual marriage!

UNITY OF BELIEF

Christians need to unite.
We need to stand on the inerrancy of scripture
And walk with the compassion of Jesus.

For Christ followers, love has its origins in relationship with God the Father, Jesus the Son, and the Holy Spirit. When we know and experience such total acceptance, we are transformed. Along with this transformation comes a deepening desire to serve the God of all creation. Christians have been at the forefront of anti-slavery movements, civil rights movements, humanitarian relief, and sex-slave release, to name a few.

This doesn't mean that longing for relationship and sexual enjoyment are thrown out the window. We were created for relationship. When God told Adam that, *"it is not good that the man should be alone"* (Genesis 2:18, KJV), He meant it and he did something about it! He created a helpmate, a companion and lover for Adam, and the two of them became one flesh. Perfect fit—perfect unity! God said it was good, very good. Then He gave them a command: be fruitful and multiply.

Notice this was God's plan—not Adam's—one biological male and one biological female. When sin entered the world, the beauty and perfection of marriage became distorted. Just read through the Bible and you'll witness all forms of degradation. It's all there. There are no punches pulled here. There are very clear descriptions of how even God's people run to the very depths of depravity when they turn away from truth. Just because they sin (can I even use that word in 2017?), it doesn't change God's mind on righteousness and holiness—or redemption! Sinners (oops, there's that word again) are continually called back to repentance and to God's plan, to live out our lives in relationship with Him.

When we love someone, especially the God of the entire universe, we have a desire to please that person. But we are a rebellious people, often deciding that we know better and leaving the safety of a healthy God relationship to pursue our own willful desires, much like teenagers that choose to engage in all kind of behaviours that disappoint and wound their parents.

There has been a continual fight throughout the centuries to maintain a standard for Godly relationship and marriage up to the current day. As a society we have now decided:

- that it is too difficult to remain celibate before marriage
- too difficult to be married
- too difficult not to give in to lustful thoughts
- too difficult not to experiment with all manner of sexual expression
- and too difficult to live up to the moral standards found in God's word and upheld by the Christian church and tradition for centuries

Giving up, giving in and fitting in with society's new norms seems far easier than adhering to an "outdated" moral standard given by a God who is viewed by unbelievers as tyrannical and selfish. It is not only those who are outside of the Church who have capitulated to "the flesh"—their sinful nature—but also those within. The fact that the Church at large is hesitant to hold believers to account for immoral behaviour has caused further disillusionment from those outside the faith. If even so-called Christians can't live up to their own standards, then why should they expect society to try?

So here's the truth: God's standards are difficult to live up to. In fact, they are impossible! Yep. That's why the Israelites had feasts and festivals, times of celebration and remembrance, sacrifices and atonements for sin. They understood that each person is guilty of some act of sin. They needed to remember, repent, and celebrate God's laws and standards. They needed sacrifices to atone for their own sins throughout the year. They were not perfect—and neither are we, but making excuses for our behaviour instead of taking responsibility for it always leads to more extreme consequences. Saying "black is white" does not change the reality of the truth claims of scripture. Not then, not now! Now we live under a new covenant. We celebrate it every Easter, as Canadians of all stripes congregate to recognize the high price Jesus paid for our sin. God has provided a substitute for our sin: Jesus, the ultimate sacrifice, the one on whom Christianity pins its hopes for redemption, deliverance, and hope of eternity. He came, not because we could live up to God's law, but because we couldn't.

We can never be "perfect" and without sin, but we can be forgiven and *choose to live and walk in freedom from sin*—even, or especially, from sexual immorality. How can this be? Well, God had a plan: Jesus's death and resurrection, after which He sent the Holy Spirit. He is our power source, our convictor, our teacher, mentor, deliverer.

As Christ followers we must never compromise on our moral convictions. We must be people of the light, striving to live in sexual purity. Maintaining solid marriages should be a priority. We must continue to walk in the truth of God's word and instruct others in it, understanding His intervention into the lives of humankind.

Although we are transformed by our relationship with God and Jesus, this doesn't mean that longing for relationship and sexual enjoyment are thrown out the window. Jesus didn't say it would be easy; in fact, He said that in this world we would experience temptation, but He also promised that we could rise above it and live according to His word.

Can it be difficult? A resounding "yes." Good things in life are difficult. When you delve into what the Bible calls immoral behaviour, like immersing yourself in alcohol or drugs, the behaviour will become more and more tracked in your brain the deeper you go, making it extremely difficult to expunge. Sexual immorality (in whatever form it takes) often leads to an addiction that is most difficult to eradicate. It takes the saving grace of God and a commitment to follow Him in righteousness to wash one's spirit, soul and body from the grime of an immoral lifestyle. Once washed, it is our decision whether we return to the compulsive sexual behaviours of the past such as:

- pornography,
- fornication,
- adultery,
- homosexuality,
- lesbianism,

- polyamorism,
- bestiality,
- or other sexual distortions.

But get this: we have the ability to choose to live above the "desires of the flesh." We are no different than the people of Jesus's day, whom he called friends and disciples. The same instructions he gave them are relevant for today, whether we choose to believe them or not!

Remember when Jesus encountered a woman brought forward to be stoned for adultery? God understands the proclivity of sin; Jesus reached down and lifted the sinner up by saying we are all sinners—no one had the right to cast the first stone (to kill her), and instead, Jesus had the right to forgive her. He then issued this instruction: go and sin no more. In other words, quit doing what you are doing.

When the Church stopped speaking this message of sin and repentance (turning away from sin), our culture responded with a free-for-all! The Christian Church must turn away from the things which God has stated are sinful and tell sinners to quit behaving in the manner they have done in the past. For those in the church, we need to quit making excuses for what God calls "sin" and call it what it is.

I believe that the initial forsaking of relationship and commitment to God, for whatever reason individuals may come up with, have led to the current demise of moral absolutes and sexual purity. Jewish and Christian theology and tradition, a five-thousand year legacy, has *now* been thrown under the bus in the name of tolerance and affirmation! Tolerance today is used to try to bury freedom of religion and conscience.[590]

The Christian church worldwide has long offered hope and healing to the outcast, the rejected, the despised, the abandoned, the lonely, the abused. You name the pain: Jesus has been the cure for hundreds of thousands of people! He never gives up on us, never lets go of us.

ENGAGING THE CULTURE

Hutchinson[591] gives us great examples of people in the past and present who have been raised up by God to engage the culture; his book *Under Siege* is well worth the read. One of those people is Miroslav Volf, a Croatian by birth, who immigrated to the US in 1991. He is the director of the Yale Center for Faith

---

[590] Ruby (2015 p. 112)
[591] Hutchinson (2017)

and Culture. The following is his position on religious political pluralism, which I believe speaks well to the issue of faith in the political forum.

Christian faith is a prophetic faith that seeks to mend the world	**Christian faith should be active in all spheres of life**
Christ was a bringer of grace	Christian faith is not to be coercive
To follow Jesus means to care for others as well as oneself	A vision of human flourishing and the common good is the main thing Christian faith brings to the public debate
The world is God's creation and the Word came to His own, even if His own did notaccept Him	The Christian stance toward culture is complex: accepting, rejecting, learning, transforming, subverting and putting various elements of a rapidly-changing culture to better use
Christian faith bears witness to Christ	Christians are to be witnesses of Christ
Christian faith offers no political blueprint	Christians desire for others the same freedoms they claim for themselves. Pluralism is embraced

Adapted from Hutchinson (2017)[592]

So, what to do? Don Hutchinson gives us these truths:[593]

- If you believe in your cause and engage it, you are likely to have an impact in its favour, regardless of the resources you do or do not have behind you—stand firm on this freedom

---

[592] Ibid (p. 180)
[593] Ibid

- The way religious freedom is defined for other religious communities (i.e. Muslims) is determinative of the way religious freedom is defined for me and my community of faith
- Religious communities tend to keep to themselves, intending their engagement with others to be inoffensive, but they will engage in a civil version of Augustine's and Aquinas's version of just war theory when attacked—battling for rights equal to those of other Canadians
- It's valuable to be intentional about thinking creatively. Thinking outside the box on freedom of religion (freedom of speech) may include consideration of matters of freedom of conscience (individual) or freedom of assembly (group)
- *Never underestimate the underdog*—particularly one who is well prepared!

The LGBT agenda, if left unabated, will have future generations looking at us with bewilderment due to today's maltreatment of religious believers in the name of sexual revolution.[594]

Longing for the ideal while criticizing the real
is evidence of immaturity.
On the other hand,
settling for the real without striving for the ideal is complacency.
Maturity is living with the tension![595]

It's time to *rise up*, Canada!

So now we come to the end of the story. Yet, the end of one thing is simply the beginning of something greater. This morning I was reading from 1 Peter chapter 4. Let me share from the New Living Translation, verses 1-6 and 14-19:

So then, since Christ suffered physical pain, you must arm yourselves with the same attitude he had, and be ready to suffer, too. For if you have suffered physically for Christ, you have finished with sin. You won't spend the rest of your lives chasing your own desires, but you will be anxious to do the will of God. You have had enough in the past of the evil things that godless people enjoy—their immorality and lust, their feasting and drunkenness and wild parties, and their terrible worship of idols.

---

[594] Ibid
[595] Warren (2012 p. 24)

Of course, your former friends are surprised when you no longer plunge into the flood of wild and destructive things they do. So they slander you. But remember that they will have to face God, who stands ready to judge everyone, both the living and the dead…so although they were destined to die like all people, they now live forever with God in the Spirit.

…If you are insulted because you bear the name of Christ, you will be blessed, for the glorious Spirit of God rests upon you. If you suffer, however, it must not be for murder, stealing, making trouble, or prying into other people's affairs. But it is no shame to suffer for being a Christian. Praise God for the privilege of being called by his name! For the time has come for judgment, and it must begin with God's household. And if judgment begins with us, what terrible fate awaits those who have never obeyed God's Good News? And also, "if the righteous are barely saved, what will happen to godless sinners?"

So if you are suffering in a manner that pleases God, keep on doing what is right, and trust your lives to the God who created you, for he will never fail you.

We, in Canada, have become soft. The Christian church has become complacent. We have not suffered extensively for our faith, in the way much of the rest of the Christian world has. When we are insulted and called such things as "homophobic" or "exporters of hate," we crumble. We melt before the radical agenda that is determined to suppress our freedom, and the freedom of parents and Christians across this land.

As believers we have a hope, a greater message than that of the world. It is the message of true freedom, but nobody has ever found true freedom in Christ without a spiritual battle ensuing. It is time for us to fall on our faces before God, confessing and turning from our own sin to pursue His truth in all things. We are not called to war as the world wars, but rather we war on our knees. When we do this, our differences and bickering fall away, and we are then strengthened to stand firm against the fiery darts of the enemy (Satan), for our battle is not against flesh and blood (Eph. 6:12). The sexually confused are not our enemy—they are simply part of a lost world in need of the love, acceptance and forgiveness of Christ, just like the rest of us. According to God's Word, they are walking in sin, as some of us have been. But Jesus said, you shall know the truth, and the truth shall set you free (John 8:32, paraphrased).

The sad news: the Gay Rights movement has a manifesto, but it is Satan who ultimately controls those who walk in sin. The Good News: it is God who sets us free from sin and death (Romans 8:2). May we heed God's call to stand out and stand firm in a lost and broken world.

I am sending you out like sheep among wolves. Therefore, be as shrewd as snakes and as innocent [gentle] as doves. (Matthew 10:16, NIV)

Jesus is still the solution for a sin-lost world.

Conclusion

I HAVE BEEN IMPACTED BY THE LGBT CULTURE FOR JUST OVER FORTY YEARS. Thankfully, I have been impacted by the life of Jesus for some forty-four years! Ultimately it is because of Jesus I am writing this book, but there have been others along the way who have impacted my life in profound ways, for whom I am forever grateful. Sometimes they have dragged me along the path of the Cross kicking and screaming; other times, I have followed willingly. What truly matters is that I continue to walk the path that Christ has set before me—that is why this book has been written.

Bibliography

Ainsworth, M. D. S. (1963). The development of infant-mother interaction among the Ganda. In B. M. Foss (Ed.), *Determinants of infant behavior* (pp. 67-104). New York, NY: Wiley.

Ainsworth, M. D. S. (1967). *Infancy in Uganda: Infant care and the growth of love*. Baltimore: Johns Hopkins University Press.

Ainsworth, M. D. S. (1989). Attachments beyond infancy. *American Psychologist, 44,* 709-716.

Ainsworth, M. D. S., & Bell, S. M. (1970). Attachment, exploration, and separation: Illustrated by the behavior of one-year-olds in a strange situation. *Child Development, 41,* 49-67.

Ainsworth, M. D. S., Bell, S. M., & Stayton, D. (1974). Infant-mother attachment and social development. In M. P. Richards (Ed.), *The introduction of the child into a social world* (pp. 99-135). London: Cambridge University Press.

Ainsworth, M. D. S., Blehar, M. C., Waters, E., & Wall, S. (1978). *Patterns of attachment: A psychological study of the strange situation*. Hillsdale, NJ: Erlbaum.

Allberry, S. (2015). *Is God anti-gay?* Blenheim House, Epsom, Surrey, UK: Good Book Company.

Amen, D.G. (1998). *Change your brain, change your life*. New York, NY: Three Rivers Press.

American Academy of Child & Adolescent Psychiatry. (2013). Sex: Talking to your child. Retrieved from www.aacap.org/AACAP/families_and_youth/facts_for_families/FFF-guide/talking-to-your-kids-about-sex

American College of Pediatricians. (2016). Gender ideology harms children. Retrieved from www.acpeds.org/the-college-speaks/position-statements/gender-ideology-harms-children

American Psychiatric Association. (2011). Sexual orientation: What causes homosexuality/heterosexuality/bisexuality? Retrieved from https://web.archive.org/web/20110722080052/http://www.healthyminds.org/More-Info-For/GayLesbianBisexuals.aspx

American Psychiatric Association. (2013). *Diagnostic and statistical manual of mental disorders* (5th ed.). Washington, DC: Author.

American Psychological Association. (2010). *Publication manual of the American Psychological Association*. Washington, DC.

The American Society of Addiction Medicine. (n.d.) Definition of Addiction. Retrieved from https://www.asam.org/quality-practice/definition-of-addiction

Arriola, K.R., Louden, T., Doldren, M.A., & Fortenberry, R.M. (2005). A meta-analysis of the relationship of child sexual abuse to HIV risk behavior among women. *Child Abuse & Neglect, 29*, 725–746.

Associated Press. (2017, July 16). Investigator found Seattle Mayor Ed Murray sexually abused foster son in 1984, report says. *Boston Globe*. Retrieved from https://www.bostonglobe.com/news/politics/2017/07/16/investigator-found-seattle-mayor-murray-sexually-abused-foster-son-report-says/J4CGjomhcOWfddafp4GnhJ/story.html

Attwood, J.D. (2006). Mommy's little angel, Daddy's little girl: Do you know what your pre-teens are doing? *The American Journal of Family Therapy, 34*, 447-467.

Austin, S.B., Roberts, A.L, Corliss, H.L., & Molnar, B.E. (2008). Sexual violence victimization history and sexual risk indicators in a community-based urban cohort of "mostly heterosexual" and heterosexual young women. *American Journal of Public Health, 98*(6), 1015-1019.

Bailey, J.M., Dunne, M.P., & Martin, N.G. (2000). Genetic and environmental influences on sexual orientation and its correlates in an Australian twin sample. *Journal of Personality and Social Psychology, 78*(3), 524–536.

Bailey, J.M., & Pillard, R.C. (1991). A genetic study of male sexual orientation. *Archives of General Psychiatry, 48*(12), 1089-1096.

Bailey, M., & Blanchard, R. (2017). Gender dysphoria is not one thing. Retrieved from https://4thwavenow.com/2017/12/07/gender-dysphoria-is-not-one-thing/

Barkai, A.R. (2017). Troubling gender or engendering trouble? *Psychoanalytic Review, 104*(1), 1-32.

Barr, A.T., & Citlau, R. (2014). *Compassion without compromise.* Bloomington, MN: Bethany House Publishers.

Batty, D. (2003). Internet grooming: the five stages. *The Guardian.* Retrieved from https://www.theguardian.com

Bauer, G.R., Hammond, R., Travers, R., Kaay, M., Hohenadel, K.M., & Boyce, M. (2009). "I don't think this is theoretical: this is our lives": How erasure impacts health care for transgender people. *Journal of the Association of Nurses in AIDS Care, 20*, 348-361.

BBC. (2014). Child abuse image investigation leads to 660 arrests. Retrieved from www.bbc.com/news/uk-28326128

Bell, A.P., & Weinberg, M.S. (1979). Homosexualities: A study of diversity among men and women. Toronto, Canada: Simon & Schuster.

Beniot, D., & Parker, K. (1994). Stability and transmission of attachment across three generations. *Child Development, 65,* 1444-1456.

Bennett, J. (2009). The Next Sexual Revolution. *Newsweek.* Retrieved from www.newsweek.com/polyamory-next-sexual-revolution-8205
Berger, J. (2013). Comments presented to the House of Commons Standing Committee on Justice and Humans Rights, regarding Bill C279.

Berton, P. (1965). *The comfortable pew: A critical look at the church in the new age.* Toronto, ON: McLelland and Steward.

Better, A. (2013). Redefining queer: Women's relationships and identity in an age of sexual fluidity. *Sexuality & Culture, 18,* 16–38.

Bibby, R. (1993). *Unknown gods: The ongoing story of religion in Canada.* Toronto, ON: Stoddard Publishing.

Bibby, R. (2015, March 26). What Canadians really believe: A surprising poll. *Macleans.*

Bieber, I., Dain H.J., Dince, P.R., Drellich, M.G., Grand H.G., Gundlach, R.H., Kremer, M.W. Rifkin,A.H., Wilbur, C.B., Bieber., T.B. (1962). *Homosexuality: A psychoanalytic study.* New York, NY: Basic Books.

Bindel, J. (2016, October 24). "I'm grateful I grew up before children who don't fit stereotypes were assumed to be transgender": Feminist activist Julie Bindel on the danger of playing gender politics with young lives. *Daily Mail.* Retrieved from http://www.dailymail.co.uk/news/article-3865632/I-m-grateful-grew-children-don-t-fit-stereotypes-assumed-transgender-Feminist-activist-Julie-Bindel-danger-playing-gender-politics-young-lives.html

Black, S.H. (2017). *Freedom realized: Finding freedom from homosexuality & living a life free from labels.* Enumclaw, WA: Redemption Press.

Blackburn, P. (2012). The sexuality research of A.C. Kinsey – 40 years later: Time for accountability. Retrieved from http://peterjblackburn.net/issues/kinsey.htm

Blackless, M., Charuvastra, A., Derryck, A., Fausto-Sterling, A., Lauzanne, K., & Lee, E. (2000). How sexually dimorphic are we? Review and synthesis. *American Journal of Human Biology, 12*(2), 151–166.

Blakemore, J.E., Berenbaum, S.A., & Liben, L.S. (2008). *Gender development.* New York; NY: Taylor & Francis.

Blanchard, R. (1997). Birth order and sibling sex ratio in homosexual versus heterosexual males and females. *Annual Review of Sex Research, 8*, 27-67.

Blanchard, R., & Bogaert, A.F. (2004). Proportion of homosexual men who owe their sexual orientation to fraternal birth order: An estimate based on two national probability samples. *American Journal of Human Biology, 16*(2), 151-157.

Blatchford, C. (2015, May 29). Three year sentence brings sad, sickening end to onetime education superstar. *National Post.* Retrieved from http://nationalpost.com/opinion/christie-blatchford-three-year-sentence-brings-sad-sickening-end-to-onetime-education-superstar/wcm/f9dea082-9ef3-4fbb-90d5-93afb5a67aa5

Bogaert, A.G., & Skorska, M. (2011). Sexual orientation, fraternal birth order and the maternal immune hypothesis: A review. *Front Neuroendocrinologist, 32*(2), 247-254.

Bonhoeffer, D. (1959). *The cost of discipleship.* New York, NY: SCM Press.

Borchgrave, A.D. (2007, March 5). Time for TV detox. *United Press International.* Retrieved from www.teradaily.com/reports/Time_For_TV_Detox_999

Bowlby, J. (1969). *Attachment and loss, vol. 1: Attachment.* New York, NY: Basic Books.

Bowlby, J. (1973). *Attachment and loss, vol. 2: Separation.* New York, NY: Basic Books.

Bowlby, J. (1979). *The making & breaking of affectional bonds.* Tavistock Publications.

Boyce, W.F., Gallupe, O., & Fergus, S. (2008). Characteristics of Canadian youth reporting a very early age of first sexual intercourse. *Canadian Journal of Human Sexuality, 17*(3), 97-105.

Bradford, et al. (1988). The heterogeneity/homogeneity of pedophilia. *Psychiatric Journal University of Ottawa, 13*, 217-26.

Braun, B.G. (1988). The BASK model of dissociation: Clinical applications. *Dissociation, 1*(2), 16-23.

Brennan, W. (1995). *Dehumanizing the vulnerable: When word games take lives.* Chicago: Loyola University Press.

Bretherton, I. (1992). The origins of attachment theory: John Bowlby and Mary Ainsworth. *Developmental Psychology, 28*, 759-775.

Bretherton, I., & Munholland, K.A. (2008). Internal working models in attachment relationships: A construct revisited. In J. Cassidy & P.R. Shaver, eds., *Handbook of attachment: Theory, research, and clinical applications*, 2nd ed., (pp. 102-127). New York, NY: Guilford Press, xix, 1020

Bridges, A.J., Wosnitzer, R., Scharrer Chyng, E., & Liberman, S.R. (2010). Aggression and sexual behavior in best-selling pornography videos: A content analysis update. *Violence against Women, 16*(10), 1065-1085.

Brizendine, L. (2006). *The female brain.* New York: Broadway.

Brown, T.M, & Fee, E. (2003). Alfred C. Kinsey: A pioneer of sex research. *American Journal of Public Health, 93*(6): 896–897.

Brown, T.N.T., & Herman, J.L. (2015). Intimate partner violence and sexual abuse among LGBT people: A review of existing research. *The Williams Institute.* Retrieved from https://williamsinstitute.law.ucla.edu/wp-content/uploads/ Intimate-Partner-Violence-and-Sexual-Abuse-among-LGBT-People.pdf

Brown University (2018, August). Brown statement, community letter on gender dysphoria study. Retrieved from https://news.brown.edu/ articles/2018/08/gender>

Bunce, M., & Rickards, A. (2004). *Working with bereaved children: A guide.* Rachel Harvey (Ed.). Retrieved from http://www.essex.ac.uk/ARMEDCON/ unit/projects/wwbc_guide/

Busseri, M. A., Willoughby, T., Chalmers, H., & Bogaert, A. F. (2008). On the association between sexual attraction and adolescent risk behavior involvement: Examining mediation and moderation. *Developmental Psychology, 44*(1), 69-80.

Butterfield, R. C. (2015). *Openness hindered.* Pittsburgh, PA: Crowne & Covenant.

Byne, W., & Parsons, B. (1993). Human sexual orientation: The biologic theories reappraised. *Archives of General Psychiatry, 50,* 235.

Cameron, P., & Cameron, K. (1996). *Homosexual Parents.* Adolescence, 31(124), 757–776.

Cameron, P., Proctor, K., Coburn, W., Forde, N., & Cameron, K. (1986). Child molestation and homosexuality. *Psychological Reports, 58,* 327-337.

Carpenter, C. (2003). Sexual orientation and body weight: Evidence from multiple surveys. *Gender Issues, 21*(3), 60–74.

Carnes, S., & Carnes, P. (2010). Understanding cybersex in 2010. *Family Therapy Magazine,* (January/February 2010), 10–17.

Carlson, K.B. (2016, July 12). The true north LGBT: New poll reveals landscape of gay Canada. *National Post*. Retrieved from nationalpost.com/news/canada/the-true-north-lgbt-new-poll-reveals-landscape-of-gay-canada/wcm/75b02fcb-8c50-45a7-a527-cdbcafeb042a

Castells, M. (1997). *The power of identity.* Malden, MA: Blackwell Publishing.

Catechism of the Catholic Church. (n.d.). Retrieved from www.vatican.va/archive/ccc_css/archive/catechism/credo.htm

CBC. (2016). OPP charge 80 linked to internet child pornography after days of raids. Retrieved from www.cbc.ca/news/canada/toronto-police.child-exploitation

Centers for Disease Control and Prevention. (n.d.). National Center for HIV, Viral Hepatitis, STD and TB Prevention. Retrieved from https://npin.cdc.gov/funding-organizations/national-center-hiv-viral-hepatitis-std-and-tb-prevention

Centers for Disease Control and Prevention. (1999). Increases in unsafe sex and rectal gonorrhea among MSM. *MMWR Morbidity Mortal Weekly, 48,* 45-48.

Centers for Disease Control and Prevention. (2004). Trends in primary and secondary syphilis and HIV infections in men who have sex with men. *MMWR Morbidity Mortal Weekly, 43,* 574-578.

Centers for Disease Control and Prevention. (2010). Sexually Transmitted Disease surveillance 2009. Atlanta: U.S. Department of Health and Human Services.

Centers for Disease Control and Prevention (2015). National Data for Chlamydia, Gonorrhea, and Syphilis. Retrieved from www.cdc.gov/std/stats14/std-trends-508.pdf

Chandra, A., Martinez, G.M., Mosher, W.D., & Jones. A.J. (2005). Fertility, family planning, and reproductive health of U.S. women: Data from 2002 National Survey of Family Growth. *National Centre for Health Statistics, Vital and Health Statistics.* 23(25).

Chapman, M.W. (2014). San Francisco's gay icon Larry Brinkin guilty of felony child porn possession. Retrieved from www.cnsnews.com/news/article/michael-w-chapman/san-francisco-s-gay-icon

Chastity Project. (n.d.). Sexual exposure chart. Retrieved from http://chastityproject.com/qa/sexual-exposure-chart/

Chemical Castration. (n.d.) Retrieved on July 28, 2017 from Wikipedia: https://en.wikipedia.org/wiki/Chemical_castration

Cheng, P.S. (2011). *Radical love: An introduction to queer theology*. Plano, TX: Bookshout Publishing.

Cheng, P.S. (2012). *From sin to amazing grace: Discovering the queer Christ*. Plano, TX: Bookshout Publishing.

Chiland, C. (2003). *Transsexualism* (P. Slotkin, Trans.). Middletown, CT: Wesleyan University Press.

The Christian and Missionary Alliance in Canada. (n.d.) Statement of faith. Retrieved from https://www.cmacan.org/statement-of-faith

Cicchetti, D., & Cohen, D.J. (2006). *Developmental psychopathology, Vol. 1: Theory and method* (2nd ed.). New Jersey: Wiley & Sons.

Cicchetti, D., & Rogosch, F.A. (1999). Conceptual and methodological issues in developmental psychopathology research. In P.C. Kendall, J.N. Butcher, & G.N. Holmbeck (Eds.), *Handbook of research methods in clinical psychology* (2nd ed.) (pp. 433-465). New York, NY: Wiley.

Clemmer, C. (2016). *The Adventures of Toni the Tampon*. Retrieved from www.tonithetampon.com

Clinton, T., & Sibcy, G. (2006). *Why you do the things you do*. Nashville, TN: Thomas Nelson.

Clutterbuck, D.J., Gorman, D., McMillan, A., Lewis, R., & Macintyre, C.C. (2001) Substance use and unsafe sex amongst homosexual men in Edinburgh. *AIDS Care, 13,* 527–535.

Cochran, S. D., & Mays, V. M. (2011). Sexual orientation and mortality among US men aged 17 to 59 Years: Results from the National Health and Nutrition Examination Survey III. *American Journal of Public Health, 101*(6), 1133–1138. Retrieved from http://doi.org/10.2105/AJPH.2010.300013

Cochran, W. G., Mosteller, F., & Tukey, J. W. (1953). Statistical problems of the Kinsey Report. *Journal of the American Statistical Association, 48*(264), 673–716. https://doi.org/10.1080/01621459.1953.10501194

Cohen, R. (2006). *Coming out straight: Understanding healing and homosexuality.* Winchester, VA: Oakhill Press.

Cohen, N.L. (2012). How the Sexual Revolution changed America forever. *News & Politics.* Retrieved from http://www.alternet.org/story/153969/how_the_sexual_revolution_changed_america_forever

Cohen-Kettenis, P.T., Owen, A., Kaijser, V.G., Bradley S.J., & Zucker, K.J. (2003). Demographic characteristics, social competence and behavior problems in children with gender identity disorder: A cross-national, cross-clinic comparative analysis. *Journal of Abnormal Psychology, 31,* 41-53.

Connor, K. (2018, January 21). Transgenders grow out of it: Doc. *The Toronto Sun.* Retrieved from http://torontosun.com/news/local-news/transgenders-grow-out-of-it-doc

Conroy, J. (2017). *Transgender kids: Who knows best?* BBC. Retrieved from http://www.bbc.co.uk/programmes/b088kxbw

Constitution Act. (1982). *Part I: The Canadian charter of rights and freedoms, section 1.*

Cotter, A., & Beaupré, P. (2012). Police-reported sexual offences against children and youth in Canada, 2012. Statistics Canada.

Covey, S. (2004). *The 7 habits of highly effective people: Powerful lessons in personal change* (2nd ed). New York, NJ: Free Press.

Craven, S., Brown, S., & Gilchrist, E. (2007). Sexual grooming of children: Review of literature and theoretical considerations. *Journal of Sexual Aggression, 12*(3), 287-299.

Dallas, J., & Heche, N. (2010). *The complete Christian guide to understanding homosexuality.* Eugene, OR: Harvest House Publishers.

Date, J. (2009). Duke U. official caught in alleged child sex sting. *ABC News.* Retrieved from www.abcnews.go.com./news/story?id=7942546

D'Augelli, A.R., Grossman, A.H., & Starks, M.T. (2006). Childhood gender atypicality, victimization and PTSD, among lesbian, gay and bisexual youth. *Journal of Interpersonal Violence, 21*(11), 1-21.

DeLamater, J., & Friedrich, W. (2002). Human sexual development. *The Journal of Sex Research, 39,* 10–14.

Denison, M. (2015). Mad Max. Retrieved from www//proudamericans.org/mad-max/

Devine, D. J. (2014). Medical policies on homosexuality alienate conservative doctors. Retrieved from https://www.christianheadlines.com/news/medical-policies-on-homosexuality-alienate-conservative-doctors.html

de Vries, A.L.C., Noens, I.L.J., Cohen-Kettenis, P.T., van Berckelaer-Onnes, I.A., & Doreleijers, T.A. (2010). Autism spectrum disorders in gender dysphoric children and adolescents. *Journal of Autism Development Disorders, 40,* 930–936.

Dhejne, C., Lichtenstein, P., Boman, M., Johansson, A.L.V., Långström, N., & Landén, M. (2011). Long-term follow-up of transsexual persons undergoing sex reassignment surgery: Cohort study in Sweden. *Plos One, 6*(2): e16885. https://doi.org/10.1371/journal.pone.0016885

Diamant, A.L., Wold, C., Spritzer, K., & Gelberg, L. (2000). Health behaviors, health status, and access to and use of health care: A population-based study of lesbian, bisexual, and heterosexual women. *Archives of Family Medicine, 9,* 1043–1051.

Diamond, L.M. (2008). *Sexual fluidity: Understanding women's love and desire.* Cambridge, MA: Harvard University Press.

Diamond, L.M. (2012). Desire disorder in research on sexual orientation in women: Contributions of dynamical systems theory. *Archives of Sexual Behavior 41,* 73-83.

Diller, R. (2014, January 15). Top secret: State reps denied request to see Planned Parenthood's graphic sex-ed curriculum. *Lifesite News.* Retrieved from https://www.lifesitenews.com/opinion/secret-state-reps-denied-request-to-see-planned-parenthoods-graphic-sex-ed

Disciples LGBTQ+ Alliance. (n.d., a) Our mission and vision. Retrieved from http://disciplesallianceq.org/about/

Disciples LGBTQ+ Alliance. (n.d., b) Resources: From sin to amazing grace: Discovering the queer Christ. Retrieved from http://disciplesallianceq.org/glad-resource/from-sin-to-amazing-grace-discovering-the-queer-christ/

Disciples LGBTQ+ Alliance. (n.d., c) Resources: Radical love: An introduction to queer theology. Retrieved from http://disciplesallianceq.org/glad-resource/radical-love-an-introduction-to-queer-theology/

Doidge, E.L. (2007). *The brain that changes itself.* New York, NY: Penguin Books.

Dörner, G., Geiser, T., Ahrens, L., Krell, L., Munz, G., Sieler, H., Kittner, E., & Muller, H. (1983). Prenatal stress and possible aetiogenetic factor homosexuality in human males. *Endokrinologie, 75,* 365–368.

Dörner, G., Götz, F., Rohde, W., Plagemann, A., Lindner, R., Peters H., & Ghanaati, Z. (2001). Genetic and epigenetic effects on sexual brain organization mediated by sex hormones. *Neuroendocrinol Letters, 22,* 403–9.

DuBay, W.H. (2001). Homosexuality: What Kinsey really said. Retrieved from http://www.queerbychoice.com/dubay_homosexuality.html

Eagle, M.N. (2013). *Attachment and psychoanalysis.* New York, NY: Guilford Press.

Eberstadt, M. (2016). *It's dangerous to believe.* New York, NY: Harper Collins.

Ehrensaft, D. (2016). Baby making: It takes an egg and sperm and a rainbow of genders. In Katie Gentile (Ed.), *The Business of Being Made: Producing Liminal Temporalities through ARTS*, chapter 7. New York: Routledge.

Eichel, E.W., & Muir, J.G. (1990). The Kinsey agenda in action. In E.W. Eichel & J.G. Muir, *Kinsey, sex and fraud: The indoctrination of people* (pp. 150–176). Vital Issues Press. Retrieved from http://www.drjudithreisman.com/meehan.html

Eisenberger, N. I., & Lieberman, M.D. (2004). Why rejection hurts: A common neural alarm system for psychical and social pain. *Trends in Cognitive Sciences, 8*(7), 294-300.

Ellis, L., & Ames, M.A. (1987). Neuro-hormonal function and sexual orientation: A theory of homosexuality-heterosexuality. *Psychological Bulletin, 101*, 233-38.

Ellis, L., Peckham, W., Ames, M.A., & Burke, D. (1988). Sexual orientation of human offspring may be altered by severe maternal stress during pregnancy. *Journal of Sex Research, 25*(1), 152-157.

Erickson-Schroth, L. (2014). *Trans bodies, trans selves: A resource for the transgender community.* New Your, NY: Oxford University Press.

Eskin, M., Kaynak-Denir, H., & Demir, S. (2005). Same-sex orientation, childhood sexual abuse and suicidal behavior in university students in Turkey. *Archives of Sexual Behavior, 34*(2), 185-195.

Evans, R. B. (1969). Childhood parental relationships of homosexual men. *Journal of Consulting and Clinical Psychology, 33*(2), 129-135.

Family Research Institute. (2009). Child molestation and homosexuality. *Family Research Institute Blog.* Retrieved from http://www.familyresearchinst. org/2009/02/child-molestation-and-homosexuality-2/

Fausto-Sterling, A. (2000). *Sexing the body: Gender politics and the construction of sexuality.* New York, NY: Basic Books.

Federer, B. (2011). Jonathan Edwards v. Max Jukes. Retrieved from www. selfeducatedamerican.com/2011/10/04/jonathan-edwards-v-max-jukes

Feldstein, A. (2015, January 14). When is my child considered an adult? Retrieved from http://www.familylawhelp.ca/child-considered-adult/

Fergusson, D., Lynskey, M., & Horwood, L. (1996). Childhood sexual abuse and psychiatric disorder in young adulthood, I: Prevalence of sexual abuse and factors associated with sexual abuse. *Journal of the American Academy of Child & Adolescescent Psychiatry, 35,* 1355–1364.

Fielder, R., & Carey, M. (2010). Predictors and consequences of sexual hookups among college students: A short-term perspective study. *Archives of Sexual Behavior, 39,* 1105-1109.

Finkelhor, D. (1979). *Sexually victimized children.* London: Collier Macmillan.

Finkelhor, D. (1993). Epidemiological factors in the clinical identification of child sexual abuse. *Child Abuse & Neglect, 17,* 67–70.

Finn, S.K., & Millican, L. (2008). Lupron: What does it do to women's health? *National Women's Health Network.* Retrieved from https://www.nwhn. org/lupron-what-does-it-do-to-womens-health/

Firth, M.T. (2014). Childhood abuse and depressive vulnerability in clients with Gender Dysphoria. *Counselling and Psychotherapy Research, 14*(4), 297-305.

Ford, C.S., & Beach, F.A. (1951). *Patterns of sexual behavior*. New York: Harper.

Fortenberry, J.D. (2002). Unveiling the hidden epidemic of sexually transmitted diseases. *Journal of the American Medical Association, 287*(6), 768-769.

Fortson, S. D., III, & Grams, R. G. (2016). *Unchanging witness: The consistent Christian teaching on homosexuality in scripture and tradition*. Nashville, TN: B&H Academic.

Fredriksen-Goldsen, I., Kim, H.J., Barkan, S.E., Balsam, K.F., & Mincer, S.L. (2010). Disparities in health-related quality of life: A comparison of lesbians and bisexual women. *American Journal of Public Health, 100*(11), 2255–2261.

Freud, S. (1965). *New introductory lectures on psycho-analysis (Complete psychological works of Sigmund Freud, vol. 22)* (J. Strachey, ed., trans.). New York, NY: W.W. Norton & Company.

Freund, K., Heasman, G., Racansky, I.G., & Glancy, G. (1984). Pedophilia and heterosexuality vs homosexuality. *Journal of Sex and Marital Therapy, 10*(3), 193-200.

Frisch, M., & Brønnum-Hansen, H. (2009). Mortality among men and women in same-sex marriage: A national cohort study of 8333 Danes. *American Journal of Public Health, 99*(1), 133–137. Retrieved from http://doi.org/10.2105/AJPH.2008.133801

Frisch, M., Smith, E., Grulich, A., & Johansen, C. (2003). Cancer in a population-based cohort of men and women in registered homosexual partnerships. *American Journal of Epidemiology, 157*, 966–972.

Gandolfo, F. (2016). What you don't know about anal sex. A gastroenterologist explains. Retrieved from www.kevinmed.com/blog/2016/03/what-you-dont-know-about-anal-sex

Garcia-Falgueras, A., & Swaab, D.F. (2010). Sexual hormones and the brain: An essential alliance for sexual identity and sexual orientation. *Endocrine Development, 17,* 22-35.

Gates, G.J. (2011). How many people are lesbian, gay, bisexual and transgender? *The Williams Institute.* Retrieved from https://williamsinstitute.law.ucla.edu/wp-content/uploads/Gates-How-Many-People-LGBT-Apr-2011.pdf

Giddens, A. (1992). The transformation of intimacy: Sexuality, love & eroticism in modern society. Stanford: Stanford University Press.

Gillies, A.E. (2013). An exploration of early childhood attachment in a sample of Christian men experiencing same-sex attraction (unpublished doctoral dissertation). Liberty University, VA.

Gillies, A.E. (2016). *Deep impact: Integrating psychology and theology in the treatment of complex traumatic stress.* Winnipeg, Canada: Word Alive Press.

Gingrich, H. D. (2013). Restoring the shattered self: A Christian counselor's guide to complex trauma. Downers Grove, IL: Inter-Varsity Press.

Goldberg, S. (1992). *When wish replaces thought: Why so much of what you believe is false.* New York: Prometheus.

Goldberg, N.G., & Meyer, I.H. (2013). Sexual orientation disparities in history of intimate partner abuse. *Journal of Interpersonal Violence, 28*(5), 1109-1118.

Golombok, S., & Tasker, F. (1996). Do parents influence the sexual orientation of their children? Findings from a longitudinal study of lesbian families. *Developmental Psychology, 32*(1), 3–11.

Grant, J.W. (1967). *The Canadian experience of church union.* London, UK: Lutterworth Press.

Green, R. (1987). *The "sissy boy syndrome" and the development of homosexuality.* New Haven, CT: Yale University Press.

Greenberg, D.F. (1988). *The construction of homosexuality.* Chicago: University of Chicago Press.

Gregor, C., Hingley-Jones, H., & Davidson, S. (2015). Understanding the experience of parents of pre-pubescent children with gender identity issues. *Child and Adolescent Social Work Journal, 32*(3), 237-246.

Greyland, M. (2017). *The last closet: The dark side of Avalon.* Winter Park, FL: Brandywine Books.

Grossman, A., & D'Augelli, A. (2007). Transgender youth and life threatening behavior. *Suicide and Life Threatening Behavior, 3,* 527-537.

Grossman, M. (2007). *Unprotected: A campus psychiatrist reveals how political correctness in her profession endangers every student.* New York, NY: Sentinel.

Grossman, M. (2009). *You're teaching my child what?: A physician exposes the lies of sex ed and how they harm your child.*

Grossman, M. (2013a). A brief history of Sex Ed: How we reached today's madness. *Witherspoon Institute.* Retrieved from http://www.the publicdiscourse.com/2013/07/10408

Grossman, M. (2013b). R18 report: Sexuality education in New Zealand: A critical review. Retrieved from www.bobmccoskrie.com/wp-content/uploads/2013/06/Miriam-Grossman-R18-Report.pdf

Gulli, C. (2016, January 7). Collapse of parenting: Why it's time for parents to grow up. *Macleans.* Retrieved from www.macleans.ca/society/the-collapse-of-parenting-why-its-time-for-parents-to-grow-up/

Gyapong, D. (2016, November 23). Churches should "tremble" at transgender agenda, professor says. Retrieved from https://www.catholicregister.org/item/23657-churches-should-tremble-at-transgender-agenda-professor-says

Haas, A.P., Rodgers, P.L., & Herman, J. (2014). Suicide attempts among transgender and gender non-conforming adults: Findings of the national transgender discrimination survey. *Williams Institute.* Retrieved from http://williamsinstitute.law.ucla.edu/wp-content/uploads/afsp

Hallman, J. (2008). *The heart of female same-sex attraction.* Downers Grove, IL: Intervarsity Press.

HALT (Humanity Against Local Terrorism). (2012) Child sexual abuse statistics. Retrieved from http://haltnow.ca/what-is-abuse/child-sexual-abuse/child-sexual-abuse-statistics

Hamilton Spectator. (2016). Hamilton dad loses fight to pull kids from school over false teachings. Retrieved from www.thespec.com/news-story/69898979-hamilton-dad

Harari, D., Bakermans-Kranenburg, M.J., & van Ijzendoorn, M.J. (2007). Attachment, disorganization and dissociation. In E. Vermetten, M. Dorahy, & D. Spiegal (eds.), *Traumatic dissociation: Neurobiology and treatment* (pp. 31-54). Arlington, VA: American Psychiatric.

Hare, L., Bernard, P., Sáncheze, J.S., Baird, P.N., Vilaine, E. Kennedy, T., & Harley, V.R. (2009). Androgen Receptor Repeat Length Polymorphism Associated with Male-to-Female Transsexualism. *Biologicial Psychiatry, 65*(1), 93-96.

Hart, D.C. (2016). Mark Regnerus finds a new bullshit study. Retrieved from http://www.slowlyboiledfrog.com/2016/06/mark-regnerus-finds-new-bullshit-study.html

Harvard Health Publications. (2010, July). Marriage and men's health. Retrieved from http://www.health.harvard.edu/newsletter_article/marriage-and-mens-health

Hassan, C., & Andone, D. (2017). "My body is awesome": Trans man expecting first child. *CNN.* Retrieved from http://www.cnn.com/2017/06/08/health/trans-man-pregnant-trnd/index.html

Hatch, L. (n.d.). Defining addiction. Retrieved from www. sexaddictionscounseling.com/defining-addiction

Haver, E.S., Yasrebi, K., Hassanzadeh, R., Moshkani, M., & Kaboos, A. (2015). Personality disorders and psychiatric comorbidity among persons with gender identity disorder. *Journal of the Indian Academy of Applied Psychology, 41*(3), 141-147.

Haverluck, M. F. (2017, May 17). Top psychiatrist smeared for debunking "transgenderism." Retrieved from https://www.onenewsnow.com/science-tech/2017/05/17/top-psychiatrist-smeared-for-debunking-transgenderism

Henton, D. (2006). Young, transgender and out in east Los Angeles. In L. Messinger & D. F. Marrow (Eds.), *Case studies on sexual orientation & gender expression in social work practice* (pp. 16-18). New York, NY: Columbia University Press.

Herkov, M. (n.d.). What is sexual addiction? Retrieved from https://psychcentral.com/lib/what-is-sexual-addiction/

Herhalt, C. (2016). Nine charged in alleged online child sex exploitation ring in Ontario. *CTV News*. Retrieved from www.toronto.ctvnews.ca/nine-charged

Hilton, D. L. (2013). Pornography addiction: A supranormal stimulus considered in the context of neuroplasticity. *Socioaffective Neuroscience & Psychology, 3*(20767). Retrieved from http://doi.org/10.3402/snp.v3i0.20767

Hodges, M. (2017, May 22). Man in threesome marriage: 'This should be the future of relationships' [daily news]. *Lifesite News*. Retrieved from https://www.lifesitenews.com/news/throuple-advocate-for-threesome-marriage-parenting

Hodges, M. (2017, July 19). Seattle's homosexual mayor faces multiple child rape allegations. *Lifesite News*. Retrieved from https://www.lifesitenews.com/news/seattles-homosexual-mayor-faces-multiple-child-rape-allegations

Hogg, R.S., Strathdee, S.A., Craib, K.J., O'Shaughnessy, M.V., Montaner, J.S., & Schechter, M.T. (1997). Modelling the impact of HIV disease on mortality in gay and bisexual men. *International Journal of Epidemiology, 26*(3), 657–661.

Hoffman, M. C. (2018). Daughter of famed sci-fi author reveals sexual horrors she suffered growing up in LGBT home. *Lifesite News.* Retrieved from https://www.lifesitenews.com/mobile/news/daughter-of-famed-sci-fi-author-reveals-sexual-horrors-she-suffered-growing

Human Rights Campaign (n.d.). McHugh Exposed: How anti-LGBTQ activists are leveraging junk science to advance their agenda. Retrieved from http://www.hrc.org/mchughexposed

Hutchinson, D. (2017). *Under siege: Religious freedom and the church in Canada at 150 (1867-2017).* Winnipeg, Canada: Word Alive Press.

Institute of Medicine (US) Committee on Lesbian, Gay, Bisexual, and Transgender Health Issues and Research Gaps and Opportunities. (2011). *The health of lesbian, gay, bisexual, and transgender people: Building a foundation for better understanding.* Washington, DC: National Academies Press. Retrieved from https://www.ncbi.nlm.nih.gov/books/NBK64806/ doi: 10.17226/13128

International Planned Parenthood Federation. (2011). Exclaim! Young people's guide to sexual rights: An IPPF declaration. Retrieved from http://www.ippf.org/sites/default/files/ippf_exclaim_lores.pdf

It's Pronounced Metrosexual. (2015). The genderbread person v. 2.0. Retrieved from http://itspronouncedmetrosexual.com/2012/03/the-genderbread-person-v2-0/#sthash.DL9ApqFb.5cqEDfM4.dpbs

James, R. (2017). Lactatia werqs Montreal at the Drag Race Show. Retrieved from http://bestkeptmontreal.com/werq-the-world-rupauls-drag-race/

Jefferys, S. (2014). *Gender hurts: A feminist analysis of the politics of transgenderism.* New York, NY: Routledge.

Jones, S.L., & Yarhouse, M.A. (2000). *Homosexuality: The use of scientific research in the church's moral debate.* Downers Grove: IL: Intervarsity Press.

Jones, S.L., & Yarhouse, M.A. (2007). *Ex gays? A longitudinal study of religiously mediated change in sexual orientation.* Downers Grove, Illinois: Intervarsity Press.

Kaltenbach, C. (2015). *Messy grace.* Colorado Springs, CO: Waterbrook Press.

Kaplin, M. (2014, October 4). Pedophilia: A disorder, not a crime. *The New York Times.* Retrieved from www.nytimes.com/2014/10/06

Keiper, A. (2016). Editor's note. *The New Atlantis: Journal of Technology and Society, 50,* 1.

Kennedy, N., & Hellen, M. (2010). Transgender children: More than a theoretical challenge. *Graduate Journal of Social Science, 7*(2), 1-19.

King C.D. (1945). The meaning of normal. *Yale Journal of Biological Medicine, 18,* 493-501.

Kinnish, K.K., Strassberg, D.S., & Turner, C.W. (2005). Sex differences in the flexibility of sexual orientation: A multidimensional retrospective assessment. *Archives of Sexual Behavior, 34,* 173-183.

Kinsey, A. C., Pomeroy, W. P., & Martin, C. E. (1948). *Sexual Behavior in the Human Male.* Bloomington, IN: Indiana University Press.

Kinsey, A. C., Pomeroy, W. P., & Martin, C. E. (1953). *Sexual Behavior in the Human Female.* Bloomington, IN: Indiana University Press.

Kinsman, S.B., Romer, D., Furstenberg, R.R., & Schwartz, D.F., (1998). Early sexual initiation: The role of peer norms. *Pediatrics, 102,* 1185-1192.

Kirk, M, & Pill, E. (1987, November). The overhauling of straight America. *Guide Magazine.*

Kirk, M., & Madsen, H. (1989). *How America will conquer its fear and hatred of gays.* New York, NJ: Doubleday.

Kirk, M., & Madsen, H. (1990). *After the ball: How America will conquer its fear and hatred of gays in the 1990s.* New York, NY: Plume.

Lab, D., Feigenbaum, J., & De Silva, P. (2000). Mental health professionals' attitudes and practices towards male childhood sexual abuse. *Child Abuse & Neglect, 24,* 391–409.

LaBarbera, P. (2017, May 15). LGBT activists slam "the most important psychiatrist of the last half-century" because he debunks transgender ideology. *Lifesite News.* Retrieved from https://www.lifesitenews.com/news/lgbt-activists-slam-the-most-important-psychiatrist-of-the-last-half-centur

LaBarbera, P. (2017, June 9). LGBT community celebrates 8 year old drag queen. Critics call it Child Abuse. *Lifesite News.* Retrieved from www.lifesitenews/lgbt-community-celebrates-8-year-old

Laflin, M.T., Wang, J., & Barry, M. (2008). A longitudinal study of adolescent transition from virgin to non-virgin status. *Journal of Adolescent Health, 42,* 228-236.

Laguipo, Angela. (2015, Nov. 25). Internet porn fuels sex addiction: study. *Tech Times.* Retrieved from http://www.techtimes.com/articles/110144/20151125/internet-porn-fuels-sex-addiction-study.htm

Laidlaw, M. (2018). The gender identity phantom: An international discussion space for clinicians and researchers. Retrieved from http://gdworkinggroup.org/2018/10/24/the-gender-identity-phantom/

Landolt, M.A., Bartholomew, K., Saffrey, C., Oram, D., & Perlman, D. (2004). Gender nonconformity, childhood rejection, and adult attachment: A study of gay men. *Archives of Sexual Behavior, 33*(2), 117–128.

Laumann, E.O., Gagnon, J.H., Michael, R.T., & Michaels, S. (1994). *The social organization of sexuality: Sexual practices in the United States* (vol. 1). Chicago: University of Chicago Press.

Laurence, L. (2015, August 20). Ontario's dangerous sex-ed is indoctrination not science says U.S. psychiatrist to large audience. *Lifesite News*. Retrieved from https://www.lifesitenews.com/news/ontarios-dangerous-sex-ed-is-indoctrination-not-science-says-u.s.-psychiatr

Laurence, L. (2017, June 29). Christian dad fights for right to remove children from LGBT classes at appeals court [daily news]. *Lifesite News*. Retrieved from https://www.lifesitenews.com/news/christian-father-fighting-for-right-to-remove-children-from-lgbt-classes-br

Lawrence, A.A. (2007). Transgender health concerns. In I.H. Myer & M.E. Northridge (Eds.), *The health of sexual miniorities: Public health perspectives on lesbian, gay, bisexual and transgender populations* (pp. 473-505). New York, NY: Springer Science & Business Media.

Leaf, C. (2009). *Who switched off my brain? Controlling toxic thoughts and emotions* (revised ed.). Nashville, TN: Thomas Nelson Publishers.

LeVay, S. (1996). *Queer science.* Cambridge, MA: MIT Press.

Littman, L.L. (2017). Rapid onset of gender dysphoria in adolescents and young adults: A descriptive study. *Journal of Adolescent Health, 60*(2), S95–S96.

Littman, L. (2018). Rapid-onset gender dysphoria in adolescents and young adults: A study of parental reports. *Plos One, 13*(8): e0202330. https://doi.org/10.1371/journal.pone.0202330

Lively, S. (2009). *Redeeming the Rainbow.* Springfield MA: Vertias Aeterna Press. Retrieved from http://www.defendthefamily.com/_docs/resources/7803765.pdf

Loche, S., Cappa, M., Ghizzoni, L., Maghnie, M., & Savage, M.O. (2010). Paediatric neuroendocrinology. *Endocrine Development, 17,* 22–35.

Love Facts. (n.d.) Sexual exposure chart. Retrieved from http://www.lovefacts.org/PDF/explanation.pdf

Luce, R. (2008). *Re-create: Building a culture in your home stronger than the culture deceiving your kids.* Ventura, CA: Gospel Light.

Lusko, L. (2017). *Swipe right: The life and death power of sex and romance.* Nashville, TN: W. Publishing.

Mandel, Michele. (2017, Nov. 15). Mandel: Depraved world view of Ben Levin continues on parole. *Toronto Sun.* Retrieved from http://torontosun.com/news/local-news/depraved-world-view-of-ben-levin-continues-on-parole

Manning, W.D., Longmore, M.A., Copp, J., & Gioranco, P.C. (2014). The complexities of adolescent dating and sexual relationships: Fluidity, meaning(s), and implications for young adults' well-being. *New Directions for Child and Adolescent Development, 144,* 53-69.

Marchiano, M. (2017) Outbreak: On transgender teens and psychic epidemics. *Psychological Perspectives, 60*(3), 345–366. DOI: 10.1080/00332925.2017.1350804

Marks, Loren. (2012). Same-sex parenting and children's outcomes: A closer examination of the American Psychological Association's brief on lesbian and gay parenting. *Social Science Research, 41*(4), 735–751. Retrieved from http://www.sciencedirect.com/science/article/pii/S0049089X12000580

Marsden, P. (1998). Memetics and social contagion: Two sides of the same coin? *Journal of Memetics: Evolutionary Models of Information Transmission, 12,* 68–79.

Marshall, J.A. (2004, May 17). Marriage: What social science says and doesn't say. Retrieved from http://www.heritage.org/marriage-and-family/report/marriage-what-social-science-says-and-doesnt-say

Maslow, A. H. (1943). A theory of human motivation. *Psychological Review, 50,* 370–396. Retrieved from psychclassics.yorku.ca/Maslow/motivation.htm

Masters, W.H., Johnson, V., & Kolodny, R. (1995). *Human sexuality* (2nd ed.). New York, NJ: Little, Brown and Company.

Mayer, K. (2011). Sexually transmitted disease in men who have sex with men. *Clinical Infectious Diseases, 53*(3), 79-83.

Mayer, L.S., & McHugh, P.R. (2016). Sexuality and gender: Findings from the biological, psychological and social sciences. *The New Atlantis: Journal of Technology and Society, 50*, 1-143.

Mayr, E. (1964). The evolution of living systems. *Proceedings of the National Academy of Sciences, 51*, 934–941.

Mayr, E. (1988). *Toward a new philosophy of biology: Observations of an evolutionist.* Cambridge, MA: Harvard University Press.

McArtor, L. (2017, February 16). Politically diverse panelists unite for women's rights, discuss dangers of transgender activism. *The Stream.* Retrieved from www.stream.org/diverse-panelists

McClintock, M.K., Bullivant, S., Jacob, S., Spencer, M., Zelano, B., & Ober, C. (2005). Human body scents: Conscious perceptions and biological effects. *Oxford Journals, Life Sciences, 30*(1), 135-137.

McCormick, J.P. (2016, September 4). This photo of trans dad breasfeeding his son tells a great story of love and acceptance. *Pink News.* Retrieved from http://www.pinknews.co.uk/2016/09/04/this-photo-of-a-trans-dad-breastfeeding-his-son-tells-a-great-story-of-love-and-acceptance/

McGroarty, E., Robbins, J., & Tuttle, E. (2017). *Deconstructing the administrative state.* Liberty Hill Publishing, American Principals Project Foundation: Washington, D.C.

McIhaney, J.S. Jr., & McKissic Bush, F. (2006). *Hooked: New science on how casual sex is affecting our children.* Chicago, IL: Northfield Publishing.

McLeod, S. (2007). The Milgram Experiment. Retrieved from https://www.simplypsychology.org/milgram.html

McWhirter, D., & Mattison, A. (1984). *Homosexuality in Perspective.* Boston, MA: Little, Brown.

Meeker, M. (2007). *Your kids at risk.* Washington, DC: Regnery Publishing.

Mercer, C.H., Fenton, K.A., Johnson, A.M., Wellings, K., Macdowall, W., McManus, S., Nanchahal, K., & Erens, B. (2003). Sexual function problems and help seeking behavior in Britain: national probability sample survey. *British Medical Journal, 327*(4212), 426-427.

Merrill, G.S., & Wolfe, V.A. (2000). Battered gay men: An exploration of abuse, help seeking, and why they stay. *Journal of Homosexuality, 39*(2), 1–30. [PubMed: 10933279]

Meyer, I.H. (2003). Prejudice, social stress and mental health in lesbian, gay and bisexual populations: Conceptual issues and research evidence. *Psychological Bulletin, 129*(5), 674-697.

Meyer, J.K. (1982). The theory of gender identity disorders. *Journal of the American Psychoanalytic Association, 30,* 381-418.

Meyer J. K., & Reter, D.J. (1979). Sex reassignment: Follow-up. *Archives of General Psychiatry, 36*(9), 1010–1015. http://dx.doi.org/10.1001/archpsyc.1979.01780090096010

Milgram, S. (1974). *Obedience to authority: An experimental view.* New York, NY: Harper Collins.

Mock, S.E., & Eibach, R.P. (2016). Stability and change in sexual orientation identity over a 10 -year period in adulthood. *Archives of Sexual Behavior, 41,* 641-648.

Monimore, M. F. (1996). *A natural history of homosexuality.* Baltimore, MD: The John Hopkins University Press.

Money, J. (1974). Two names, two wardrobes, two personalities. *Journal of Homosexuality, 7*(1), 65-70.

Morehead, D. (1999). Oedipus, Darwin, and Freud: One big, happy family? *Psychoanalytic Quarterly, 68*(3), 347-375.

Morgan, Joe. (2017, January 6). There are fears a BBC documentary on trans children will be "blatant transphobic propaganda." *Gay Star News*. Retrieved from http://www.gaystarnews.com/article/fears-bbc-documentary-trans-children-will-blatant-transphobic-propaganda/#gs.BopEuKg

Morris, Alex. (2006, February 6). The cuddle puddle of Stuyvesant High School. *New York Magazine*. Retrieved from http://nymag.com/nymag/toc/20060206/

Mullen, P., Martin, J., Anderson, J., Romans, S., & Herbison, G. (1993). Childhood sexual abuse and mental health in adult life. *British Journal of Psychiatry, 163*, 721–732.

National Coalition of Gay Organizations. (1972). The 1972 gay rights platform: platform created at the National Coalition of Gay Organizations Convention held in Chicago in 1972. Retrieved from http://www.rslevinson.com/gaylesissues/features/collect/onetime/bl_platform1972.htm

National Post. (2015, April 13). Former Ontario deputy education minister met parent he had swapped child sexual fantasies with, court told. Retrieved from www.news.nationalpost.com/news/canada/sentencing-hearing

National Post. (2015, April 14). Ex-Ontario deputy minister claimed to have had sex with his own daughters, in online chat, court hears.

Net Doctor. (2012, March 12). Problems with oral and anal sex. Retrieved from http://www.netdoctor.co.uk/ask-the-expert/sexual-health/a1514/problems-with-oral-and-anal-sex/

Newport, Frank. (2015). Americans greatly overestimate percent gay, lesbian in U.S. *Gallup*. Retrieved from http://www.gallup.com/poll/183383/americans-greatly-overestimate-percent-gay-lesbian.aspx?g_source=adults+estimate+americans+gay+lesbian&g_medium=search&g_campaign=tiles

Nyhus, N. (2015). Medical concerns about the new sex ed curriculum. Unpublished article.

O'Carroll, T. (1980). *Paedophilia: The radical case*. London, UK: Owen Publishing.

Ogawa, J.R., Sroufe, L.A., Weinfield, N.S., Carson, E.A., & England, B. (1977). Development and the fragmented self: Longitudinal study of dissociative symptomatology in a nonclinical sample. *Development and Psychopathology, 9,* 855-879.

Oppenheimer, A. (1991). The wish for a sex change: A challenge to psychoanalysis? *The International Journal of Psychoanalysis, 72,* 221-321.

Orenstein, A. (2001). Substance use among gay and lesbian adolescents. *Journal of Homosexuality, 41,* 1–15.

Oxford Dictionaries. (2016, November). Word of the year 2016 - Post truth. Retrieved from https://en.oxforddictionaries.com/word-of-the-year/word-of-the-year-2016

Paglia, C. (1994). *Vamps and Tramps*. New York, NY: Random House.

Parents of 4thWaveNow. (2017, January 27). Shriveled raisins: The bitter harvest of "affirmative" care. *4thWaveNow*. Retrieved from https://4thwavenow.com/2017/01/26/shriveled-raisins-the-bitter-harvest-of-affirmative-care/

Parfitt, A. (2007). Fetishism, transgenderism and the concept of castration. *Psychoanalytic Psychotherapy, 21,* 61-89.

Pasterski, V., Gilligan, L., & Curtis, R. (2014). Traits of autism spectrum disorders in adults with gender dysphoria. *Archive of Sexual Behaviour. 43*(2), 387–93. doi: 10.1007/s10508-013-0154-5. Epub 2013 Jul 18.

Perry, B.D. (2003). Effects of traumatic events on children. *The Child Trauma Academy*. Retrieved from wwwchildtrauma.org

Pinos, H., Collado, P., Rodrequez-Zafra, M., Rodriguez, C., Segovia, S., & Guillamon, A. (2001). The development of sex differences in the locus coeruleus of the rat. *Brain Research Bulletin, 56,* 73-78.

Plummer, K. (1991). Understanding childhood sexualities. *Journal of Homosexuality, 20*(1-2), 231-249.

Pollack, M. (1985). Male homosexuality. In P. Aries & A. Bejin (Eds.), *Western sexuality: Practice and precept in past and present times* (pp. 40-61). New York, NY: Blackwell.

Polusny, M., & Follette, V. (1995). Long term correlates of child sexual abuse: Theory and review of the empirical literature. *Applied and Preventative Psychology, 4,* 143–166.

Pomeroy, W.B. (1972). *Dr. Kinsey and the Institute for Sex Research.* New York, NY: Harper & Row.

Pomeroy, W.B. (1976, November). A new look at incest. *Penthouse Forum,* 9-13.

Postmedia Network. (2017, March 2). Man spends $50,000 on plastic surgery on way to becoming "sexless alien." *Toronto Sun.* Retrieved from http://www.torontosun.com/2017/03/02/man-spends-50000-on-plastic-surgery-on-way-to-becoming-sexless-alien

ProCon.org. (2011). Percentage of men (by country) who paid for sex at least once: The johns chart. Retrieved from www.prostitution.procon.org/view.resource.php?resourceID=004119

Psychology Today. (2018). Pedophilia. Retrieved from https://www.psychologytoday.com/ca/conditions/pedophilia

The Public Discourse. (2016). State vs family: The tyranny of the emerging orthodoxy. Retrieved from www.thepublicdiscourse.com/2016/12/18403

Putnam, F.W. (2003). Ten-year research update review: Child sexual abuse. *Journal of Child and Adolescent Psychiatry, 42,* 3.

Rainbow Flag. (n.d.) Retrieved on July 29, 2017 from Wikipedia: https://en.wikipedia.org/wiki/Rainbow_flag

Rector, R.E., Johnson, K.A., & Noyes, L.R. (2003). Sexually active teenagers more likely to be depressed and to attempt suicide. *Heritage Center for Data Analysis.* Retrieved from http://www.heritage.org/education/report/sexually-active-teenagers-are-more-likely-be-depressed-and-attempt-suicide

ReCAPP. (2013). Statistics: Sexual activity. Retrieved from www.recapp.etr.org/recapp/index/.cfm

Regnerus, M. (2012). How different are the adult children of parents who have same-sex relationships? Findings from the New Family Structures Study. *Social Science Research, 41,* 752–770.

Regnerus, M. (2016). The data on children in same-sex households get more depressing. *Witherspoon Institutute.* Retrieved from http://www.thepublicdiscourse.com/2016/06/17255/

Religion in Canada. (n.d.). Retrieved in 2017 from Wikipedia: https://en.wikipedia.org/wiki/religion_in_Canada.

Reisman, J. (1998). *Kinsey: Crimes and consequences.* Crestwood, KY: The Institute for Media Education.

Reisman, J. (2003). *Stolen honor, stolen innocence.* Orlando, FL: New Revolution Publishers.

Reisman, J. (2013). Stag films as sex research. Chapter 4 in *Stolen honor, stolen innocence.* 4th edition. Orlando, FL: New Revolution Publishers.

Reisman, J. (2017). About Judith Gelerner Reisman, Ph.D. Retrieved from http://www.drjudithreisman.com/about_dr_reisman.html

Reisman, J., & Eichel, E.W. (1990). *Kinsey, sex and fraud: The indoctrination of people.* J.H. Court & J.G. Muir, eds. Lafayette, LA: Lochinvar-Huntington.

Reisman, J., & Fink, D. (1990). Female child sexuality. In J.H. Court & J.G. Muir, eds., *Kinsey, sex and fraud: The indoctrination of people* (pp. 58–82), Lafayette, LA: Lochinvar-Huntington.

Reisman, J.G., McAlister, M.E., & Gallagher, D.M. (2016). *Natural vs novel sexuality.* Retrieved from https://www.scribd.com/document/312404476/NATURAL-vs-NOVEL-SEXUALITY

Resnick, M.D., Bearman, P.S., & Blum, R.W. (1997). Protecting adolescents from harm: Findings from the national longitudinal study on adolescent health. *Journal of the American Medical Association, 278*(10), 823-832.

Ridge, S.R., & Feeney, J.A. (1998). Relationship history and relationship attitudes in gay males and lesbians: Attachment style and gender differences. *Australian and New Zealand Journal of Psychiatry, 32,* 848-859.

Riittakerttu, K. H., Sumia, M., Työläjärvi, M, & Lindberg,N. (2015). Two years of gender identity service for minors: Overrepresentation of natal girls with severe problems in adolescent development. *Child and Adolescent Psychiatry and Mental Health, 9,* 9. DOI 10.1186/s13034-015-0042-y. https://capmh.biomedcentral.com/articles/10.1186/s13034-015-0042-y

Robbins, J., & Tuttle, E. (2018). What's wrong with the new NIH study on transgender kids? The Witherspoon Institute: Public Discourse. Retrieved from http://www.thepublicdiscourse.com/2018/01/20844/

Roberts, A.L., Austin, S.B., Corliss, H.L., Vandermorris, A.K., & Koenen, K.C. (2010). Pervasive trauma exposure among US sexual orientation minority adults and risk of posttraumatic stress disorder. *American Journal of Public Health, 100*(12), 2433-2439.

Roberts, A.L., Rosario, M., Corliss, H.L., Koenen, K.C., & Austin, S. B. (2012). Childhood gender nonconformity: A risk indicator for childhood abuse and posttraumatic stress in youth. *American Academy of Pediatrics.* Retrieved from http://pediatrics.aappublications.org/content/early/2012/02/15/peds.2011-1804

Roller, C., Martsolf, D.S., Draucker, C.B., & Ross, R. (2009). The sexuality of childhood sexual abuse survivors. *International Journal of Sexual Health, 21,* 49-60.

Rosenthal, S.M. (2014). Approach to the patient: Transgender youth: Endocrine considerations. *Journal of Clinical Endocrinol Metabolism, 99*(12), 4379-4389.

Rotenberg, C. (2017). Police-reported sexual assaults in Canada, 2009 to 2014: A statistical profile. Canadian Centre for Justice Statistics.

Ruby, G. (2015). *The global sexual revolution.* Kettering, OH: Angelico Press.

Sandfort, T.G.M. (1997). Sampling male homosexuality. In J. Bancroft (Ed.), *Researching sexual behavior: Methodological issues* (pp. 261-275). Bloomington, IN: Indiana University Press.

Sandfort, T.G.M., Bakker, F., Schellevis, F.G., & Vanwesenbeeck, I. (2006). Sexual orientation and mental and physical health status: Findings from a Dutch population survey. *American Journal of Public Health, 96*(6), 1119-1125.

Sandfort, T., Brongersma, E. & van Naerssen, A. (1991). *Male intergenerational intimacy.* New York, NY: Haworth Press.

Sandfort, T.G.M., de Graaf, R., Bijl, R., & Schnabel, P. (2001). Same-sex sexual behavior and psychiatric disorders: Findings from the Netherlands Mental Health Survey and Incidence Study (NEMESIS). *Journal of American Medical Association, 58*(1), 85-90.

San Diego District Attorney. (n.d.). Protecting children online. Retrieved from http://www.sdcda.org/preventing/protecting-children-online/facts-for-parents.html

Savage, D. (2015). Savage love: Resolving deception in a monogamish relationship. Retrieved from http://www.straight.com/life/579231/savage-love-resolving-deception-monogamish-relationship

Savin-Williams, R.C. (2001). Suicide attempts among sexual-minority youths: population and measurement issues. *Journal of Clinical Psychology, 69*(6); 983-991.

Savin-Williams, R.C., & Ream, G.L. (2007). Prevalence and stability of sexual orientation components during adolescence and young adulthood. *Archives of Sexual Behavior, 36,* 385-394.

Sax, L. (2002). How common is intersex: A response to Anne Fausto-Sterling. *The Montgomery Center for Research in Child and Adolescent Development.* Maryland, NY. Retrieved from http://www.leonardsax.com/how-common-is-intersex-a-response-to-anne-fausto-sterling

Sax, L. (2015). *The collapse of parenting: How we hurt our kids when we treat them like grown-ups.* New York, NY: Basic Books.

Schallhorn, K. (2017, June 29). Colorado baker: Death threats and hate for refusing to make gay wedding cake. *Fox News.* Retrieved from http://www.foxnews.com/politics/2017/06/29/colorado-baker-describes-harassment-after-refused-to-bake-cake-for-gay-wedding.html

Scott, J.P., Stewart, J.M., & De Ghett, V.J. (1974). Critical periods in the organization of systems. *Developmental Psychobiology, 7,* 489-513.

Scott, S.K. (2015). *Jesus speaks: 365 days of guidance and encouragement, straight from the words of Christ.* New York, NY: Waterbrook Press.

Segal, C. (2017). Trans patients, looking for fertility options, turn to cancer research. *PBS Newshour.* Retrieved from http://www.pbs.org/newshour/updates/trans-patients-looking-fertility-options-turn-cancer-research/

Seper, Franjo Cardinal. (1975). Sacred Congregation for the Doctrine of Faith, Persona Humana: Declaration on certain questions concerning sexual ethics. Retrieved from http://www.vatican.va/roman_curia/congregations/cfaith/documents/rc_con_cfaith_doc_19751229_persona-humana_en.html)

Serritellia, A.P. (2016). *Transgenda: Abuse and regret in the sex-change industry.* Morgan Hill, CA: Bookstand Publishing

Sex and Love Addicts Anonymous. (n.d.). Retrieved from https://slaafws.org/

Sexual Fluidity. (n.d.). Retrieved in 2017 from Wikipedia: https://en.wikipedia.org/wiki/Sexual_fluidity

Sheff, S.A. (2014). Seven forms of non-monogamy. *Psychology Today.* Retrieved from www.psychologytoday.com/blog/the-polyamorists-next-door/201407

Siegal, et al. (1987). The prevalence of childhood sexual assault. *American Journal of Epidemiology, 126,* 1141.

Siegelman, M. (1974). Parental background of male homosexuals. *Journal of Consulting Psychology, 29,* 558-564.

Singal, J. (2016). How the fight over transgender kids got a leading sex researcher fired. *New York Magazine: Science of Us.* Retrieved from http://nymag.com/scienceofus/2016/02/fight-over-trans-kids-got-a-researcher-fired.html

Singal, J. (2017). BBC's controversial documentary on the gender-dysphoria researcher: Kenneth Zucker. *New York Magazine: Science of Us.* Retrieved from http://nymag.com/scienceofus/2017/01/you-should-watch-the-bbcs-kenneth-zucker-documentary.html

Singh, S., & Darroch, J.E. (2000). Adolescent pregnancy and childbearing: Levels and trends in developed countries. *Family Planning Perspectives, 32*(1), 14-23.

Sisk, C.L. (2006). New insights into the neurobiology of sexual maturation. *Sexual and Relationship Therapy, 21*(1), 5-14.

Sisk, C.L. & Zehr, J.L. (2005). Pubertal hormones organize the adolescent brain and behavior. *Frontiers in Neuroendocrinology, 26,* 163–174.

Smith, N. (2013). The 20th anniversary of the LGBT march on Washington: How far have we come. *Huffington Post.* Retrieved from http://www.huffingtonpost.com/nadine-smith/the-20th-anniversary-of-the-lgbt-march-on-washington_b_3149185.html

Socarides, C. (1970). A psychoanalytic study of the desire for sexual transformation (transsexualism): The plaster-of-Paris man. *The International Journal of Psychoanalysis, 51,* 341-349.

The Society of Obstetricians and Gynecologists of Canada. (n.d.). Sexuality and childhood development: An overview of healthy childhood sexual development. Retrieved from http://www.sexualityandu.ca/parents/sexuality-child-development

Sperber, J., Landers, S., & Lawrence, S. (2005). Access to health care for transgendered persons: Results of a needs assessment in Boston. *International Journal of Transgenderism, 8,* 75-91.

Sprigg, P., & Dailey, T. (Eds.) (2004). *Getting it straight: What research shows about homosexuality.* Washington, DC: Family Research Council.

Sroufe, L.A., Cofffino, B., & Carlson, E.A. (2010). Conceptualizing the role of early experience: Lessons from the Minnesota Longitudinal Study. *Developmental Review, 30*(1), 36-51.

Sroufe, L.A., Egeland, B., Carlson, E., & Collins, W. A. (2005). Placing early attachment experiences in developmental context. In K. E. Grossmann, K. Grossmann, & E. Waters (Eds.), *Attachment from infancy to adulthood: The major longitudinal studies* (pp. 48-70). New York, NY: Guilford Publications.

Stall, R., Paul, J.P., Greenwood, G., et al. (2001). Alcohol use, drug use and alcohol-related problems among men who have sex with men: the Urban Men's Health Study. *Addiction, 96,* 1589–1601.

Starr, P. (2011). HHS: Children are "sexual beings." *CNS News*. Retrieved from http://www.cnsnews.com/news/article/hhs-children-are-sexual-beings

Statistics Canada. (2012). Police reported sexual offences against children. Retrieved from http://www.statcan.gc.ca/pub/85-002-x/2014001/article/14008-eng.htm

Stoleru, S., Grégoire, M.C., Gérard, D., Decety, J., Lafarge, E., Cinotti L., Lavenne F, Le Bars, D., Vernet-Mauray E., Rada, H., Collet, C., Mazoyer, B., Forest, M.G., Magnin, F., Spira, F., & Comar, D., (1999). Neuroanatomical correlates of visually evoked sexual arousal in human males. *Archives of Sexual Behavior, 28,* 1-21.

Strang, J.F., Kenworthy, L., Dominska, A., Sokoloff, J., Kenealy, L.E., Berl, M., Walsh, K., Menvielle, E., Slesaransky-Poe, G., Kim, K.E., Luong-Tran, C., Meagher, H., & Wallace, G.L. (2014). Increased gender variance in autism spectrum disorders and attention deficit hyperactivity disorder. *Archive of Sexual Behaviour. 43*(8), 1525–33. doi: 10.1007/s10508-014-0285-3.

Stroumboulopoulos, G. (2013). 12 Facts and figures about having a disability in Canada. *CBC*. Retrieved from www.cbc.ca/strombo/news/by-the-numbers-international -day-of-persons-with-disabilities

Struthers, W., & Wolf, N. (2016). How pornography has rendered men less sexually responsive to real women. *Worth a Second Thought*. Retrieved from https://worthasecondthought.wordpress.com/.../william-struthers-naomi-wolf

Swaab, D.F. (2008). Sexual orientation and its basis in brain structure and function. *Proceedings of the National Academy of Sciences, 105*(30), 10273 – 10274.

Swift, M. (1987). The gay manifesto. *Free Republic*. Retrieved from http://www.freerepublic.com/focus/news/3023834/posts

Tang, H., Greenwood, G.L., Cowling, D.W., Lloyd, J.C., Roeseler A.G., & Bal, D.G. (2004). Cigarette smoking among lesbians, gays, and bisexuals: How serious a problem? (United States). *Cancer Causes Control, 15,* 797–803.

Tate, T. (1998). *Secret History: Kinsey's Paedophiles.* Yorkshire Television Production.

Tavistock and Portman Foundation. (2017). GIDS referrals increase slows in 2016/17. Retrieved from https://tavistockandportman.nhs.uk/about-us/news/stories/gids-referrals-increase-slows-201617/

Teen Health Source. (n.d.). Anal Play. Planned Parenthood International. Retrieved from http://teenhealthsource.com/sex/anal-play/

Tix, A.P., & Frazier, P.A. (1998). The use of religious coping during stressful life events: Main effects, moderation and meditation. *The Journal of Consulting and Clinical Psychology, 66*(2), 411-422.

Trafton, A. (2015). Neuroscientists reveal how the brain can enhance connections. *Massachusetts Institute of Technology News.* Retrieved from http://news.mit.edu/2015/brain-strengthen-connections-between-neurons-1118

Trans Student Educational Resources. (2017). The gender unicorn. Retrieved from www.transstudent.org/gender

Trocmé, N., Fallon, B., MacLaurin, B., Sinha, V., Black, T., Fast, E., Felstiner, C., Hélie, S., Turcotte, D., Weightman, P., Douglas, J., & Holroyd, J. (2008). *Canadian Incidence Study of Reported Child Abuse and Neglect (CIS-2008): Major Findings.* Ottawa, ON: Public Health Agency of Canada.

Turrell, S.C. (2000). A descriptive analysis of same-sex relationship violence for a diverse sample. *Journal of Family Violence, 15*(3); 281-293.

University of Michigan Lesbian, Bisexual, Gay, and Transgender Resource Center. (n.d.). LGBTQ glossary. Retrieved from http://lbgtrc.msu.edu/educational-resources/glossary-of-lgbtq-terms/

Urban, R. (2017, February 7). *The Australian.* Gender theory banned in New South Wales classrooms. Retrieved from http://www.theaustralian.com.au/national-affairs/education/gender-theory-banned-in-nsw-classrooms/news-story/eeb40f3264394798ebe67260fa2f5782

Valanis, B.G., Bowen, D.J., Bassford, T., Whitlock, E., Charney, P., & Carter, R.A. (2000). Sexual orientation and health: Comparisons in the women's health initiative sample. *Archives of Family Medicine, 9,* 843–853.

Valente, S.M. (2005). Sexual abuse of boys. *Journal of Child and Adolescent Psychiatric Nursing, 18*(1), 10-16.

Valleroy, L.A., MacKellar, D.A, Karon, J.M., Rosen, D.H., McFarland, W., Shehan, D.A., Stroyanoff, S.R., LaLota, M., Celentano, D.D., Koblin, B.A., Thiede, H., Katz, M.H., Torian, L.V., & Janssen, R.S. (2000). HIV Prevalence and associated risks in young men who have sex with men. *Journal of the American Medical Association, 284*(2), 198-204.

Van Beijsterveldt, C.E., Hudziak, J.J. & Boomsma, D.I. (2006). Genetic and environmental influences on cross-gender behavior and relation to behavior problems: A study of Dutch twins at ages 7 and 10 years. *Archives of Sexual Behavior, 35*(6): 647-658.

Van Den Aardweg, G. J. M., (1984). Parents of homosexuals: Not guilty? Interpretation of childhood psychological data. *American Journal of Psychotherapy, 38*(2), 181-89.

Van de Ven, P., Roden, P., Crawford, S., & Kippax, S. (1997). A comparative demographic and sexual profile of older homosexually active men. *The Journal of Sex Research, 34*(4), 349-360.

VanderLaan, D.P., Leef, J.H., Wood, H., Hughes, S.K., & Zucker, K.J. (2015).Autism spectrum disorder risk factors and autistic traits in gender dysphoric children. *Journal of Autism and Developmental Disorders, 45*(6), 1742–1750.

Voltaire. (1765). Retrieved from http://izquotes.com/quote/191107

Von Bruch, H. (n.d.). To be like Jesus. Retrieved from http://breadsite.org/lyrics/628.htm

Voon, V., Mole, T.B., Banca, P., Porter, L., Morris, L., Mitchell, S., et al. (2014). Neural correlates of sexual cue reactivity in individuals with and without compulsive sexual behaviors. *Plos ONE, 9*(7): e102419. https://doi.org/10.1371/ journal pone.0102419.

Vrangalova, Z., & Savin-Williams, R.C. (2010). Correlates of same-sex sexuality in heterosexually identified young adults. *Journal of Sex Research, 47*(1), 92-102.

Walters, M.L., Chen, J., & Breinding, M.J. (2013). The national intimate partner and sexual violence survey (NISVS): 2010 findings on victimization by sexual orientation. Atlanta: National Center for Injury Prevention and Control, Centers for Disease Control and Prevention. Retrieved from www.cdc.gov/ violenceprevention/pdf/nisvs_sofindings.pdf

Warner, J., McKeown, E., Griffin, M., Johnson, K., Ramsay, A., Cort, C., & King, M. (2004). Rates and predictors of mental illness in gay men, lesbians and bisexual men and women: Results from a survey based in England and Wales. *British Journal of Psychiatry, 185,* 274-485.

Warren, R. (2012). *The Purpose driven life: What on earth am I here for.* Grand Rapids, MI: Zondervan.

Weatherbe, S. (2016). Gay British actor warns against sex change for children. *Lifesite News.* Retrieved from www.lifesitenews.com/news/gay-british-actor-warns-against-gender-confusion-for-children

Web MD. (n.d.) Anal sex safety and health concerns. Retrieved from http:// www.webmd.com/sex/anal-sex-health-concerns#1

Weinrich, J., & Pillard, R. (1986). Evidence of familial nature of male homosexuality. *Archives of General Psychiatry, 43,* 808-812._

What Is Gender Dysphoria? (n.d.). Retrieved from https://www.psychiatry. org/patients-families/gender-dysphoria/what-is-gender-dysphoria

Whitehead, N., & Whitehead, B. (1999). *My genes made me do it!* Huntington House Pub.

Winograd, W. (2014). The wish to be a boy: Gender Dysphoria and identity confusion in a self-identified transgender adolescent. *Psychoanalytic Social Work, 21,* 55-74. http://www.tandfonline.com/doi/pdf/10.1080/15228878.2013.840 245

Winship, A.D. (2005). *Jukes-Edwards: A study in education and heredity.* Retrieved from https://www.gutenberg.org/files/15623/15623-h/15623-h.htm

Wolf, N. (2003). The porn myth. *New York Magazine.* Retrieved from http:// nymag.com/nymetro/news/trends/n_9437/

WRAL News. (2010). Durham man faces long prison term for sex crimes against adopted child. Retrieved from www.wral.com/news/local/story/7330467

Xiridou, M., Geskus, R., de Wit, J., Coutinho, R., & Kretzschmar, M. (2004). Primary HIV infection as source of HIV transmission within steady and casual partnerships among homosexual men. *AIDS, 18,* 1311–1320.

Yarhouse, M.A. (2010). *Homosexuality and the Christian.* Minneapolis, MN: Bethany House.

Yarhouse, M.A., & Tan, E.S.N. (2004). *Sexual identity synthesis.* Lanham, MD: University Press of America.

Youth Trans Critical Professionals. (n.d.). Professionals Thinking Critically about the Youth Transgender Narrative. Retrieved from https://www. youthtranscriticalprofessionals.org/about/

YouTube (2015). The Children of Table 34. Retrieved from https://www. youtube.com/watch?v=JtElwdCUTc

Zerrilli, J. (2010). Christians, homosexuality and the same-sex marriage question. *The Humanist.* Retrieved from https://thehumanist.com/magazine/ may-june-2010/features/christians-homosexuality-and-the-same-sex-marriage- question

Zucker, K. (2004). Gender identity development and issues. *Child Adolescent Psychiatric Clinics of North America, 13,* 551-568.

Zucker, K.J. (2018): The myth of persistence: Response to "A critical commentary on follow-up studies and desistance theories about transgender and gender non-conforming children" by Temple Newhook et al. (2018). *International Journal of Transgenderism, 19*(2), 231-245, DOI: 10.1080/15532739.2018.14682

Zucker, K.J., & Bradley, S.J. (1995). *Gender Identity Disorder and psychosexual problems in children and adolescents.* New York, NY: Guildford Press.

Zucker, K.J., Bradley, S.J., & Sanikhani, M. (1997). Sex differences in referral rates of children with gender identity disorder: Some hypotheses. *Journal of Abnormal Child Psychology, 25,* 217-227.

Zucker, K.J, Owen, A., Bradley, S.J, & Ameeriar, L. (2002). Gender-dysphoric children and adolescents: A comparative analysis of demographic characteristics and behavioral problems. *Clinical Child Psychology & Psychiatry, 7,* 398–411.

Zukerman, W., & Purcell, A. (2011). Brain's synaptic pruning continues into your 20s. Retrieved from https://www.newscientist.com/article/dn20803-brains-synaptic-pruning-continues-into-your-20s/

About the Author

ANN AND HER HUSBAND, BOB, HAVE A BLENDED FAMILY OF SIX ADULT children, and are the proud grandparents of nine beautiful grandchildren. Professionally, Dr. Gillies has trained jointly in psychology and theology, with a primary therapeutic focus on survivors of Complex Trauma. She is an ordained pastor, former adjunct professor, psychotherapist, and author. Ann is also a chaplain coordinator with the Billy Graham Rapid Response Team in Canada, leading chaplaincy teams into places of disaster and teaching "Sharing Hope in Crisis" courses. Ann is a gifted speaker and presents an extensive range of workshops, seminars, and conferences.